Words and Phrases for the TOEIC® Test

新TOEIC®テスト ズバリ出る英単語ファイル

三原 京 著

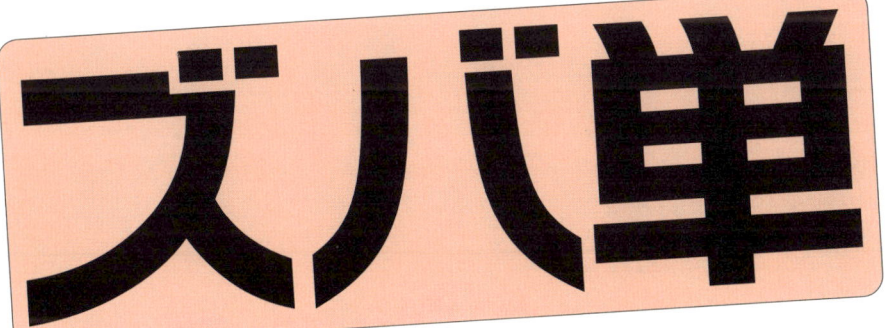

TOEFL is a registered trademark of Educational Testing Service (ETS).
This publication is not endorsed or approved by ETS.

南雲堂

はしがき

　ボキャブラリーをコツコツと蓄積すれば、英語力はグーンと伸びます。この本はTOEIC®テスト講座を担当している筆者が、その経験を生かし効果的に単語力を強化できるように、800点以上のスコアアップを目指す人だけでなく、TOEIC®テストにはじめてチャレンジする人のためにも作成しました。

　TOEIC®テストの3つの特徴は、①リスニングが50％あること ②問題数が200問と多いこと ③出題内容は日常生活とビジネス関連のトピックが中心であることが挙げられますが、これに対処するには、集中力、持続力、スピードが必要です。実際、2時間で200問という長丁場を乗り切るには、集中力と持続力がなければなりません。また、1つの問題にあまり長い時間をかけずに問題を解くスピードが求められます。そのために必要なのが、単語力なのです。

　さてTOEIC®テストで必要な単語力とは、
　①音を聞いて、その単語を認識でき意味が解る力
　②目で見て、その単語を認識でき意味が解る力
のことです。単語をマスターするには、見たり、聞いたりした瞬間にその意味が浮かぶまで、トレーニングすることが大切です。いわゆる単語認識の瞬発力を養うのです。繰り返し同じ単語に出会えば出会うほど、その瞬発力は増します。

　TOEIC®テストはビジネス語句、日常生活語句を中心に問題が作成されているため、ある程度の単語力がないと問題を解くことができません。そこで、まず基本的なレベルの単語力をつけ、その上に未知の単語を推測できる力をつけましょう。単語を覚えるのは大変ですが、それをクリアーすれば、英語の世界は大きく変わります。2000語程度の基本単語をきちんと身につけてください。さらに加えて1000語程度をマスターすれば、TOEIC®テストで知らない単語はぐんと減ります。

　とにかくTOEIC®テスト攻略で不可欠なことは、リスニングとリーディングの要となる単語力をつけることです。目標スコアを取った将来の自分の姿を頭に思い描きながら、しっかりとした単語力を身につけて、大きく飛躍してください。

　最後に、本書の作成にあたり、南雲堂編集部の青木泰祐編集部長、また英文の校閲をしていただいたJim Knudsen氏に大変お世話になりました。心から感謝の意を表したいと思います。

筆者

本書の使い方

1 本書の6つの特徴

1. **精選されたTOEIC®テスト頻出単語・イディオム**
   必ず身につけておきたい厳選したTOEIC®テスト頻出単語・イディオムを、見出し語として選んでいます。
2. **レベル別・テーマ別**
   単語をマスターしやすいように、リスニングはレベル別（Level 1とLevel 2）、ビジネス語句と日常生活語句はテーマ別に示しています。
3. **単語と例文が対応**
   見出し語を含む例文を示しています。TOEIC®テスト必須単語を例文の中で確認し、覚えることが可能です。
4. **赤シート学習**
   赤シートを使用することで、単語の意味の理解度をチェックできます。
5. **文法チェック**
   TOEIC®テストでよく出題される文法基礎事項を簡潔にまとめています。文法の弱点を補強し、確実に攻略するための助けとなるはずです。
6. **CDでリスニング力のアップ**
   本書に添付されているCDには、【リスニング語句】の見出し語と例文の音声が入っています。

2 本書で使用している記号

1. （ ）：意味の補足
2. （反）：反意語　（類）：類義語
3. （動）：動詞　（名）：名詞　（形）：形容詞　（副）：副詞
4. 《米》：アメリカ英語　《英》：イギリス英語

CONTENTS

◆リスニング頻出語句

動詞
 1. 情報・調査 　　　　・・・・・・・・・16
 2. 動作・移動 　　　　・・・・・・・・・22
 3. 操作 　　　　　　　・・・・・・・・・31
 4. 使用・取得 　　　　・・・・・・・・・34
 5. 感情・気持 　　　　・・・・・・・・・42

＜文法のまとめ１＞：比較、接続詞　　　・・・・・47

名詞
 1. 人物 　　　　　　　・・・・・・・・・50
 2. 仕事 　　　　　　　・・・・・・・・・54
 3. 移動 　　　　　　　・・・・・・・・・60
 4. 物 　　　　　　　　・・・・・・・・・64
 5. 暮らし 　　　　　　・・・・・・・・・70
 6. 風景 　　　　　　　・・・・・・・・・77
 7. 情報 　　　　　　　・・・・・・・・・83

＜文法のまとめ２＞：分詞、to 不定詞(1)(2)、動名詞(1)(2)　・・・93

形容詞、副詞　　　　　　　　　　　・・・・・・98

＜文法のまとめ３＞：時制、受動態、助動詞・・・・・・・・112

◆ビジネス頻出語句

1. 会社　　　　　：組織・支店・部局、経営・展開　・・・118
2. 人材・キャリア：幹部・役員、社員・職種、昇進・異動、
      採用・資格、労働・条件　・・・・・・・122
3. オフィスワーク：業務、財務会計、事務用品　・・・・・130
4. 取引・契約　　：交渉、契約、国際取引、履行条件　・・・137
5. 広告・販売　　：広告、販売、注文・商品、請求・支払、
      物流・運送　・・・・・・・・・・・・・141

6.	通信	：コンピューター、インターネット、セキュリティー、メール、ソフト、パソコン利用と姿勢、電話、郵便・ファックス・宅配 ・・・・・・	149
7.	待遇制度	：給与・手当、保険・年金 ・・・・	158
8.	マネー	：銀行、金融、投資 ・・・・・・・	162
9.	マーケティング	：市場、生産、顧客サービス ・・・	166
10.	会議・プレゼンテーション	：会議、会議進行、プレゼン心構え、スピーチ・ことば、提案・・・・・	170
11.	経済状況	：産業、科学・技術、景況感 ・・・	176
12.	通勤・交通	：通勤、道路、交通、車関係 ・・・	182
	<文法のまとめ 4>	：冠詞、名詞・代名詞、関係詞(1)(2)・・・・	188

◆日常生活頻出語句

1.	気象	：天気・予報、地理、雲の形状 ・・・・	194
2.	旅行	：海外旅行、空港、フライト ・・・	199
3.	環境	：大気、自然、環境保全、食品、ゴミ・リサイクル ・・	205
4.	健康・医療	：健康、症状・病気、医療、薬、禁煙・アルコール、感情・気持 ・・・・・・・	211
5.	映画・DVD	：映画、映画館・劇場、DVD・ゲーム ・・・	224
6.	教育・スポーツ	：指導、課程、スポーツ・レジャー、芸術 ・	230
7.	マスコミ・メディア	：報道、紛争、政治、法律 ・・・・・・	239
8.	不動産・引越し	：不動産、引越し、契約、家電 ・・・・	247
9.	社交・パーティー	：社交、パーティー、食事、食材・調味、料理法・	253
10.	日常生活	：生活、家庭、社会、ファッション、風景、休日・	261
	<文法のまとめ 5>	：形容詞、副詞、前置詞、仮定法、強調・・・	270

索引（見出し語）・・・・・・・275

TOEIC®テスト Q&A

1. TOEIC® テストとは？

TOEIC（トーイック）とは Test of English for International Communication の略称で、英語によるコミュニケーション能力を評価するテストです。TOEIC® テストには公開テストと団体特別受験制度（IP = Institutional Program）があります。公開テストは TOEIC 運営委員会の定めた日時・場所で実施するものです。IP は学校、企業などで任意に実施するものです。IP テストでは公開テストで発行される Official Score Certificate（公式認定証）は発行されませんが、IP テストの結果の有効性は通常、公開テストと同等と判断されます。

2. TOEIC® テストの構成は？

1. 問題はリスニングセクション（45分間、100問）と、リーディングセクション（75分間、100問）で構成され、2時間で200問に答えます。
2. リスニングセクションの放送は1回のみ流されます。
3. 途中休憩はありません。リスニング終了後、すぐにリーディングを開始します。
4. すべてマークシート方式のテストです。

2006年5月より、TOEIC® テストがリニューアルされ問題形式は次のように変更されました。

	Name of each part	パート名	問題数	時間
リスニング	1 Photographs	写真描写問題	10	45分
	2 Question-Response	応答問題	30	
	3 Short Conversations	会話問題	30	
	4 Short Talks	説明文問題	30	
リーディング	5 Incomplete Sentences	短文穴埋め問題	40	75分
	6 Text Completion	長文穴埋め問題	12	
	7 Reading Comprehension	読解問題		
	Single passage	・1つの文書	28	
	Double passage	・2つの文書	20	
計			200問	120分

各パートの内容
- **1. 写真描写問題：** 写真を正しく説明している英文を選ぶ。
- **2. 応答問題：** 質問と応答を聞き、正しい応答を選ぶ。
- **3. 会話問題：** 2人の会話を聞き、3つの質問を読んで正しい答えを選ぶ。設問は3題ずつ設定。（質問は放送される。印刷もされている）
- **4. 説明文問題：** 説明文を聞き、3つの質問を読んで正しい答えを選ぶ。設問は3題ずつ設定。（質問は放送される。印刷もされている）
- **5. 短文穴埋め問題：** 短文の中の空所に語句を補充。
- **6. 長文穴埋め問題：** 長文の中に複数ある空所に語句を補充。
- **7. 読解問題：** 文を読んで、質問に対する答えを選ぶ。新TOEICでは2つの文章を読んで設問に答える問題を追加。

3. 受験上の留意点
1. 携帯電話は使用禁止です。電源はオフにします。
2. 試験教室は禁煙で、飲食（ペットボトル、ガム、飴など）は禁止されています。
3. 試験中の退室は原則として認められません。
4. 問題用紙への書き込みは禁止です。書き込みとはメモ、線、○・×・✓などの印も含みます。

4. TOEICスコアとは？
5点きざみの配点で、リスニング（5点〜495点）とリーディング（5点〜495点）で評価されます。TOEIC®テストの結果はトータルで、最低10点〜最高990点のスコアで表示されます。

（TOEICスコアと英語コミュニケーション能力の相関表）

TOEICスコア	レベル	評価（ガイドライン）
860〜990	A	**Non-native**として十分なコミュニケーションができる。
730〜855	B	どんな状況でも適切なコミュニケーションができる素地を備えている。
470〜725	C	日常生活のニーズを充足し、限定された範囲内では業務上のコミュニケーションができる。
220〜465	D	日常会話で最低限のコミュニケーションができる。
215以下	E	コミュニケーションができるまでに至っていない。

5. 目標スコアと単語力
(A) リスニングと単語力

目標スコア：495〜375

- 短い会話において、幅広い単語（あまり使われていない単語、あるいは様々なトピックで用いられている単語）を使用した話の主旨、目的、基本的な文脈が推測できるようにする。
- 短い会話文において、難しい単語が使われている場合でも詳細が理解できるようにする。
- 長い聴解文において、幅広い単語が使用されていても話の主旨、目的、基本的な文脈が推測できるようにする。
- 難しい単語を含め、幅広く様々なトピックの単語を聞き取れるようにする。

目標スコア：370〜275

- 短い会話において、特に単語が難しくないときは、話の主旨、目的、基本的な文脈が推測できるようにする。
- 短い会話文において、簡単な、または中級レベルの単語が使用されているときは、話の詳細が理解できるようにする。
- 長い聴解文において、情報の繰り返しや言い換えがあるときは、話の主旨、目的、基本的な文脈が推測できるようにする。
- 中級レベルの単語や、慣用語句を聞き取れるようにする。

目標スコア：270

- 短い会話や写真描写において、単語が簡単で、話のごく一部を理解すればよいときは、話の詳細や写真に関する記述が理解できるようにする。
- 長い聴解文において、情報が何度も繰り返されたり、単語が簡単で、話のごく一部を理解すればよいときは、話の詳細や写真に関する記述を理解できるようにする。
- やや難しい単語が使用されているときは、話の主旨、目的、基本的な文脈を理解できるようにする。
- 基礎的な単語、イディオムを聞き取れるようにする。またリスニング攻略に必要な音声的な特徴を理解する。

(B) リーディングと単語力

目標スコア：495〜425

・幅広い単語（あまり使われていない単語、あるいは様々なトピックで用いられている単語）をマスターする。
・よく使用されている難しい単語の例外的な意味、慣用句的な使い方が理解できるようにする。
・似たような意味で使われる難しい複数の単語を区別できるようにする。

目標スコア：420〜325

・文章に使用されている単語や文法が難しいときでも、文章の限られた範囲内では情報を関連付けることができるようにする。
・文脈中の難しい単語、よく使用される単語の例外的な意味、慣用句的な使い方が理解できるようにする。
・似たような意味で使われる複数の単語を区別できるようにする。
・中級レベルの単語が理解できるようにする。

目標スコア：320〜225

・簡単な単語だけでなく、中級レベルの単語も少し理解できるようにする。
・文法以外の言語的要素（難しい単語が使われている、情報を関連付ける必要がある）がある場合でも、文法的に正しい選択肢を選べるようにする。

目標スコア：220

・事実に基づく情報の、言い換え表現が理解できるようにする。
・基本的な単語、よく使用される語句が理解できるようにする。

6. アメリカ英語とイギリス英語の違い
覚えておきたいアメリカ英語とイギリス英語の違い50語

アメリカ英語	イギリス英語	意味
apartment	flat	アパート
baggage	luggage	手荷物
be busy	be engaged	電話で話し中である
be laid off	be made redundant	解雇される
bill	note	紙幣
bulletin board	notice board	掲示板
can	tin	缶
cookie	biscuit	クッキー
crosswalk	pedestrian crossing	横断歩道
downtown	city centre	市街地
drugstore	pharmacy	薬局
elevator	lift	エレベーター
exit	way out	出口
fall	autumn	秋
first floor	ground floor	1階　イギリス英語で2階は　first floor
freeway / turnpike	motorway	高速道路
French fries	chips	フライドポテト
garbage / trash	rubbish	ゴミ
garbage can	dustbin	ゴミ箱
gas	petrol	ガソリン
give ... a ride	give ... a lift	車で送る
last name	surname	名字
laundry	washing	洗濯物
license plate	number plate	ナンバープレート
line	queue	列
mail	post	投函する
mailbox	letter box	郵便受け
major in	specialise in	〜を専攻する
movie	film	映画
nothing / zip	nil	（競技の得点で）ゼロ

11

one-way ticket	single ticket	片道切符
pants	trousers	ズボン
parking lot	car park	駐車場
potato chips	crisps	ポテトチップス
purse	handbag	ハンドバッグ
railroad	railway	鉄道
round-trip ticket	return ticket	往復切符
salesclerk	shop assistant	店員
schedule	timetable	時刻表
sidewalk	pavement	歩道
soccer	football	サッカー
stove	oven / cooker	コンロ
subway	underground / tube	地下鉄　イギリス英語でsubwayは地下通路
sweater	jumper	セーター
takeout	takeaway	持ち帰り用の
train station	railway station	鉄道の駅
truck	lorry	トラック
trunk	boot	（車の）トランク
windshield	windscreen	（車の）フロントガラス
zip code	postcode	郵便番号

7. アメリカ英語とイギリス英語の発音

　新 **TOEIC®** テストのリスニングでは、アメリカ英語の他に、イギリス英語、カナダ英語、オーストラリア（ニュージーランドを含む）英語の発音が、それぞれ25％の割合で出題されます。リスニング対策として、4ヶ国語の発音に慣れておく必要があります。

　単語の発音として、カナダ英語はほとんどアメリカ英語と同じで、オーストラリア英語（ニュージーランド英語）はイギリス英語とほぼ同じ発音を共有しています。

　つまり、アメリカ英語とイギリス英語の発音の違いを理解すれば、カナダ英語やオーストラリア英語の違いも分かり、聞き取れるようになります。例として、次のような違いが見られます。

1. car:　　　アメリカ英語「カァー」 [r] を舌を丸めてしっかり発音します。
　　　　　　イギリス英語「カー」[r] をほとんど発音しない傾向があります。
2. can:　　　アメリカ英語「キャン」
　　　　　　イギリス英語「カン」
3. butter:　　アメリカ英語「バラー / バダー」
　　　　　　イギリス英語「バター」

アメリカ英語では、母音に挟まれた [t] は、[r] や [d] のように聞こえる傾向があります。
一方イギリス英語では、[t] ははっきりと正確に発音される傾向があります。

4. secretary:　アメリカ英語「セクレタリ」
　　　　　　イギリス英語「セクレトリ」

アメリカ英語では、[t] の後の母音をはっきり発音します。一方イギリス英語では、[t] の後ろの母音をほとんど発音しない傾向があります。

8. オーストラリア英語とカナダ英語の特徴

【オーストラリア英語】
＜発音の特徴＞
・「エイ [ei]」を「アイ [ai]」と発音します。**today** は「トゥダイ」、**say** は「サイ」のように聞こえます。
・2重母音を長母音で発音する傾向があります。**here, year, tour** は、それぞれ「ヒー[hi:]」、「イー[yi:]」、「トー[tu:]」と聞こえます。
・「アイ [ai]」を「オイ [ɔi]」と発音し、**time** が「トイム」と聞こえることがあります。

＜典型的な表現＞
・挨拶として、**Good day, mate / G'day, mate**「こんにちは」があります。**Good day** が「グッダイ」、**mate**（友達）を「マイト」と発音するので「グッダイマイト」と聞こえます。
・**No worries, mate!**「ノーウォーリーズマイト（心配ないよ）」は、**Thank**

you や Sorry に対する応答として使われます。
・Ta「ター」は、Thank you のくだけた表現です。
・Sorry? は、Pardon (me)?「何とおっしゃいました」の表現です。
・Cheers「チャーズ」は、Thanks や Bye の表現で使われます。

【カナダ英語】
＜発音の特徴＞
・[i] の発音が [e] に近く、English は「イングレッシュ」、link は「レンク」のように聞こえます。
・[z] は、アメリカ英語は「ズィー」ですが、カナダ英語は「ゼット」と聞こえます。

＜典型的な表現＞
・文末に eh?「〜でしょ？」をつける特徴があります。発音は「エィ？」と聞こえます。
　たとえば How's it going, eh? とか、It's hot, eh? と言います。
・Ya「ヤー」をよく言います。Yes という時、Ya-Ya-! と言うのがカナダの特徴です。
・単語のつづりは、イギリス英語つづりです。
　　アメリカ英語：　　　　　　　　center　color　favorite　theater
　　カナダ英語(イギリス英語)：centre　colour　favourite　theatre
・カナダ英語はトイレを washroom と言います。アメリカ英語では bathroom、イギリス、オーストラリア英語では toilet / loo と言います。

9. TOEIC® テストに出る単語

　実用的でビジネス志向の TOEIC® テストでは、ビジネスコミュニケーションに不可欠な会社、人材、オフィスワーク、契約、広告、コンピューター、待遇、マネー、マーケティング、会議などが頻出トピックです。当然、TOEIC® テストに出る単語はビジネスに関連したものが多くなります。

　また、ビジネストピックに加え、天気、旅行、環境、映画、教育、マスコミ、不動産、社交といった日常生活にかかわるトピックも TOEIC® テストでは頻繁に出題されます。頻出トピックに合わせて、これらの分野の頻出単語もマスターしておく必要があります。

◆リスニング頻出語句

動詞　1. 情報・調査
　　　2. 動作・移動
　　　3. 操作
　　　4. 使用・取得
　　　5. 感情・気持
　　　＜文法のまとめ１＞
名詞　1. 人物　　5. 暮らし
　　　2. 仕事　　6. 風景
　　　3. 移動　　7. 情報
　　　4. 物
　　　＜文法のまとめ２＞
形容詞
副詞
　　　＜文法のまとめ３＞

1 情報・調査（Level 1）

1. **advertise** [ǽdvərtàiz]　　広告する
"Is that guitar you advertised in Sunday's *Observer* still available?"
"I'm afraid it's already been sold."
「日曜日の『オブザーバー』紙に広告したギターはまだ入手できますか」
「すでに売れていると思います」

2. **appear** [əpíər]　　現れる、載る
The ads will appear in commuter trains throughout the metropolitan area.
その広告は首都圏の通勤電車に現れるでしょう。

3. **call** [kɔ́:l]　　電話をかける
I'm calling about the room you advertised in today's paper.
今日の新聞の広告に出ていた部屋について電話をしています。

4. **chat** [tʃǽt]　　雑談する
The guests are chatting over food and drinks.
来客は飲食物を味わいながら雑談しています。

5. **choose** [tʃú:z]　　選ぶ
The successful applicant will be chosen based on experience and performance on an in-company test.
合格する応募者は経験と社内試験の成績に基づいて選ばれるでしょう。

6. **explain** [iksptéin]　　説明する
The woman is using her hands to explain something.
女性は何かを説明するのに手を使っています。

7. **inform** [infɔ́:rm]　　知らせる
We regret to inform you that there are no openings in the department at this time.
残念ですが、今はその部局には空きがないことをお知らせします。

16

8 **inquire** [inkwáiər]　　　　尋ねる
To inquire about our mileage plan, press 2 now.
マイル・プランについてのお尋ねは2を押してください。
　　　inquiry [inkwái(ə)ri]〔名〕問い合わせ

9 **notice** [nóutəs]　　　　気づく
I didn't notice the error until Janice at work showed it to me.
職場でジャニスが私に見せるまで、その間違いに気づきませんでした。

10 **plan** [plǽn]　　　　計画する
What's the old manager planning to do now?
今、前部長は何を計画していますか。(old=former)

11 **prepare** [pripéər]　　　　準備をする
The woman is preparing to take a trip to Southeast Asia.
女性は東南アジアへ旅行する準備をしています。

12 **realize** [ríːəlàiz]　　　　知る
Sorry, I didn't realize this table was taken.
すみません、このテーブルがふさがっているのを知らなかったのです。

13 **record** [rikɔ́ːrd]　　　　記録する、書き留める
I'm going to record everything in my journal.
すべてのことを日誌に書き留めるつもりです。

14 **report** [ripɔ́ːrt]　　　　報告する、告げ口する
Do you want me to report you to the manager?
経営者にあなたのことを報告してほしいのです。

15 **show** [ʃóu]　　　　上映される
There are several good films showing at the mall cineplex.
モールのシネコンで何本かの良い映画が上映されています。

16 **talk** [tɑ́ːk]　　　　話す
I'm sorry, but he is talking on the phone right now.
すみませんが、ただ今彼は電話で話しています。

17 **warn** [wɔ́ːrn]　　　　警告する

If something goes wrong, the system warns you right away.
何かがうまく行かなければ、システムがすぐにあなたに警告します。

1 情報・調査（Level 2）

Disc 1
3

18 **adjourn** [ədʒə́ːrn]　　　　　延期する
I would like to propose that we adjourn the meeting until Monday.
月曜日まで会議を延期することを提案したいと思います。

19 **alert** [ələ́ːrt]　　　　　通報する
The robot can feed patients and alert staff to emergency.
ロボットは患者に食事をさせ、緊急事態をスタッフに通報することができます。

20 **bow** [báu]　　　　　負ける、屈服する
The Mariners lost their fifth straight, bowing to the Los Angeles Angels 6-5.
マリナーズは5試合連続で負け、ロサンゼルス・エンジェルスに6対5で負けました。

21 **combine** [kəmbáin]　　　　　組み合わせる
This fun new sport combines kicking with the art of boxing.
このおもしろい新しいスポーツはキックとボクシングの技を組み合わせています。

22 **consult** [kənsʌ́lt]　　　　　相談する
I guess she should consult a pediatrician.
彼女は小児科医に相談すべきだと思います。

23 **decide** [disáid]　　　　　決める
Have you decided who you're going to go to next week's costume party as?
誰に変装をして来週の仮装パーティーに行くのか決めましたか。

24 **define** [difáin]　　　　　明らかにする、定義する
This new dictionary defines words much more clearly and simply.
この新しい辞典は単語をよりはっきりと定義しています。

25 **deteriorate** [ditíəriərèit]　　　　　悪化する

18

The environment is deteriorating to a critical point.
環境は危機的状況に悪化しています。

26 **focus** [fóukəs] 　　　　　焦点を合わす
Why not focus on one or two writers that you think are especially important?
特に重要と思う1人か2人の作家に焦点を合わせたらどうですか。

27 **forbid** [fərbíd] 　　　　　禁じる
On-line gambling and shopping are strictly forbidden in the office.
オフィスではオンラインでのギャンブルや買い物は堅く禁じています。

28 **improve** [imprúːv] 　　　　改善させる、向上させる
It gives me a chance to think about what I need to do to improve my life.
それは私の生活を改善させるのに必要なことについて考える機会を与えます。

29 **permit** [pəːrmít] 　　　　　許す、許可する
No parking is permitted on the airport concourse.
空港のコンコースでは駐車は許可されません。

30 **prove** [prúːv] 　　　　　　証明する
The theory has never been proven to be established fact.
その理論は決して確立した事実として証明されていません。

31 **reduce** [ridjúːs] 　　　　　減らす
Regular exercise helps reduce body fat.
規則正しい運動は体脂肪を減らす手助けをします。

32 **relieve** [rilíːv] 　　　　　解消する、減らす
A good massage relieves stress in a hurry.
よいマッサージはすぐにストレスを解消します。

33 **ruin** [rúːin] 　　　　　　台なしにする
Just look at my new white skirt! It's totally ruined.
ちょっと私の新しい白いスカートを見てください。まったく台なしです。

34 **soak** [sóuk] 　　　　　　びしょぬれになる

I was caught in a downpour and got soaked through.
大雨に会い、びしょぬれになりました。

35 **sponsor** [spánsər]　　　提供する
The clinic sponsors a variety of mental health services.
その診療所はさまざまな精神的健康サービスを提供しています。

36 **stress** [strés]　　　〜を強調する
Let me stress once again the importance of service and aftercare.
サービスとアフターケアの重要性をもう一度強調しましょう。

イディオム

37 **be supposed to**　　　〜することになっている
"How hot is it supposed to get today?"
"Not as hot as yesterday, thank goodness."
「今日はどれほど暑くなるでしょうか」
「ありがたいことに昨日ほど暑くはならないですよ」

38 **be unfamiliar with**　　　よく知らない
The new secretary is unfamiliar with online research methods.
新しい秘書はオンライン・リサーチ方法をよく知りません。

39 **bring up**　　　話題にする、持ち出す
Why don't you bring it up at the next meeting?
次の会合で話題にしたらどうですか。

40 **call for**　　　予報する
The forecast calls for intermittent showers later this afternoon.
天気予報は今日の午後遅くに降ったりやんだりの雨を予報しています。

41 **catch a movie**　　　映画を見る
Shall we catch a movie tonight?
今夜、映画を見ましょうか。

42 **come up**　　　やって来る
My vacation is coming up next month.

私の休暇は来月に来ます。

43 **come up with** 〜を考え出す
Have you come up with a slogan for your new language school yet?
もう新しい語学学校のスローガンを考えましたか。

44 **die out** 絶滅する
Many bird species are dying out.
多くの種の鳥が絶滅しかかっています。

45 **give away** 寄付する
"I have a lot of old clothes I want to give away."
"Call a charity organization. They'll be happy to take them."
「寄付したいたくさんの古い服があります」
「慈善団体に電話しなさい。喜んで引き取ってくれるでしょう」

46 **have nothing to do with** 〜と関係がない
She insists that she had nothing to do with the kidnapping.
彼女はその誘拐に関係がなかったと主張しています。

47 **let out** 終わる
The movie is just letting out.
映画はちょうど終わりかけています。

48 **look alike** 似ているように見える
This fridge and that one may look alike, but they are quite different.
この冷蔵庫とあの冷蔵庫は似ているように見えるかもしれないが、まったく違っています。

49 **look for** 探す
It looks as if I'll be looking for a new job soon.
すぐに新しい仕事を探すことになりそうです。

50 **look over** 〜を(ざっと)調べる
The customer is looking over our new pamphlet.
その客は私たちの新しいパンフレットを調べています。

51 **look through** 〜を細かく調べる
The assistant is looking through the file cabinet.

その店員はファイルキャビネットを細かく調べています。

52 **look up** 〜を調べる
Can you show me how to look up book reviews on the Internet?
インターネットで書評を調べる方法を教えてくれますか。

53 **be rained out** 雨で中止になる
What a shame! Tonight's game has been rained out.
ついていない！ 今夜の試合は雨で中止になりました。

54 **stand for** 表す
The pyramid on the U.S. dollar stands for something that lasts forever, like America itself.
アメリカのドル紙幣のピラミッドは、アメリカそのもののように永遠に続くものを表しています。

55 **sum up** 要約する
George summed up the new novel by saying, "I loved the book, but hated the ending."
ジョージは「この本は好きだが、終わりが嫌いだ」と、新しい小説を要約しました。

56 **take the day off** （会社を）休む
I'll have to take the day off from work.
仕事を休まなければならないでしょう。

57 **take up** 取り上げられる
War news takes up almost all the paper these days.
近ごろ戦争のニュースがほとんどすべての新聞に取り上げられています。

58 **take ... up with** 〜と話し合う、相談する
I'll have to take it up with personnel.
人事課と相談しなければならないでしょう。

2 動作・移動（Level 1）

Disc 1
5

59 **bike** [báik] 自転車に乗る

22

"Have you thought about biking to work?"
"I would if there were a shower in the office."
「仕事に行くのに自転車に乗ることを考えたことがありますか」
「会社にシャワーがあれば、そうするでしょう」

60 **breathe** [brí:ð]   吸う
Doesn't it feel great to breathe some clean, fresh air for a change?
気分転換にきれいで新鮮な空気を吸うのは最高の気分ではないですか。

61 **brew** [brú:]   醸造する
It's not really a beer. It's brewed from peas.
それは本当はビールではありません。エンドウ豆を醸造しています。

62 **brush** [brʌʃ]   磨く
"Shouldn't you turn the water off while you're brushing your teeth?"
"Sorry. It's an old habit."
「歯を磨いている間、水を止めるべきではないですか」
「すみません、昔からの習慣です」

63 **chase** [tʃéis]   追跡する
The police chased the speeding car for 50 miles along the freeway.
警察は高速道路を50マイル、スピード違反の車を追跡しました。

64 **clap** [klǽp]   (手を) たたく
When the children finish singing, clap your hands.
子供たちが歌い終えたとき、拍手をしてください。

65 **climb** [kláim]   登る
The fireman climbed the tree to rescure the cat.
消防士はネコを救出するために木に登りました。

66 **destroy** [distrɔ́i]   破壊する
A massive earthquake destroyed the entire town.
巨大地震がその町全体を破壊しました。

67 **dig** [díg]   掘る
Why is our neighbor digging up his backyard?
なぜ近所の人は裏庭を掘り起こしているのですか。

68 **drive** [dráiv] 　　　　　車で送る
"Why don't you let me drive you home?"
"Thanks, but I'll just call a taxi."
「家まで車で送らせてくれませんか」
「ありがとう、でもタクシーを呼びます」

69 **exercise** [éksərsàiz] 　　　　運動する
I enjoy exercising at the fitness center three times a week.
私は週3回、フィットネスセンターで運動することを楽しみます。

70 **lie** [lái] 　　　　　横になる、寝る
The boy is lying on his back gazing at the stars.
男の子は星を見ながら仰向けに寝ています。

71 **load** [lóud] 　　　　　積む
The truck is loaded with cardboard boxes.
トラックは段ボール箱を積んでいます。

72 **move** [mú:v] 　　　　　引っ越す
I'll move somewhere else that's quieter and safer.
私は、より静かでより安全などこか他の場所へ引っ越すでしょう。

73 **pack** [pǽk] 　　　　　詰める、荷造りする
"How many boxes do you think I'll need to pack all these books in?"
"I would say 15, at least."
「これらのすべての本を詰めるのにどれほど箱がいると思いますか」
「少なくとも15箱はいるでしょう」

74 **point** [pɔ́int] 　　　　　指さす
The teacher is pointing at something on the blackboard.
教員が黒板の何かを指さしています。

75 **pose** [póuz] 　　　　　ポーズをとる
The seniors are posing for a class photograph.
最上級生たちがクラス写真のためにポーズをとっています。

76 **remove** [rimú:v] 　　　　　取り除く
They are removing a notice from the bulletin board.

彼らは掲示板から掲示を取り除いています。

77 **serve** [sə́ːrv]　　　　　　（飲食物を）出す
"How should this wine be served?"
"It's best at room temperature."
「このワインはどのように出すべきですか」
「常温が最高です」

78 **speed** [spíːd]　　　　　　急ぐ
The ambulance is speeding towards the scene of the accident.
救急車が事故現場へ急いでいます。

79 **stop** [stáp]　　　　　　止める
Could you please stop talking and listen to me?
話すのを止めて、聴いていただけますか。

80 **sunbathe** [sʌ́nbèið]　　　　　　日光浴をする
Hundreds of people are sunbathing on the beach.
何百人もの人がビーチで日光浴をしています。

81 **sweep** [swíːp]　　　　　　さっと通過する、吹く
High winds swept across a field where a baseball game was in progress.
激しい風が野球の試合が行われているフィールドに吹きました。

82 **tap** [tǽp]　　　　　　打つ
The woman is tapping the keyboard with a pencil.
女性は鉛筆でキーボードを打っています。

83 **toss** [tɔ́ːs]　　　　　　投げる
The tourists are tossing coins into the fountain.
旅行者は泉にコインを投げています。

84 **type** [táip]　　　　　　タイプ〔入力〕する
I have to finish typing up this letter first.
まずこの手紙をタイプすることを終えねばなりません。

85 **walk** [wɔ́ːk]　　　　　　歩く

I was walking along the sidewalk when a big dog bit me.
歩道を歩いていると、大きな犬が私にかみつきました。

86 **wave** [wéiv] （手を）振る
I saw someone waving at me from across the street.
誰かが通りの向こう側から私に手を振っているのを見ました。

87 **wear** [wéər] 着る
The new employees are all wearing skirts.
新入社員はみんなスカートをはいています。

88 **work** [wə́ːrk] 動く
One of the escalators is now working.
エスカレーターの一つは今、動いています。

2 動作・移動（Level 2）

Disc 1
6

89 **abandon** [əbǽndən] 捨てる
Infants who have been abandoned often die for lack of love and human contact.
捨てられた幼児は、愛と人間的触れ合いがないためによく死にます。

90 **absorb** [əbzɔ́ːrb] 夢中になる
My roommate is absorbed in reading the newspaper.
ルームメイトは新聞を読むのに夢中です。

91 **clip** [klíp] 切り取る
The professor is clipping an article from the newspaper.
教授は新聞から記事を切り取っています。

92 **conduct** [kəndʌ́kt] 実施する、行う
The library conducts 8-week courses for immigrants who want to become U.S. citizens.
図書館は米国市民になりたいと思う移民のために8週間コースを実施します。

93 **depart** [dipɑ́ːrt] 出発する

His flight is about to depart from Gate 157.
彼の便は157ゲートから出発しようとしています。

94 **downshift** [dáunʃìft]　　減速する
We can downshift to a better, simpler way of life.
より良く、より簡素な生活様式に減速することができます。

95 **explore** [ikspló:r]　　散策する
You're all free to explore the city on your own.
自分でまったく自由に街を散策できます。

96 **interrupt** [ìntərʌ́pt]　　妨げる、中断する
Construction was interrupted by several accidents.
建設はいくつかの事故で中断されました。
　interruption [interrruption] 〔名〕妨害、中断

97 **overdo** [òuvədú:]　　やりすぎる
You shouldn't overdo exercise at first.
最初は運動をやりすぎるべきではありません。

98 **overwork** [òuvəwə́:rk]　　働き過ぎる
Don't overwork yourself so soon after your operation.
手術のあとすぐに働き過ぎないようにしてください。

99 **pack** [pǽk]　　混む、いっぱいである
"The freeway is always packed at this time of day."
"Shall we take another route then?"
「高速道路は一日のこの時間はいつも混んでいます」
「では別のルートにしましょうか。」

100 **pat** [pǽt]　　なでる
The little girl is patting the dog on the head.
幼い女の子が犬の頭をなでています。

101 **quit** [kwít]　　止める
"Have you managed to quit smoking yet?"
"No, but I'm down to ten cigarettes a day."
「なんとかもうタバコを吸うのをやめましたか」

「いいえ、でも1日10本に減らしています」

102 **slip** [slíp]   すべる
The pedestrian slipped on the icy sidewalk.
歩行者が凍った歩道ですべりました。

103 **spank** [spǽŋk]   （尻を）たたく
I don't think you should spank your kids like that.
そのように子供のお尻をたたくべきではないと思います。

104 **transfer** [trænsfə́:r]   転勤させる
I don't mind being transferred again.
また転勤してもかまいません。

105 **transport** [trænspɔ́:rt]   輸送する、運ぶ
The subway transports a daily average of 4.5 million passengers.
地下鉄は一日平均450万人の乗客を運びます。

イディオム

Disc 1
7

106 **cut up**   切断する
I'm going to have to cut up your credit card.
クレジットカードを切断しなければならないでしょう。

107 **do the dishes**   皿洗いをする、食器を洗う
You take it easy on the sofa and I'll do the dishes.
ソファーでのんびりしてください。私が食器を洗います。

108 **drop out**   身を引く、辞退する
I'll let you know as soon as someone drops out.
誰かが辞退するとすぐ、あなたに知らせます。

109 **get oneself posted to**   〜配属される
How did you get yourself posted to such a dream assignment?
どうしてこんな夢のような仕事に配属されたのですか。

110 **get rid of**   廃棄する、取り除く

28

Do you have an old car or truck you'd like to get rid of?
廃車したい古い車やトラックがありますか。

111 **get to**　　　　　　　　〜に到着する
My bus pulled out just as I got to the stop.
私が停留所に着くと、バスは出て行きました。

112 **get together**　　　　　会う
Shall we get together for a drink sometime?
いつか一杯飲むために会いましょうか。

113 **go for**　　　　　　　　〜に行く
It's a beautiful day. Let's go for a drive.
いい日ですね。ドライブに行きましょう。

114 **go out**　　　　　　　　外へ出る
Aren't you going out for lunch today?
今日は昼食に出かけませんか。

115 **go to bed**　　　　　　　寝る
"Have you tried drinking warm milk before going to bed?"
"Yes, but I still have trouble falling asleep."
「寝る前に温かいミルクを飲んでみたことがありますか」
「ええ、でもやはり眠れません」

116 **have ... on board**　　〜を（組織に）入れる
I'm very pleased to have him on board.
彼がここに来てくれてとてもうれしいです。

117 **lay off**　　　　　　　　解雇する、休む
My father was laid off when the company downsized.
会社が人員削減したとき、父は解雇されました。

118 **let ... go**　　　　　　　〜を解雇する
I'm going to have to think seriously about letting you go.
君を解雇することを真剣に考えなければならないでしょう。

119 **pack with**　　　　　　〜でおおう

The roads are already packed with ice, and chains are required.
道路はすでに氷で覆われていて、チェーンが必要です。

120 **pick up** 片付ける
The busboys are picking up food and plates from the tables.
バスボーイが食卓の食べ物と皿を片付けています。
　busboy「男性のレストラン食器片付け係」

121 **pull out** 出る
The car pulled out onto the highway and was hit from behind.
車は幹線道路に出て、うしろから追突されました。

122 **put back** 戻す
Could you help me put these books back on the shelf?
これらの本を棚に返すのを手伝ってくれますか。

123 **run an errand** 使いに行く
I've been running errands all over town today.
今日は町まで使いに行っていました。

124 **settle down** ゆったり座る
My son cannot seem to sit still or settle down.
息子はじっと座るか、ゆったり座ることができないように思えます。

125 **shake hands** 握手をする
The little boy is shaking hands with the tennis champion.
幼い男の子はテニスのチャンピオンと握手をしています。

126 **stop off** 立ち寄る
How about stopping off for a drink after work?
仕事の後、飲みに行くのはどうですか。

127 **strike out** 三振をとる
He struck out 313 batters last season, a new record.
彼は昨シーズン、新記録の313人のバッターを三振にとりました。

128 **take a walk** 散歩する
The office worker always takes a walk during her lunch hour.

会社員はいつも昼食時に散歩しています。

129 **take part in** 　　　　参加する
The institute is seeking volunteers to take part in a research study on insomnia.
研究所は不眠症の調査研究に参加するボランティアを探しています。

130 **take up** 　　　　～を始める
Do you think I should take up jogging, then?
それでは私がジョギングを始めるべきだと思いますか。

131 **turn off** 　　　　切る、消す
Passengers standing near the Priority Seats are requested to please turn off their cellphones.
優先座席の近くに立っているお客様は、どうか携帯を切ってくださいますようお願いいたします。

132 **turn around** 　　　　振り向く
He heard a loud noise and quickly turned around.
彼は大きな音を聞き、すばやく振り向きました。

133 **wait for** 　　　　～を待つ
I'm tired of waiting for the elevator. Let's take the stairs.
エレベーターを待つのに飽きました。階段で行きましょう。

3 操作（Level 1）

134 **check** [tʃék] 　　　　点検する
The woman is checking the headlights on her car.
女性は車のヘッドライトを点検しています。

135 **e-mail** [íːmèil] 　　　　Eメールで送る
Is the photograph you e-mailed me last time really you?
この前、Eメールで送ってくれた写真は本当にあなたですか。

136 **fax** [fǽks] 　　　　ファックスする

31

Just call or fax us with a list of the titles you want.
希望するタイトルのリストから電話かファックスをしてください。

137 **land** [lǽnd] 着陸する
One airplane is about to land on Runway 5.
一機の飛行機が第5滑走路に着陸しようとしています。
　　landing〔名〕着陸

138 **lift** [líft] 持ち上げる
You look great! Have you been lifting weights?
すてきですね！　重量挙げをしたことがあるのですか。

139 **operate** [ápərèit] 操作する
I would like to learn to operate a bulldozer.
ブルドーザーを操作することを学びたいです。

140 **tow** [tóu] 牽引する
The car is towing a mobile delicatessen.
車が移動式デリカテッセン（売店）を牽引しています。

3 操作（Level 2）

Disc 1
9

141 **convert** [kənvə́:rt] 変える、換算する
To convert Celsius to Fahrenheit, multiply the temperature by 1.8 and add 32.
摂氏を華氏に換算するには、温度に1.8を掛けて32を加えてください。

142 **download** [dáunlòud] ダウンロードする
Would you mind showing me how to download TV programs from the Net?
ネットからTV番組をダウンロードする方法を教えてくれますか。

143 **install** [instɔ́:l] 取り付ける
Technicians install wireless cameras in the home.
技術者はワイヤレスカメラ（防犯カメラ）を家に取り付けます。
　　installation [instəléiʃən]〔名〕設置

144 **pump** [pʌ́mp] （ポンプで）入れる
They pump your gas for you at this station.
彼らはあなたのためにガソリンスタンドでガソリンを入れます。

145 **re-heat** [rihíːt] 暖め直す
All you have to do is re-heat it in the microwave.
あなたがしなければならないことは電子レンジで暖め直すことだけです。

146 **shoot** [ʃúːt] 撮影する
She is shooting a new picture in South Africa.
彼女は南アフリカで新しい映画を撮影しています。

147 **skip** [skíp] スキップする、飛び越える
I skip from site to site and have no idea where the time goes.
サイトからサイトへスキップし、時間が経つのが分かりません。

イディオム

Disc 1
10

148 **break down** 故障する
The hospital computer system just broke down.
病院のコンピュータシステムがちょうど故障しました。

149 **take off** 離陸する
The planes are taking off despite the snow.
雪にもかかわらず、飛行機は離陸しています。

150 **tow away** 撤去する
Vehicles parked on the concourse will be towed away at the owner's expense.
コンコースに駐車している車は持ち主の費用で撤去されるでしょう。

151 **turn down** （温度、音などを）弱くする、下げる
Consumers are requested to turn down the heat this winter.
消費者はこの冬は暖房を弱くすることを求められています。

152 **turn out** （電気を）消す
If you turn out the lights, it's almost as good as sitting in a theater.

もし電気を消すなら、ほとんど映画館で座っているようです。
as good as 「〜も同然」

153 **work out** うまくいく
How's your new computer working out?
新しいコンピューターはうまくいっていますか。

4 使用・取得（Level 1）

Disc 1
11

154 **accept** [əksépt] 受理する
Are you accepting job applications right now?
ちょうど今、出願を受け付けているところですか。

155 **allow** [əláu] 許可する
No meat products or fruits are allowed to enter the country.
肉製品や果物は、その国に持ち込むことを許可されていません。

156 **apply** [əplái] 応募する
Who can apply for the new position?
誰がその新しい職に応募できますか。

157 **book** [búk] 予約する
"Is it possible to book a DVD that's not on the shelf?"
"Sure. We'll call you when it comes back in."
「棚にない DVD を予約することはできますか」
「もちろん、戻ってきたら電話します」

158 **break** [bréik] 破る
Anyone caught smoking in the lavatories will be breaking a United States federal law.
トイレでタバコを吸っているのを見つけられた人はだれでも、米国連邦法を破っていることになるでしょう。

159 **cancel** [kǽnsəl] 取り消す、中止する
All classes will be cancelled on Founder's Day.
創立記念日はすべての授業が休みになるでしょう。

34

160 **cook** [kúːk] 料理する
"Are you sure you want to cook for 25 people?"
"You're right. Let's order some pizzas."
「25人分の料理を望んでいるのは確かですか」
「その通りです。ピザを注文しましょう」

161 **depend** [dipénd] 〜による
The rate depends on where you're calling from.
通話料金はあなたがどこから電話をかけているかによります。

162 **earn** [ə́ːrn] もうける、得る
Telemarketers have to earn a living, too, so don't be so rude.
電話セールスをする人もまた生計を立てねばなりません。だから、そんなに無礼にしてはいけません。

163 **eat** [íːt] 食べる
The doctor told me not to eat fried foods.
医者は私に油で揚げた食物を食べないように言いました。

164 **fit** [fít] 合う
You can send the sweaters back if they don't fit right or you don't like them.
合わなかったり気に入らなかったりすれば、セーターを返送できます。

165 **include** [inklúːd] 含む
"How many meals does the tour include each day?"
"It includes a full English breakfast."
「ツアーには1日、何度の食事が含まれていますか」
「完全な英国風朝食が含まれています」

166 **involve** [inválv] 含む
Does your job involve much traveling?
仕事には多くの旅行も含まれていますか。

167 **join** [dʒɔ́in] 加わる
"Do you mind if I join you?"
"Sorry, but I'm waiting for someone."
「ご一緒してもよろしいですか」

「すみませんが、人を待っています」

168 **keep** [kíːp]　　　　　　持ち続ける、借りる
How long can I keep this CD for?
このCDはどれくらいの期間借りることができますか。

169 **offer** [ɔ́(ː)fər]　　　　　　提供する
The university offers two MBA programs that allow you to continue to work while you study.
この大学は、勉強しながら働き続けられる２つの経営学修士プログラムを提供します。

170 **order** [ɔ́ːrdər]　　　　　　〜を注文する
I'd like to order the salmon, please.
サーモンを注文したいです。

171 **pay** [péi]　　　　　　払う
The woman is paying for some DVDs at the cash register.
女性はレジでDVDのお金を払っています。

172 **purchase** [pə́ːrtʃəs]　　　　　　買う
I purchased the camera at one of your other branches.
他の支店の一つでカメラを買いました。

173 **repair** [ripéər]　　　　　　修理する
My wife is repairing the computer herself.
妻は自分でコンピューターを修理しています。

174 **select** [silékt]　　　　　　選ぶ
You must be very sharp to have been selected for this team.
このチームに選ばれたので、あなたはとても頭が切れるにちがいありません。

175 **use** [júːz]　　　　　　使う
No one's using the copy machine right now.
ただ今、誰もコピー機を使っていません。

4 使用・取得 (Level 2)

Disc 1
12

176 **accompany** [əkʌ́mpəni]　　添える
All entries must be accompanied by a maximum 300-word essay.
すべての応募作品には300語以内のエッセイを添えなければなりません。

178 **adopt** [ədɑ́pt]　　養子にする
"Have you thought about adopting a child?"
"I want to, but my husband isn't so sure."
「子供を養子にすることを考えたことがありますか」
「私はそうしたいですが、夫はそれほど確信がありません」

179 **approve** [əprúːv]　　認可する
The mayor approved the building plan.
市長はその建築プランを認可しました。

180 **cater** [kéitər]　　提供する、食事を出す
Planning a party?　Let FunFoods cater to all your needs.
パーティーを計画していますか。ファンフーズに必要なものをすべて提供させてください。

181 **charge** [tʃɑ́ːrdʒ]　　請求する
We charge five cents per book per day.
1日、1冊につき5セントを請求します。

182 **complete** [kəmplíːt]　　終わらせる、完成する
The course allows early-career managers to complete their MBA in three years.
そのコースは、3年間で下級管理職者が経営学修士を終えることができるようにしています。

183 **consume** [kənsúːm]　　消費する
This oven consumes less electricity than any other product of its kind on the market.
このオーブンは、市場に出ている同じ種類のどの製品よりも、電気を消費しません。

184 **donate** [dóunèit]　　寄付する
The proceeds from the sale will be donated to various charities.

37

販売の収益はさまざまな慈善団体に寄付されるでしょう。

185 **equip** [ikwíp] 　　　　　備え付ける
The beautiful kitchen is fully equipped with the most up-to-date appliances.
きれいな台所は最新の器具が完全に備え付けられています。

186 **expire** [ikspáiər] 　　　　期限が切れる、終わる
Your membership card will expire soon.
あなたの会員証はまもなく期限が切れるでしょう。

187 **handle** [hǽndl] 　　　　　扱う、対処する
"Do you think you can handle the ad campaign?"
"I'm your man."
「あなたは広告キャンペーンを扱えると思いますか」
「私は適任者です」

188 **inspire** [inspáiər] 　　　　刺激する
We should invite real working scientists to come to class and talk to and inspire students.
本物の現役の科学者たちを授業に招いて、学生に話をしたり刺激を与えてもらうべきです。

189 **invest** [invést] 　　　　　預ける
Where do you recommend that I invest my inheritance?
どこに遺産を預けたらよいか推薦してくれますか。

190 **prohibit** [prouhíbət] 　　　禁止する
Smoking anywhere on the aircraft is strictly prohibited.
喫煙は機内のどこでも固く禁止されています。

191 **register** [rédʒistər] 　　　登録する
There is no need to register for the workshop.
講習会の登録は必要ありません。

192 **renew** [rinjúː] 　　　　　～を更新する
The star centerfielder renewed his contract yesterday.
センターを守るスター選手が昨日、契約を更新しました。

193 **retire** [ritáiər] 退職する
Since my husband retired last month, he seems bored.
夫は先月退職したので、退屈そうです。

194 **stage** [stéidʒ] 上演する
The theater is staging a science fiction fantasy.
その映画館は SF ファンタジーを上演しています。

195 **submit** [səbmít] 提出する
All proposals must be submitted to the Planning Department by May 31.
すべての提案は 5 月 31 日までに企画部に提出されなければなりません。

196 **subscribe** [səbskráib] 〜を定期購読する
Do you subscribe to the *Times* or the *Herald*?
タイムズかヘラルドを定期購読していますか。

イディオム

Disc 1
13

197 **be prone to** 〜を起こしやすい
Drivers who speak into hands-free devices are prone to accidents as well.
ハンドフリーの装置で話すドライバーも事故を起こしやすいです。

198 **be required to** 〜するよう義務づけられている
All our bus drivers are required to take a drug test.
すべてのバスの運転手は麻薬検査を受けるよう義務づけられています。

199 **check out** 借りる
I'm afraid the book is checked out. Shall I reserve it for you?
その本は借り出されていると思います。予約しましょうか。

200 **get off** 切り上げる
They are planning to get off work at lunchtime on Friday.
彼らは金曜日の昼食時に仕事を切り上げることを計画しています。

201 **go over very well** とても受けが良い

With so many women drivers, the new ads should go over very well.
たくさんの女性ドライバーがいるので、新しい広告はとても受けがよいはずです。

202 **go with** 〜に合う
Would you like some ketchup or mustard to go with that?
それに合うケチャップかカラシが欲しいですか。

203 **have ... in common** 共通して〜を持つ
All the members of the tour have one big thing in common.
その旅行のメンバーは全員、一つの大きな共通点があります。

204 **keep up** ついていく
"Why didn't you answer my last e-mail?"
"You write five or six times a day! I can't keep up."
「どうしてこの前のEメールに返事をくれなかったのですか」
「あなたは1日に5、6回書きます！ ついていけません」

205 **keep up with** 〜に遅れないでついていく
We should try to keep up with what's going on around the world.
世界中で起こっていることに遅れないように努力すべきです。

206 **make one's way** 進出する
Robots are making their way into homes, hospitals and nursing care facilities.
ロボットは家庭、病院、介護施設へ進出しています。

207 **make use of** 〜を利用する
You can make use of our facilities as often as you like.
好きなだけ私たちの施設を利用できます。

208 **opt for** 〜を選ぶ
We opted for the quieter, simpler lifestyle of rural England.
イングランドの田舎の、より静かでより単純な生活スタイルを選びました。

209 **pick out** 選ぶ
"Could you help me pick out a new board?"
"I'd be happy to. Right this way."
「新しいサーフボードを選ぶのを手伝ってくれますか」

「喜んで。さあこちらへどうぞ」

210 **pick up** 〜を身につける
Since moving to the country, we've had to pick up new living skills.
田舎へ引っ越して以来、新しい生活術を身につけなければなりませんでした。

211 **point out** 指摘する
As you pointed out in your lecture, Harry Potter is no longer just for kids.
あなたが講義で指摘したように、ハリー・ポッターはもはや子供だけの読み物ではありません。

212 **put up** （広告を）出す
This is an ad put up by someone who is moving out of the dormitory.
これは寮から引っ越そうとしている人によって出された広告です。

213 **rack up** 得る
Shops rack up huge sales each time a tour group goes through a community.
店は旅行団体が地域を通過するたびに莫大な売り上げを得ています。

214 **reserve for** 〜のために取っておく
The purple Priority Seats are reserved for elderly and physically challenged passengers.
紫の優先座席は、お年寄りや身体の不自由な人のためのものです。

215 **result from** 〜の結果として生ずる
The flood resulted from heavy rains and melting snow.
洪水は豪雨と雪解けのために起きました。

216 **run out** 期限が切れる
My membership card will run out this week.
私の会員証は今週期限が切れるでしょう。

217 **sign up** 署名する、申し込む
Sign up now at the reference desk.
今、レファレンスデスクで申し込んでください。

218 **sort through** 〜を仕分けして整理する
Could you give me a hand sorting through last week's sales records?
先週の販売記録を仕分けして整理するのを手伝ってくれますか。

219 **take care of** 支払いを引き受ける
Here, let me take care of that. Lunch is on me.
さあ、その支払いを引き受けさせてください。昼食は私のおごりです。

220 **take over** 引き継ぐ
He has been transferred here to take over the late Mr. Dilman's duties.
彼は故ディルマンさんの職務を引き継ぐためにここに転勤しました。

221 **try one's hand at** 〜をやってみる
"Would you like to try your hand at bungee jumping?"
"Not me! I'm afraid of heights."
「バンジージャンプをやってみたいですか」
「私はごめんです！ 高いところが怖いです」

222 **wait tables** ウェーターをする
All I'm doing this summer is waiting tables at Denny's.
この夏に私がすることは、デニーズでウェーターをすることだけです。

5 感情・気持（Level 1） Disc 1　14

223 **bother** [bάðər] 〜を悩ます
"Which tooth did you say is bothering you?"
"On the bottom, in the back, on the right."
「あなたはどの歯で悩んでいると言いましたか」
「下の奥の右です」

224 **envy** [énvi] うらやむ
I envy you your happy childhood.
あなたの幸せな子供時代がうらやましいです。

225 **feel** [fiːl] 感じる

Why don't you tell your colleague how you feel?
どのように感じているか同僚に言ったらどうですか。

226 **forget** [fərgét] 忘れる
Sorry. I guess I forgot to check the arrival date.
すみません、到着日時をチェックするのを忘れたと思います。

227 **mind** [máind] 気にする、いやがる
I don't mind if I do. It looks delicious.
いやではありません。おいしそうですね。

228 **miss** [mís] 〜がなくて寂しい
Frankly speaking, I missed the nightlife of the big city.
率直に言って、大都市の夜の歓楽がなくて寂しかったです。

229 **prefer** [prifə́:r] 〜の方を好む
Wouldn't you prefer to own your own home?
自分の家を持つ方を好まないのですか。

230 **satisfy** [sǽtisfài] 満足させる
He was quite satisfied with his performance as King Lear.
彼は自分のリア王の演技にとても満足しました。

231 **sound** [sáund] 〜のように思われる
From the symptoms you've described, it sounds like sciatica.
あなたが述べた症状から坐骨神経痛のように思われます。

5 感情・気持（Level 2） Disc 1 15

232 **addict** [ədíkt] 夢中になる、中毒になる
I think I may have become addicted to the Internet.
インターネット中毒になったのかもしれないと思います。

233 **apologize** [əpálədʒàiz] わびる、あやまる
She's already apologized, so let's forget it.
彼女はすでにあやまっているのだからそのことは忘れましょう。

234 **disappoint** [dìsəpɔ́int]　　失望する
We were disappointed to hear that you have dropped out of college.
あなたが大学を中途退学したことを聞いて、私たちは失望しました。

235 **expect** [ikspékt]　　期待する
The game was a lot better than I expected.
試合は私が期待していたよりもずっとよかったです。

236 **overcome** [òuvərkʌ́m]　　克服する
"How about taking a speech class to help you overcome your shyness?"
"Only if you promise to take the class with me."
「恥ずかしさを克服する手助けをするため会話の授業を取るのはどうですか」
「あなたが一緒に授業を取ることを約束してくれたらね」

237 **reprimand** [réprəmæ̀nd]　　叱責する
The boss reprimanded the receptionist again this morning.
今朝また上司が受付係を叱責しました。

238 **upset** [ʌpsét]　　動揺する、うろたえる
Voters are really upset about that new tax law Congress passed.
有権者は議会が通過させた新しい税法について本当に動揺しています。

イディオム

Disc 1
16

239 **back up**　　支持する
You propose your ideas, and I'll back you up.
あなたがアイデアを提案したら、支持しますよ。

240 **be exposed to**　　〜に触れる
Being exposed to another culture will be good for your children.
異文化に触れることは、子供にとって良いでしょう。

241 **be in trouble**　　困っている
The president's sudden departure was seen by many employees as a sign that the company was in trouble.
社長の突然の退社は、多くの社員に会社が困っている兆候として見られました。

44

242 **care for** ～を好む
Most people don't care for the movie, but I enjoyed it.
ほとんどの人はその映画が好きではないが、私は楽しみました。

243 **feel like** ～のような気がする
Yoga has made me feel like a new person already.
ヨガで私はすでに生まれ変わったような気がしました。

244 **get along** 暮らしていく
My husband and I have had to learn to get along on far less money.
夫と私はずっと少ないお金で暮らしていくことを学ばねばなりません。

245 **get along with** ～とうまくやっていく
You seem to be getting along well with your colleagues.
あなたは同僚ととてもうまくやっているように見えます。

246 **get down** 憂うつにさせる
Are the pressures and stresses of modern life getting you down?
現代生活のプレッシャーとストレスがあなたを憂うつにしているのですか。

247 **get fed up with** ～に飽き飽きしている、うんざりしている
I'm getting fed up with standing on a crowded train every day.
私は毎日混んだ列車で立っていることにうんざりしています。

248 **get it off one's chest** それを打ち明ける
If you have complaints about your job, let's get it off your chest right now.
もし仕事に不満があるなら、今それを打ち明けてください。

249 **get sick of** ～にいやになる、うんざりする
I'm getting pretty sick of driving back and forth by myself every day.
毎日自分で車を運転して行き帰りすることが、かなりいやになっています。

250 **get tired of** ～にうんざりする、疲れる
I'm getting tired of all these telephone sales calls.
私はこれらすべての電話セールスにうんざりしています。

251 **get used to** 慣れる

45

I'm finally starting to get used to my new responsibilities.
私はやっと新しい責任に慣れ始めているところです。

252 **keep in mind** 　　　　心に留める
Please keep in mind that Hi-Hop Video has a three-dollar charge per day per DVD.
ハイホップビデオは DVD 1 枚につき 1 日あたり 3 ドルの料金を請求することを心に留めてください。

253 **look forward to** 　　　　～を楽しみに待つ
I'm looking forward to hearing from you.
あなたからの便りを楽しみに待っています。

254 **make up one's mind** 　　　　決める
I haven't made up my mind about your proposal yet.
まだあなたの提案について決めていません。

255 **mean business** 　　　　本気である
Always stand up straight, offer a friendly smile, and show the clerk that you mean business.
いつも背筋をのばして立ち、やさしい笑みを浮かべ、本気であることを店員にに示してください。

256 **sleep on** 　　　　（一晩寝て）～をよく考える
I think we should sleep on it over the weekend.
週末によく考えるべきだと思います。

257 **think twice** 　　　　よく考える、慎重に考える
Those of you who are planning to drive today might think twice about setting out in this snow.
あなた方の中で今日ドライブを計画している人は、この雪の中で出かけることについてよく考えた方がいいかもしれません。

＜文法のまとめ１＞

比較

原級の比較表現

1. 同等比較：A … as + 原級 + as B「A は B と同じくらい〜だ」(A=B)
   Therapy is as effective as drugs in treating depression.
   （心理療法はうつ病の治療には薬と同じくらい効果的です）

2. A … not as [so] + 原級 + as B「A は B ほど〜ではない」(A<B)
   This car is not as elegant as that one.
   （この車はあの車ほどエレガントではありません）

3. as + 原級 + as possible / as + 主語 + can「できるだけ〜」
   We want to sell our products as quickly as possible.（=as quickly as we can）
   （できるだけ早く製品を売りたく思います）

4. as + 原級 + as any + 単数名詞「どんな…にも劣らない」
   The design is as good as that of any cellphone on the market.
   （そのデザインは市場のどんな携帯電話のデザインにも劣りません）

5. 倍数の表現 A … times as + 原級 + as B「A は B の〜倍である」
   ２倍は twice, 半分は half
   This dining room set costs three times as much as that one.
   （このダイニングルームセットは、あちらのセットの３倍の値段です）

比較級の比較表現

6. A … + 比較級 + than B「A は B よりも〜だ」
   The town was much friendlier than the other places we visited.
   （その町は私たちが訪れた他のどんな所よりずっとフレンドリーです）
   比較級を強めるのは much, far, still, even, etc.

7. superior, inferior, senior, junior は than でなく to
   The new computer is superior to the old one in several ways.
   （新しいコンピューターは、いくつかの点で古いものより優れています）

8. the + 比較級 …, the + 比較級「〜すればするほど、ますます」
   The more you know, the more you want to learn.
   （知れば知るほど、ますます学びたくなります）

9. 比較級 + and + 比較級「だんだん、ますます」
   The situation is growing more and more complicated.
   (情況はますます複雑になってきています)

最上級の比較表現

10. the + 最上級 + of [in]「〜の中で最も…だ」副詞の最上級には the をつけない
    This is the oldest movie theater in the city.
    (これは町で一番古い映画館です)
    Who runs fastest in your class?
    (あなたのクラスで一番走るのが速いのは誰ですか)

11. one of + the + 最上級 + 複数名詞「一番〜の１つ」
    He took us to dinner at one of the best Italian restaurants in town.
    (彼は私たちを町で一番良いイタリアレストランの１つに連れて行ってくれました)

12. 最上級の慣用表現
    at least「少なくとも」at (the) most / at the very most「せいぜい」
    make the best of, make the most of「〜をできるだけ利用する」not in the least「少しも〜ない」

接続詞

等位接続詞：対等の関係

and「AとB」　or「AかB」　but「AだがB」
for「とういのは〜だからだ」　so「それで」

相関語句：他の語と関連して

1. 命令文 + and [or] …「〜しなさい。そうすれば［さもないと］…」
   Make dinner, and I'll take care of the children.
   (夕食を作ってください。そうすれば私が子供の世話をします)
   Hurry up, or you'll be late.
   (急ぎなさい、さもないと遅れますよ)

2. both A and B「AもBも両方とも」
   Both he and his brother now live in New Zealand.
   (彼も彼の弟も今ニュージーランドに住んでいます)

3. not A but B「A ではなく B」
   It's not coffee but tea that she ordered.
   (彼女が注文したのはコーヒーではなく紅茶です)

4. not only but also B「A だけでなく B も」
   Not only he but also I believe that it's time for change.
   (彼だけでなく私も変化のときだと信じます)

5. either A nor B「A か B のどちらか」
   Either my husband or I am going to the meeting.
   (夫か私が会合に行きます)

6. neither A nor B「A も B も〜ない」
   Neither the council members nor the mayor has yielded on the issue.
   (議会議員も市長もその問題について大声では言いませんでした)

   ＊4,5,6 では相関語句が主語のとき、動詞は B に一致

従属接続詞：主従の関係

7. 名詞節を導く
   that「〜が…するということ」
   whether, if「〜が…するかどうか」

8. 副詞節を導く
   時： after, before, once, since, till, until, when
   原因・理由： as, because, since
   条件： if, suppose, unless,
   譲歩： though, while
   結果： so … that, such … that

9. 接続詞句：数語で１つの接続詞の働き
   as soon as「〜するとすぐに」 … as well as 〜「〜だけでなく … も」
   as if「まるで〜であるかのように」 even if「たとえ〜であっても」
   etc.

名詞

1 人物 (Level 1)

258 **actress** [ǽktris] 　　　　女優
This year's Oscar for an actress in a leading role goes to Belinda Wise.
今年の主演女優オスカー賞はベリンダ・ワイズです。

259 **agent** [éidʒənt] 　　　　代理人
I'll make you an appointment with a literary agent.
あなたのために著作権代理業者に予約をしておきます。

260 **bride** [bráid] 　　　　花嫁
I'm not sure if I should tell the story in front of his bride.
彼の花嫁の前でその話をするべきかどうか確信がもてません。

261 **caller** [kɔ́:lər] 　　　　電話をかける人
Did the caller leave a contact number?
電話をかけてきた人は連絡用の電話番号を残しましたか。

262 **carpenter** [ká:rpəntər] 　　　　大工
The carpenters are hard at work putting in the staircase.
大工は階段を取り付ける作業を一生懸命しています。

263 **cashier** [kæʃíər] 　　　　レジ係
I've worked as a cashier in a convenience store.
私はコンビニでレジ係として働いています。

264 **counselor** [káunsələr] 　　　　カウンセラー
If you would like to make an appointment to see one of our counselors, call 9876-4321.
カウンセラーの 1 人に会う予約をしたいなら、9876-4321に電話ください。

265 **grown-up** [gróunʌp] 　　　　大人
The movie is as much for grown-ups as it is for children.

その映画は子供用であると同様に、大人のためのものです。

266 **housewife** [háuswàif]　　主婦
She became bored with being a housewife and started her own blog.
彼女は主婦であることが退屈になり、自身のブログを始めました。

267 **junior** [dʒúːnjər]　　（大学）3年生
I'm a junior at the University of Ballard and a non-smoker with no pets.
私はバラード大学の3年生でタバコも吸わないし、ペットも飼っていません。

268 **member** [mémbər]　　メンバー、会員
Club members get a 50% discount on all meals for four guests or more.
クラブ会員は、4人以上の客に対して、すべての食事に50%の割引があります。

269 **passenger** [pǽsəndʒər]　　乗客
This bus is specially equipped for physically challenged passengers.
このバスは身障者の乗客に特別な設備があります。

270 **patient** [péiʃənt]　　患者
Emergency medical technicians rushed the patient into the hospital.
緊急医療専門家がその患者を病院へ運びました。

271 **salespeople** [séilzpìːpl]　　店員
Negotiating with salespeople for a lower price is becoming increasingly popular.
値段を下げてもらうために店員と交渉することが、だんだん人気になっています。

272 **secretary** [sékrətèri]　　秘書
"Who does Mr. Jennings' new secretary think she is?"
"I guess she thinks she's the boss herself."
「ジェニングズの新しい秘書は自分が誰だと思っているのでしょうか」
「彼女は自分が上司だと思っている、と私は推測します」

273 **senior** [síːnjər]　　お年寄り
Seniors like yourself need a strong network of friends and family.
あなた自身のようなお年寄りは友達と家族の強いネットワークが必要です。

274 **stranger** [stréindʒər]　　知らない人
I like the idea of spending nine days with a group of complete strangers.
9日間、全然知らない人のグループと一緒に過ごすという考えは好きです。

278 **youth** [júːθ]　　若者
In fact, it has become the number one illness among the nation's youth.
実際、それはその国の若者の中で第一の病気になりました。

279 **waitress** [wéitrəs]　　ウェートレス
I thought the waitress did a nice job.
そのウェートレスはいい仕事をすると思いました。

1 人物 (Level 2)

Disc 1
18

280 **colleague** [káliːg]　　同僚
The new hire is shaking hands with all her colleagues.
新入社員は彼女の同僚全員と握手をしています。

281 **critic** [krítik]　　批評家
You can't always put much stock in what the critics say.
批評家が言うことは、いつも信用できるとは限りません。

282 **dweller** [dwélər]　　住民
A few years ago, like so many stressed-out city dwellers, we moved out to the countryside.
数年前、多くのストレスのたまった都市住民のように、私たちは田舎へ移り住みました。

283 **expert haggler**　　値切るのがうまい人
You can become an expert haggler if you follow these simple steps.
これらの簡単な手順に従うなら、あなたは値切り上手な人になれます。

284 **finalist** [fáinəlist]　　決勝進出者
Two finalists have been selected from each French, German, and Spanish class.

フランス語、ドイツ語、スペイン語のクラスからそれぞれ2人の決勝進出者が選ばれました。

285 **home caregiver**　　　　在宅介護人
"Why are you interested in becoming a home caregiver?"
"I really like working with elderly people."
「なぜ在宅介護人になることに関心があるのですか」
「お年寄りの人を相手に仕事をすることが本当に好きです」

286 **live-alone senior**　　　　一人暮らしのお年寄り
The proportion of live-alone seniors is rising rapidly.
一人暮らしのお年寄りの割合は急激に増加しています。

287 **low-seniority** [lóusi:njɔ́:rəti]　　若年者
They say 30 low-seniority employees could be downsized next month.
来月30人の若年者が人員削減されるそうです。

288 **mid-career manager**　　　　中堅管理職者
The program is a two-year course for mid-career managers who hope to become top-level leaders.
そのプログラムはトップレベルの指導者になりたいと思う中堅管理職者のための2年間のコースです。

289 **nurse's helper**　　　　看護ヘルパー
This robot is designed to work as a nurse's helper.
このロボットは看護ヘルパーとして働くように設計されています。

290 **office personnel**　　　　社員
I want all office personnel to be informed of the new policy immediately.
すべての社員にすぐに新しい政策を知らせることを望んでいます。

291 **passerby** [pǽsərbái]　　通行人
The striking workers are handing out newsletters to passersby.
ストライキをしている労働者は通行人にニュースレターを配っています。

292 **personnel** [pɑ̀:rsənél]　　社員

53

Attention all personnel. Please report to the main conference room.
すべての社員に申し上げます。メイン会議室に来てください。

293 **representative** [rèprizéntətiv] 代表者、担当者
If you would like to speak with one of our representatives, please stay on the line.
担当者の一人と話したいなら、電話を切らずにそのままお待ちください。

294 **retailer** [rí:tèilər] 小売商人
Haggling is becoming a respected way to get better deals from retailers.
値切ることは、小売商人とより良い取引をする尊敬すべき方法になりつつあります。

295 **retiree** [ritàiərí:] 退職者
The club's members are retirees who love flowers and gardens.
クラブの会員はみんな花と庭が好きな退職者である。

296 **telemarketer** [téləmɑ̀ːrkətər] 電話セールスの人
A telemarketer for an office-cleaning service is on the line, Mr. Gluckman.
グルックマンさん、オフィス掃除サービスの電話セールスの人が電話に出ています。

297 **witness** [wítnəs] 看取る人、目撃者
Life without a friend is like death without a witness.
友人のいない人生は看取る人のいない死のようなものです。

2 仕事 (Level 1)

Disc 1
19

298 **ability** [əbíləti] 能力
Your work is far below the level we expect from a man of your abilities.
君の仕事は君のような能力のある人に、私たちが期待しているレベルのはるか下になっています。

299 **advantage** [ædvǽntidʒ] 利益
What advantages do you think you would bring to our business?

わが社にどんな利益をもたらすとお考えですか。

300 **branch** [bræntʃ]　　　　支社
"Have you ever worked in the Singapore branch before?"
"No, and I'm really excited about it."
「以前にシンガポール支社で働いたことがありますか」
「ありませんが、そのことについて本当にわくわくしています」

301 **cash register**　　　　レジ
You will get an additional 25% discount at the cash register.
レジでさらに25%の割引してもらえるでしょう。

302 **chance** [tʃǽns]　　　　チャンス
I'm afraid I can't give you any more chances.
もうチャンスは与えられないと思います。

303 **convenience** [kənvíːnjəns]　　都合、便利
We would like you to come in for an interview at your earliest convenience.
できるだけ早く都合のつくときに面接に来てもらいたいと思います。

304 **deal** [díːl]　　　　取引
Our agency will get you the best possible deal.
代理店はあなたとできるだけ良い取引をするでしょう。

305 **dental** [déntəl]　　　　歯科
Does the company health insurance include dental?
会社の健康保険は歯科を含んでいますか。

306 **department** [dipɑ́ːrtmənt]　　部、課
I think we should have some plants in our department.
私たちの部に植木をおくべきだと思います。

307 **eye contact**　　　　アイコンタクト
The most important thing is maintaining eye contact with the person you are dealing with.
最も重要なことは、取引している人とアイコンタクトを維持することです。

308 **front desk** フロントデスク
I want you all back here in front of the front desk no later than 5 p.m.
午後5時までにフロントデスク前のここに戻ってきてもらいたいと思います。
no later than「〜までに」

309 **lunch break** 昼休み
There will be a one-hour lunch break starting at 11:30.
11時30分に始まる昼休みが1時間あるでしょう。

310 **note** [nóut] メモ、ノート
The better notes you take, the better you'll do on the test.
良いノートをとればとるほど、ますますテストでうまくいくでしょう。

311 **notice** [nóutəs] （退職）通知
"Shouldn't you at least give two weeks' notice?"
"I don't want to work here another day!"
「少なくとも2週間前に退職通知を申し出るべきではないですか」
「もう一日もここで働きたいとは思わないのです」

312 **stock** [sták] ストック、蓄え
We have a large stock of classic as well as recently-released DVDs.
最近発売されたDVDだけでなく古典もたくさんのストックがあります。

313 **TV ads** テレビ広告
Half of last year's PR budget went to TV ads.
昨年の宣伝予算の半分はテレビ広告に使われました。

2 仕事 (Level 2)

Disc 1
20

314 **advertising agency** 広告代理店
The men in the corner work for an advertising agency.
角にいる男性たちは広告代理店で働いています。

315 **affiliated station** 系列局
David has been working at affiliated station KLMN as a reporter for

the past five years.
デービッドはこの5年間レポーターとして系列局の KLMN で働いていました。

316 **benefit** [bénəfit]　　　手当
The salary is $55,000 a year, with full benefits.
年収は5万5千ドルで、十分な手当があります。

317 **budget** [bʌ́ʤit]　　　予算
Thanks to the recession, we're on a pretty tight budget these days.
不況のせいで、このごろ予算はかなり限られています。

318 **conference room**　　　会議室
The seminar is held every Thursday at 7:00 p.m. in the conference room.
セミナーは会議室で毎週木曜日の午後7時に開催されます。

319 **contract** [kɑ́ntrækt]　　　契約
Let us represent you the next time you negotiate a new contract.
今度、新たな契約を交渉するときは、あなたを代理人にしましょう。

320 **credit** [krédit]　　　功績
Mr. Alexander has several local television awards to his credit.
アレクサンダー氏はその功績で地元のテレビ放送賞をいくつか持っています。

321 **day off**　　　休日、非番の日
I'll have to take the day off from work to attend my son's open house.
息子の授業参観に出席するため、仕事の休みをとらなければならないでしょう。
open house (= school event when the classrooms are "opened" for parents to observe)

322 **document** [dɑ́kjumənt]　　　書類
Copies of the document will be made available to all employees.
書類のコピーはすべての社員が利用できるようにされるでしょう。

323 **evaluation** [ivæljuéiʃən]　　　評価
Your evaluation shows that your performance level is dropping.
評価はあなたの業績レベルが落ちていることを示しています。

324 **executive** [igzékjutiv]　　　幹部、経営者、重役
　　It is time top exccutives like you had an agent to go to bat for you.
　　あなたのような最高経営者は、あなたの代理をする代理人を持ってもよいころです。
　　　　go to bat for(= represent)

325 **hyperlink** [háipərlìŋk]　　　ハイパーリンク
　　When a site visitor clicks the hyperlink, the destination is displayed on the Web.
　　サイトの訪問者がハイパーリンクをクリックすると、目的地がウェブに示されます。

326 **industrial purpose**　　　産業目的
　　Robots for industrial purposes have been around for decades already.
　　産業目的のロボットは、すでに何十年もの間普及しています。

327 **law enforcement**　　　法執行機関
　　Law enforcement is always a challenging profession.
　　法執行機関はいつもやりがいのある仕事です。

328 **layout** [léiaùt]　　　レイアウト、配置
　　What do you think of the layout of this poster?
　　このポスターのレイアウトをどう思いますか。

329 **line** [láin]　　　セリフ
　　The movie has a couple of funny lines, but that's about all.
　　その映画は2，3のおもしろいセリフがあるが、それがほぼすべてです。

330 **maternity leave**　　　産休
　　Would it be all right if I extended my maternity leave for one month?
　　1ヶ月間、産休を延ばしても良いでしょうか。
　　　　annual leave 年次休暇　　take a leave 休暇を取る

331 **military** [mílitèri]　　　軍隊
　　My father was in the military in Japan when I was in high school.
　　私が高校生であったとき、父は日本で軍隊にいました。

332 **overtime** [óuvətàim]　　　残業
　　You wouldn't be available for overtime, then?

それでは残業はできないのですね。

333 **personal ad**　　　　個人広告
How many times have you placed a personal ad on the Internet?
インターネットに個人広告を載せたことが何回ありますか。

334 **previous position**　　　前の勤め先
Would you mind telling me why you left your previous position?
前の勤め先をなぜ辞めたのか言ってくれますか。

335 **promotional idea**　　　販売促進のアイデア
Mr. James loved your promotional ideas.
ジェームズさんはあなたの販売促進のアイデアを気に入りました。

336 **provider**　[prəváidər]　　プロバイダー
What made you change your provider all of a sudden?
どうして突然、プロバイダーを変えたのですか。

337 **public relation department**　広報部
A new copy editor position is opening up in the public relations department.
広報部で新しい編集係の職があります。

338 **résumé**　[rézəmèi]　　履歴書
We received your résumé this morning and found it very interesting.
今朝あなたの履歴書を受け取り、とても興味深いことが分かりました。

339 **retirement age**　　　退職年齢
What is the retirement age in your company?
あなたの会社では退職年齢は何歳ですか。

340 **screenplay**　[skrí:nplèi]　映画脚本
"How's that new screenplay of yours coming along?"
"I sent it off to my agent yesterday."
「あなたの新しい映画脚本の進み具合はどうですか」
「昨日代理人に送りました」

341 **small part**　　　　わき役

You've been offered a small part as a nurse in a new TV series.
あなたは新しい TV シリーズで看護師としてのわき役が与えられています。

342 **special effect**　　　特殊効果
"Weren't those special effects amazing?"
"Sure, but there wasn't much of a story."
「それらの特殊効果は驚くべきものではありませんでしたか」
「ええもちろん。でもストーリーはたいしたことなかったです」

343 **the yen**　　　円相場
"What's the yen today?"
"Up against the dollar, but down against the euro."
「今日の円（相場）はどうですか」
「ドルに対して円高だが、ユーロに対しては円安です」

344 **translation** [trænsléiʃən]　　　翻訳
Don't worry; as always, translations will be provided.
心配しないで、いつものように翻訳が与えられるでしょう。

345 **workshop** [wə́ːrkʃàːp]　　　ワークショップ、研修会
A workshop on how to teach reading is held every Monday.
リーディングの教え方に関する研修会が毎月曜日に開かれます。

3 移動 (Level 1)　　　Disc 1　21

346 **aircraft** [érkræft]　　　飛行機
Please remain seated until the aircraft comes to a complete stop.
どうか飛行機が完全に止まるまで座ったままでいてください。

347 **ambulance** [ǽmbjuləns]　　　救急車
How long will it take for the ambulance to get here?
救急車がここに着くにはどれくらいかかりますか。

348 **boat** [bóut]　　　ボート
You can rent a boat by the hour or the day.
時間決めか日割りでボートを借りることができます。

349 **car** [káːr]　　　　　車、自動車
"What kind of warranty does the car have?"
"It's for five years, or 50,000 miles."
「車にはどんな種類の保証がありますか」
「5年間か5万マイルです」

350 **driver** [dráivər]　　　ドライバー、運転手
I think drunk drivers should go to prison.
酔っ払い運転手は投獄されるべきだと思います。

351 **ferry** [féri]　　　　　フェリー
The ferries aren't running today because of the strong winds.
フェリーは強風のため今日は出航しません。

352 **flight** [fláit]　　　　フライト、便
I have decided to take an early flight back to Atlanta this afternoon.
今日の午後アトランタへ戻る早い時間の便に乗ることに決めました。

353 **garage** [gəráːʒ]　　　（車の）修理工場、ガレージ
The family car is in the garage for repairs.
自家用車は修理のために修理工場にあります。

354 **gas station**　　　　　ガソリンスタンド
Prices at self-service gas stations are a few cents lower per gallon.
セルフサービスのガソリンスタンドの料金はガロンあたり数セント安いです。
（類）filling [service] station《英》petrol station

355 **gasoline** [gǽsəlíːn]　　ガソリン
Supreme unleaded gasoline has the highest octane rating.
高無鉛ガソリンはオクタン価が一番高いです。

356 **go for a ride**　　　　車に乗って出かける
How about going for a ride and looking at the Christmas lights?
車で出かけてクリスマス・イルミネーションを見るのはどうですか。

357 **reservation** [rèzərvéiʃən]　予約
For flight reservations or to reconfirm, press 3.
フライトの予約や再確認には、3を押してください。

358 **stoplight** [stɑ́:plàit]　　　停止信号
They were stopped at a stoplight when the earthquake hit.
地震が発生したとき、彼らは停止信号で止まりました。

359 **track** [trǽk]　　　路線、線路
The city's first subway line carried 15,000 people per day along its 9-mile track.
その都市の最初の地下鉄線は9マイルの路線で1日に1万5千人の人を運びました。

360 **traffic** [trǽfik]　　　交通
Take the bus and avoid getting caught in traffic.
バスに乗って交通に巻き込まれるのを避けてください。

361 **train** [tréin]　　　電車、鉄道
In the city I come from, there are no trains or subways.
私の出身の都市では電車も地下鉄もありません。

362 **public transportation**　　　公共輸送機関
The only means of public transportation are the buses.
公共輸送機関の唯一の手段はバスです。

363 **vehicle** [ví:əkl]　　　車、乗物
Why not donate your used vehicle to charity?
チャリティーにあなたの中古車を寄付したらどうですか。

364 **walk** [wɔ́:k]　　　歩行距離
The nearest bus stop is a 15-minute walk away.
一番近くのバス停は歩いて15分です。

365 **wheels** [hwi:lz]　　　車輪
This is a library on wheels that serves the surrouding rural areas.
これは周辺の農村地域にサービスをする移動式図書館です。

❸ 移動（Level 2）

366 **antifreeze** [ǽntifrì:z]　　　不凍液

You'd better make sure there's plenty of antifreeze in your car's radiator.
車のラジエーター（冷却装置）にたくさん不凍液が入っていることを確かめた方がよいです。

367 **car pool** [kɑ́:rpùːl]　　カープール（通勤などで１台の車に相乗りすること）
This lane is for car pools only.
このレーンはカープールだけのものです。

368 **clean driving record**　　（交通違反のない）きれいな運転記録
You must have a clean driving record to qualify for this job.
この仕事に適任であるためには、きれいな運転記録を持っていなければなりません。

369 **commute time**　　通勤時間
Thanks to the new super express, my commute time has been cut in half.
新しい超特急のおかげで、通勤時間は半分に短縮しました。

370 **dashboard** [dǽʃbɔ̀ːrd]　　（車の）ダッシュボード
What's that monitor that's on your dashboard?
ダッシュボードにある、あのモニターは何ですか。

371 **drive-through** [dráivθrúː]　　ドライブスルー
Let's go to a drive-through and get something to eat.
ドライブスルーへ行って、何か食べ物を買いましょう。

372 **go-kart** [góukàːrt]　　ゴーカート
The go-karts are for children aged six and over.
ゴーカートは６歳以上の子供用です。

373 **home-delivery service**　　宅配サービス
We would like to remind you of our new home-delivery service.
私たちの新しい宅配サービスを心に留めておいてください。
　（類）door-to-door service

374 **parking ticket**　　駐車違反切符
You have not so much as a parking ticket on your record.
あなたの記録には駐車違反切符もありません。

375 **stroller** [stróulər]　　　　ベビーカー
Where can I buy a stroller for triplets?
三つ子用のベビーカーをどこで買うことができますか。

376 **traffic jam**　　　　交通渋滞
This device tells me if there are any traffic jams I should avoid.
この装置は避けるべき交通渋滞があるかどうかを教えます。

377 **traffic light**　　　　交通信号
All the traffic lights were out because of the power shortage.
すべての交通信号は電力不足のため消えました。

4 物 (Level 1)

Disc 2
2

378 **balloon** [bəlúːn]　　　　風船
The child has some balloons in her hand.
子供は手にいくつかの風船を持っています。

379 **bill** [bíl]　　　　紙幣
Someone has written something on the back of this dollar bill.
誰かがこのドル紙幣の裏面に何かを書きました。

380 **billboard** [bílbɔːrd]　　　　掲示板
The huge billboard was distracting drivers.
大きな掲示板が運転手の気をそらせました。

381 **booklet** [búklət]　　　　パンフレット、小冊子
The booklet gives a lot of useful tips on finding a hotel in London.
そのパンフレットはロンドンでホテルを見つけるのに、多くの役立つ情報を提供しています。

382 **bookshelf** [búkʃèlf]　　　　本棚
The books on his bookshelf are all hardbacks.
彼の本棚の本はすべてハードカバーです。

383 **bottle** [bátl]　　　　ボトル

The wine bottles are stacked on wooden shelves.
ワインボトルが木製の棚に積まれています。

384 **cash** [kǽʃ] 現金
You can pay in cash if you like.
よろしければ現金で払うことができます。

385 **catalog** [kǽtəlɔ̀(ː)g] カタログ
I have a catalog of our latest models right here with me.
ちょうどここに最新型のカタログがあります。

386 **cellphone** [sélfòun] 携帯電話
Everyone in the coffee shop was talking on their cellphones.
喫茶店では誰もがみんな携帯電話で話しています。

387 **coat** [kóut] コート
You had better wear a warm coat today.
今日は暖かいコートを着たほうがいいです。

388 **costume** [kástjuːm] 衣装、コスチューム
Yours should win the prize for best costume.
あなたのものがベストコスチューム賞をとるはずです。

389 **cupboard** [kʌ́bərd] 戸棚
Shall I put the dishes in the cupboard for you?
戸棚に皿を置きましょうか。

390 **dish** [díʃ] お皿、料理
There's a dish of leftover lasagna in the freezer.
フリーザーに残り物のラザーニャ（パスタの一種）のお皿があります。

391 **dishwasher** [díʃwɔ̀(ː)ʃər] 食器洗い機
The kitchen is equipped with a powerful microwave oven and built-in dishwasher.
台所は強力な電子レンジと、はめ込み式の食器洗い機が備え付けられています。

392 **envelope** [invéləp] 封筒
We stock a wide range of envelopes, postal cards and stationery.

広範囲におよぶ封筒、はがき、文房具の在庫があります。

393 **flag** [flǽg]　　　　　　　　旗
The flags of several countries are displayed outside the hotel.
いくつかの国の旗がホテルの外に掲げられています。

394 **ladder** [lǽdər]　　　　　　　はしご
The firefighter is climbing the ladder.
消防士がはしごを登っています。

395 **luggage** [lʌ́gidʒ]　　　　　　手荷物
Workers are unloading the luggage from the airplane.
労働者は飛行機から荷物を降ろしています。

396 **machine** [məʃíːn]　　　　　　機械
This ATM machine is open 24-7.
このATM機械はいつも開いています。
　　24-7 (= twenty-four hours a day, seven days a week)

397 **mobile** [móubəl]　　　　　　携帯電話
Would you please phone me on my mobile as soon as you get this message?
このメッセージを受け取ったらすぐ、携帯に電話をいただけますか。

398 **phone** [fóun]　　　　　　　電話、電話機
Many people no longer have regular phones in the homes.
多くの人は家ではもはや通常の電話機を持っていません。

399 **plug** [plʌ́g]　　　　　　　　栓
Don't forget to pull the plug and let the water out.
栓を抜き、水を出すことを忘れないでください。

400 **price** [práis]　　　　　　　価格
All the items in this bin are half price.
この箱のすべての商品は半額です。

401 **purse** [pə́ːrs]　　　　　　　財布
The customer is looking in her purse for her checkbook.

顧客は小切手帳を探して財布の中を見ています。

402 **quarter** [kwɔ́ːrtər] 　　　25セント硬貨
It's only 25 cents a cup, so just drop a quarter in the little can.
1カップ25セントだけですので、小さなカンに25セント硬貨を入れてください。

403 **raincoat** [réinkòut] 　　　レインコート
The children are wearing raincoats and carrying umbrellas.
子供はレインコートを着て傘をさしています。

404 **refrigerator** [rifrídʒərèitər] 　冷蔵庫
Never put bananas in the refrigerator.
絶対にバナナを冷蔵庫に入れないでください。

405 **shelf** [ʃélf] 　　　　　　　棚
Everything on the shelf crashed to the floor.
棚のすべてのものが床に落ちました。

406 **sunglasses** [sʌ́nglæ̀sis] 　　サングラス
He has to wear sunglasses day and night.
彼は毎日サングラスをかけなければなりません。

407 **sweater** [swétər] 　　　　セーター
Make sure you take along a nice, warm sweater in case it turns cold.
寒くなるといけないので、必ずとても暖かいセーターを持って行きなさい。

408 **washer** [wɑ́ʃər] 　　　　洗濯機
It would cost as much to repair the washer as it would to buy a new one.
洗濯機を修理するのは、新しいものを買うのと同じほど費用がかかるでしょう。

4 物 (Level 2)

Disc 2
3

409 **appliance** [əpláiəns] 　　器具、装置
The kitchen is equipped with energy-saving appliances.
台所はエネルギー節約器具が備え付けられています。

67

410 **ATM (=automated teller machine)**　現金自動支払機、ATM
The cash withdrawal limit for this ATM is $200.
このATMの現金引き出し限度は200ドルです。

411 **battery**　バッテリー
You can take this computer with you anywhere, thanks to our powerful battery.
強力なバッテリーのおかげで、どこでもこのコンピューターを持って行くことができます。

412 **bulletin board**　掲示板
Just put an announcement on the office bulletin board.
ちょっと社内掲示板に通知を出してください。

413 **coffee maker**　コーヒーメーカー
"What time did you set the coffee maker for?"
"6:30.　Is that too early?"
「コーヒーメーカーを何時にセットしましたか」
「6時30分です。早過ぎますか」

414 **cologne**　[kəlóun]　オーデコロン
I think the commercial is for some sort of new men's cologne.
コマーシャルは何か新しい男性用オーデコロンのようなものだと思います。

415 **currency**　[kə́:rənsi]　通貨
The currency of Japan rose dramatically against the euro.
日本の通貨はユーロに対して劇的に高騰しました。

416 **electric blanket**　電気毛布
Would you like me to get you an electric blanket?
電気毛布を買ってきてあげましょうか。

417 **electricity**　[ilèktrísəti]　電気
"Do you prefer cooking with gas or electricity?"
"I think gas is more efficient."
「ガス、それとも電気で料理するのが好きですか」
「ガスがより効率的であると思います」

418 **folk arts and crafts**　　民芸品
My mother is interested in folk arts and crafts.
私の母は民芸品に関心があります。

419 **microwave** [máikrəwèiv]　　電子レンジ
Just pop the leftover stew in the microwave for about 5 minutes.
残りもののシチューを約5分間電子レンジに入れてください。

420 **nicotine gum**　　ニコチンガム
Those smokers who turn to nicotine gum succeed in quitting more often.
ニコチンガムに頼る喫煙者は、しばしば禁煙に成功します。

421 **MP3 player**　　エムピースリープレイヤー
Step up and get a good close look at this amazing new MP3 player from Universal Electric.
ユニバーサル・エレクトリック社のこの驚くべき新型エムピースリープレイヤーを近づいてよく見てください。

422 **plastic** [plǽstik]　　ビニール袋
"Paper or plastic, ma'am?"
"Neither. I always bring my own bag."
「奥様、紙袋とビニール袋のどちらになさいますか」
「どちらもいりません。いつも自分の袋を持っています」

423 **rice cooker**　　炊飯器
A rice cooker can be used to make cakes, too.
炊飯器はケーキを作るのにも使用できます。

424 **slow cooker**　　スロークッカー（電気煮込み鍋）
This slow cooker is the perfect timesaver for working mothers.
このスロークッカーは働いている母親にとって完璧な時間節約器です。

425 **utility** [ju:tíləti]　　光熱費
"Does the rent include cable TV and the Internet?"
"Yes, and all utilities, too."
「賃貸料はケーブルＴＶ、インターネットを含んでいますか」
「はい、すべての光熱費もです」

426 **vacuum cleaner** 　　　　掃除機
　　 This vacuum cleaner can reach into narrow spaces and corners.
　　 この掃除機は狭いスペースや角に届くことができます。

427 **visual aids** 　　　　視聴覚教材
　　 "Have you prepared any visual aids to support your talk?"
　　 "Yes, I have some maps and charts."
　　 「あなたの話を支える視聴覚教材を準備したのですか」
　　 「はい、地図と図表を準備しました」

5 暮らし（Level 1）　　　　　　　　　Disc 2　4

428 **bill** [bíl] 　　　　請求書
　　 On-line banking is the quick, easy way to pay your bills.
　　 オンライン・バンキングは請求書を払うための速くて簡単な方法です。

429 **blood** [blʌ́d] 　　　　血液
　　 The hospital is asking people to give blood for the accident victims.
　　 病院は事故の犠牲者のために、血液を提供することを人々に求めています。

430 **break** [bréik] 　　　　休憩
　　 Let's take a short break and get a cup of coffee.
　　 短い休憩をとり、コーヒーを飲みましょう。

431 **calory** [kǽləri] 　　　　カロリー
　　 Does this device tell you how many calories you burn?
　　 この装置はどれほど多くのカロリーを燃焼するかを示すのですか。

432 **cheese** [tʃíːz] 　　　　チーズ
　　 The store is known for its selection of French and British cheeses.
　　 その店はフランスとイギリスのチーズの品ぞろえで知られています。

433 **cure** [kjúər] 　　　　治療法、（治療）薬
　　 Is there a cure for anorexia nervosa?
　　 拒食症の治療法はありますか。

434 **diet** [dáiət] 食事、ダイエット
The doctor says I have to change my diet and get more exercise.
食事を変えて、もっと運動しなければならないと医者は言います。

435 **dinner** [dínər] 夕食
I'm afraid I won't be able to have dinner with you tonight as planned.
予定していたように今夜あなたと夕食をとれないのではないかと思います。

436 **discount** [dískaunt] 割引
During our Year End Sale, you can get the discounts you want on the things you need.
歳末セール中、あなたが必要とするものに希望の割引をすることができます。

437 **doubles** [dʌ́blz] （テニスの）ダブルス
Get yourself a partner and we'll play doubles.
パートナーを見つけてください、そうすればダブルスをしましょう。

438 **drink** [dríŋk] 飲み物
Coffee is the only drink available for breakfast.
コーヒーは朝食で飲める唯一の飲み物です。

439 **game** [géim] ゲーム
What party games do you think we should play?
どんなパーティーのゲームをすべきだと思いますか。

440 **grade** [gréid] 成績、評価
You could get better grades if you tried harder.
もし一生懸命するなら、いい成績をとることができるでしょう。

441 **journal** [dʒɚ́ːrnl] 日誌
I use the time on the train to write in my journal.
日誌を書くために列車の中で時間を使います。

442 **lease** [líːs] リース
The new apartments are for rent or lease only.
新しいアパートは賃貸か、リースだけです。

443 **menu** [ménju:]　　　　　メニュー
We offer a full menu of party foods for up to 50 people.
50人までのパーティーの食事として完全なメニューを提供します。

444 **monthly** [mʌ́nθli]　　　　毎月の、１か月の
Does the monthly rent include the maintenance fee?
毎月の家賃は管理費を含んでいますか。

445 **overweight** [òuvərwéit]　　太りすぎ
Being overweight can lead to various ailments.
太りすぎることは、さまざまな病気につながることになります。

446 **package** [pǽkidʒ]　　　　パッケージ、箱
I have five packages of beef jerky and two bottles of bourbon.
5箱のビーフ・ジャーキーと2本のバーボンがあります。

447 **party** [pá:rti]　　　　　パーティー
Let's have your birthday party at the beach.
ビーチであなたの誕生パーティーをしましょう。

448 **play** [plei]　　　　　　劇
The students plan to put on a play by Shakespeare.
学生たちはシェークスピアの劇を上演することを計画しています。

449 **portion** [pɔ́:rʃən]　　　（食べ物の）一人前
The portions in America are usually too large for Japanese.
アメリカでの一人前は、たいてい日本人には多すぎます。

450 **purchase** [pə́:rtʃəs]　　　買い物
Delivery is free for purchase of $250 or more.
配達は、250ドル以上の買い物なら無料です。

451 **receipt** [risí:t]　　　　レシート、領収書
I can exchange the camera only if you have your receipt.
レシートがありさえすれば、カメラを交換できます。

452 **sale** [séil]　　　　　　販売
The houses won't be for sale until late June or early July.

家は6月下旬か7月上旬まで販売されないでしょう。

453 **science** [sáiəns] 科学、自然科学
Our students don't seem to be as interested in science these days.
学生たちはこのごろ自然科学に関心がないように思えます。

454 **smoke-free** [smóukfrì:] 禁煙の
The entire building is smoke-free now.
今、全館禁煙です。

455 **steak** [stéik] ステーキ
How many calories are there in a steak like this?
このようなステーキにはどれほどのカロリーがありますか。

456 **tip** [típ] チップ
Aren't you going to leave the waitress a tip?
ウエートレスにチップを置かないのですか。

457 **veggie / vegetable** [védʒi]/[védʒtəbl] 野菜
There's some lettuce and other veggies in the refrigerator.
冷蔵庫にレタスと他の野菜があります。

458 **vote** [vóut] 投票
You in the audience will be asked to cast your vote for your favorite speakers.
聴衆の中のあなたは好きな講演者に投票することを求められるでしょう。

459 **weight** [wéit] 体重
If I eat out here too often, I'm sure I'll put on weight.
ここであまりにもよく外食するなら、きっと体重が増えるでしょう。

5 暮らし (Level 2)

Disc 2
5

460 **abuse** [əbjú:s] 虐待
Child abuse is everyone's business.
児童虐待はみんなの関心事です。

461 **action** [ǽkʃən]　　　　作業、動作
Parents get an opportunity to let their children see Mom and Dad in action.
両親は働いている父母を子供たちに見せる機会を得ます。

462 **activity** [æktívəti]　　　活動
The senior citizen center offers various outdoor and indoor activities.
高齢者センターは、さまざまな野外と屋内活動を提供します。

463 **allergy** [ǽlərdʒi]　　　アレルギー
People with pollen allergies really suffer at this time of year.
1年のこの時期に花粉アレルギーの人々は本当に苦しみます。

464 **asthma** [ǽzmə]　　　ぜん息
More and more American children are coming down with asthma.
だんだん多くのアメリカの子供たちがぜん息を患っています。

465 **award** [əwɔ́ːrd]　　　賞
Look at all those awards the young actress has won already.
若い女優がすでに受賞したあのすべての賞を見てください。

466 **bacteria** [bæktíəriə]　　バクテリア、細菌
The immune system fights against bacteria and viruses that come from outside.
免疫システムは、外から来るバクテリアやウイルスと戦います。

467 **bug** [bʌ́g]　　　ウイルス
Get your flu shots today before the flu bug starts going around.
インフルエンザ・ウイルスが広まる前にインフルエンザ予防注射をしなさい。

468 **delivery charge**　　　配達料
Is there a delivery charge for furniture and electric appliances?
家具と電気器具には配達料がありますか。

469 **directory** [diréktəri]　　　電話帳
Do you have a business directory for South King County?
サウス・キング郡の職業別電話帳がありますか。

470 **donation** [dounéiʃən] 寄付
Clothing and food donations are especially appreciated.
衣類と食料の寄付は特にありがたく思います。

471 **flu shot** インフルエンザ予防注射
The clinic is offering flu shots at no charge next Monday.
診療所は来週の月曜日インフルエンザ予防注射を無料で行います。

472 **get-together** [géttəgèðər] 会合
Next month's get-together will be held at Martha's house on the 15th.
来月の会合は15日にマーサの家で行われるでしょう。

473 **harmless** [háːrmləs] 無害の
The body can sometimes produce antibodies against outside substances that are in fact harmless.
身体はときどき実際には無害である外の物質に対して抗体をつくることができます。

474 **immune system** 免疫組織
The immune system protects our bodies from disease by producing antibodies.
免疫組織は抗体を作ることで病気から身体を守ります。

475 **kidney infection** 腎臓感染症
"Are you on any medications at the moment?"
"Yes, for a kidney infection."
「今、薬物治療中ですか」
「はい、腎臓感染症で」

476 **lap** [lǽp] 1往復
How many laps did you swim today?
今日は何往復泳ぎましたか。

477 **medication** [mèdəkéiʃən] 薬、医薬品
"Are you taking your medications as I directed?"
"Every day, just as you told me to."
「私が指示した薬を飲んでいますか」
「毎日言われたようにしています」

478 **performance** [pərfɔ́ːrməns]　上演
　　Performances are at 7 p.m. every evening except Monday.
　　月曜日を除き、上演は毎晩午後7時です。

479 **regular mail**　　　　　普通郵便
　　All contest entries should be sent in by regular mail.
　　コンテストの応募作品はすべて普通郵便で送らなければなりません。

480 **section** [sékʃən]　　　コーナー
　　This movie doesn't belong in the comedy section.
　　この映画はコメディーのコーナーにはありません。

481 **snapshot** [snǽpʃὰːt]　　スナップ写真
　　You are invited to enter your favorite digital snapshot in our photo contest.
　　写真コンテストに好きなデジタルスナップ写真を投稿することをお勧めします。

482 **tab** [tǽb]　　　　　　勘定、費用
　　"Shall we split the tab?"
　　"That sounds like a fair deal."
　　「勘定を割りましょうか」
　　「公平な取り決めのようです」

483 **treatment** [tríːtmənt]　治療、治療法
　　New treatments for nervous system disorders are being developed all the time.
　　神経系障害の新しい治療はいつも進歩しています。

484 **used title**　　　　　　中古のタイトル
　　Buy three used DVD titles and get an additional one absolutely free.
　　3つの中古のDVDタイトルを買って、無料でもう1つ手に入れてください。

485 **vital signs**　　　　　　生命徴候
　　"How are the patient's vital signs?"
　　"Pulse 100, blood pressure, 180 over 90, respiration 40."
　　「患者の生命徴候はどうですか」
　　「脈拍は100、血圧は上が180で下が90、呼吸は40です」

486 **workout** [wə́ːrkàut]　　　働き、運動
This rowing machine gives your heart and lungs an excellent workout.
（こぎ方練習用の）ローイングマシンは心臓と肺にすばらしい働きを与えます。

6　風景（Level 1）　　　Disc 2　6

487 **change** [tʃéindʒ]　　　気分転換
"Doesn't this clear mountain air taste good for a change?"
"You said it!"
「この澄んだ山の空気は気分転換に良い味でないですか」
「あなたの言うとおりです」

488 **cinema** [sínəmə]　　　映画館
The cinema is closed for repairs until further notice.
さらなる通知まで、映画館は修理のため閉められています。

489 **clinic** [klínik]　　　診療所
The shots will be given in the company clinic by nurses from County General Hospital.
注射は会社の診療所で郡総合病院の看護師によって行われるでしょう。

490 **cloud** [kláud]　　　雲
There's not a cloud in the sky today.
今日は空に雲がありません。

491 **countryside** [kʌ́ntrisàid]　　　田舎
We moved out to the countryside to escape the noise and pollution.
騒音と公害からのがれるため田舎へ引っ越しました。

492 **court** [kɔ́ːrt]　　　コート
The park's clay tennis courts are being resurfaced.
公園のクレーテニスコート（土のテニスコート）は表面が新しくされています。

493 **dolphin** [dɑ́lfin]　　　イルカ
"Did you read the story in yesterday's paper about the dolphins?"

"No, I didn't see that."
「イルカに関する昨日の新聞の記事を読みましたか」
「いや、見なかったです」

494 **downtown** [dàuntáun]　　ダウンタウン、(町の) 中心部
"Shall we do our shopping downtown or at the mall?"
"Parking downtown is such a bother."
「ダウンタウンかあるいはモールで買い物をしましょうか」
「ダウンタウンでの駐車はとても難しいですよ」

495 **factory** [fǽktəri]　　工場
The cell becomes a kind of factory that produces more viruses.
その細胞は多くのウイルスを生産する一種の工場になります。

496 **farmhouse** [fάːrmhàus]　　農家
They live in a farmhouse 50 miles outside of Boston.
彼らはボストン郊外50マイルの農家に住んでいます。

497 **film** [fílm]　　映画
Are there any good films coming out this weekend?
今週末公開される良い映画はありますか。

498 **fog** [fɔ(ː)g]　　霧
"Can you see all right in this fog?"
"I think I'd better pull over for a while."
「この霧の中でちゃんと見えますか」
「しばらく車を寄せて止めた方がいいと思います」

499 **gym** [dʒím]　　ジム、体育館
I've been to the gym every day for two months.
2ヶ月間毎日ジムに通いました。

500 **hospital** [hάspitl]　　病院
The hospital is to the left about a half mile straight ahead.
病院はまっすぐ前方約半マイル行ったところの左手にあります。

501 **hurricane** [hə́ːrəkèin]　　ハリケーン
"What's the differnce between a typhoon and a hurricane?"

"One's in the Pacific Ocean, the other in the Atlantic."
「台風とハリケーンの違いは何ですか」
「一つは太平洋にあり、もう一つは大西洋にあります」

502 **location** [loukéiʃən] ロケ地
The best actress winner is filming on location in Rwanda.
最優秀女優賞受賞者はルワンダのロケ地で撮影しています。

503 **market** [má:rkit] マーケット、市場
The market is especially crowded on organic produce Tuesdays.
マーケットは特に有機産物の火曜日には混んでいます。

504 **neighborhood** [néibərhùd] 近隣、近所
This neighborhood is the safest in the city.
この都市ではこの近隣が一番安全です。

505 **pavement** [péivmənt] 歩道
My husband is busy shoveling snow off the pavement.
夫はシャベルで忙しく歩道の雪かきをしています。

506 **restaurant** [réstərənt] レストラン
I learned to speak the language while working at a Mexican restaurant.
メキシコレストランで働きながら言葉を話すことを学びました。

507 **shark** [ʃá:rk] サメ
A pod of dolphins gathered around some swimmers to protect them from a large shark.
イルカの群れが、泳いでいる人を巨大サメから守るために集まりました。

508 **star** [stá:r] 星
I've never seen so many stars in my life.
私の人生でそんなに多くの星を見たことがありません。

509 **studio** [stjú:diòu] スタジオ、撮影所
The tour takes you inside an actual film studio.
ツアーは実際の映画撮影所の中へ連れて行ってくれます。

510 **suburb** [sʌ́bəːrb] 郊外
Life in the suburbs is too bland for me.
郊外での生活は私にはあまりにも味気がありません。

511 **subway** [sʌ́bwèi] 地下鉄
Construction of the subway took nearly four years to complete.
地下鉄建設は完成するのにほぼ4年かかりました。

512 **theater** [θíːətər] 劇場
There's a long line in front of the theater.
劇場の前に長い列ができています。

513 **trout** [tráut] マス
"What's the biggest trout you ever caught?"
"A little over 15 pounds."
「かつて釣った最大のマスはどれくらいですか」
「15ポンドを少し超えたものです」

514 **wave** [wéiv] 波
I'd like to challenge some bigger waves this year.
今年はより大きな波に挑戦したいです。

6 風景 (Level 2)

Disc 2
7

515 **aisle** [áil] 通路
I'd prefer sitting on the aisle, if you don't mind.
よかったら、私は通路側に座るのが好きなのです。

516 **auditorium** [ɔ̀ːdətɔ́ːriəm] 講堂
The speech contest will be held in the main auditorium.
スピーチコンテストはメイン講堂で開催されるでしょう。

517 **blizzard** [blízərd] 大吹雪
The weatherman predicts blizzard conditions starting as early as 10 a.m.
天気予報官は早くも午前10時には大吹雪の状態が始まると予報しています。

518 **break room**　　　　休憩室
The new coffee machine in the break room makes the best coffee I've ever tasted.
休憩室の新しいコーヒー自動販売機は、私が今までに味わった中で最高のコーヒーを作ります。

519 **condominium** [kàndəmíniəm]　　分譲マンション
The best thing about a condominium is that there's no yard to take care of.
分譲マンションについて最も良いことは、手入れをする庭がないことです。

520 **construction** [kənstrʌ́kʃən]　建設
We're living here temporarily while our new home is under construction.
新しい家を建設中、一時的にここに住んでいます。

521 **daycare center**　　　　託児所、保育園
"Who watches your son while you're attending class?"
"I drop him off at the college daycare center."
「授業に出ている間、誰が息子の面倒をみるのですか」
「大学の託児所に預けます」

522 **development** [divéləpmənt]　開発
Logging and land development are destroying many animals' habitats.
木材の伐採、土地開発が多くの動物の生息地を破壊しています。

523 **downpour** [dáunpɔ̀ːr]　　どしゃ降り
I had to bicycle all the way home in a downpour.
どしゃ降りの中、家までずっと自転車に乗って帰らねばなりませんでした。

524 **eco-tour** [ìːkoutúər]　　エコツアー
This time I'm joining an eco-tour to Costa Rica.
今度はコスタリカのエコツアーに参加するでしょう。

525 **environment** [inváiərənmənt] 環境
The environment as a whole is under increasing stress and strain.
全体として環境はストレスと緊張の高まりを受けています。

526 **extinction** [ikstíŋkʃən]　　絶滅
Scientists say that over 300 bird speecies are threatened with extinction.
科学者は300種以上の鳥が絶滅の危機にあると言います。

527 **fitness center**　　フィットネスセンター
I haven't seen you at the fitness center for a couple of weeks.
2、3週間、フィットネスセンターであなたを見かけませんでした。

528 **multiplex** [mʌ́ltəplèks]　　シネコン、複合映画館
Did you hear about the new multiplex theater they're going to build in the mall?
モールに造る予定の新しいシネコンについて聞きましたか。

529 **natural resources**　　天然資源
Help us preserve our natural resources by dressing warmly and turning down the heat.
温かい服装をし、暖房を弱くすることで天然資源を守る手助けをしてください。

530 **natural surroundings**　　自然環境
All photograph entries must be of wild birds in their natural surroundings.
すべての応募写真は自然環境の中にいる野鳥のものでなければなりません。

531 **nightfall** [náitfɔ̀:l]　　日暮れ、日没
At least 15 inches of snow are expected to accumulate by nightfall.
少なくとも15インチの積雪が日没までにあると予報されています。

532 **North Star**　　北極星
You can just see the North Star above the top of the mountain.
ちょうど山頂の上に北極星を見ることができます。

533 **research vessel**　　調査船
My professor got me a job on an environmental research vessel.
教授は環境調査船に乗る仕事を私にくれました。

534 **site** [sáit]　　場所
Every year the organization designates certain areas as world

heritage sites.
毎年その組織は世界遺産地として、ある地域を指定します。

7 情報 (Level 1)

Disc 2
8

535 **ad** [ǽd]　　　　　　広告
I'd like to place an employment ad in the classified section of your magazine.
あなたの雑誌の項目別広告欄に求人広告を載せたいと思います。

536 **article** [ά:rtikl]　　　記事
He's written many books and articles on science and technology topics.
彼は科学と技術のトピックについて多くの本と記事を書きました。

537 **attendance** [əténdəns]　出席
Attendance at the lecture series is mandatory for all executives.
講演シリーズへの出席はすべての役職者に必須です。

538 **average** [ǽvəridʒ]　　平均
Japanese women live an average of 85 years, while the life expectancy of Japanese men is 78.
日本人女性は平均85歳まで生き、一方日本人男性の平均寿命は78歳です。

539 **blog** [blάg]　　　　　ブログ
This year's most-used new word was "blog," a shortened version of "Web log."
今年最も使われた新語は「ウェブ・ログ」の短縮形「ブログ」でした。

540 **commercial** [kəmə́:rʃəl]　コマーシャル
I have no idea what this commercial is supposed to be advertising.
このコマーシャルは何を宣伝しようとしているのか分かりません。

541 **condition** [kəndíʃən]　状態
All the items have been tested to make sure they are in perfect condition.

83

すべての品目は完全な状態であることを確かめるために検査されました。

542 **degree** [digríː] 度
Normal body temperature is 98.6 degrees Fahrenheit.
平常体温は華氏98.6度です。

543 **direction** [dirékʃən] 道順
Let's ask that police officer for directions.
あのおまわりさんに道を尋ねましょう。

544 **display** [displéi] 展示
The museum has a large display of early model "flying machines."
博物館には初期モデルの「航空機」の大規模な展示があります。

545 **experience** [ikspíəriəns] 経験
Do you have any experience in the hotel management field?
ホテル経営の分野に経験がありますか。

546 **fault** [fɔ́ːlt] ミス、過失
How could it be my fault since I wasn't even there?
そこにいなかったのに、どうして私の過失なのでしょうか。

547 **forecast** [fɔ́ːrkæst] 天気予報
The forecast says the temperature's going to drop down to at least 15 below freezing tonight.
天気予報は、今夜は気温が少なくとも氷点下15度まで下がると言います。

548 **grief** [gríːf] 悲しみ
Some people need counseling to deal with their grief.
悲しみに対処するのにカウンセリングを必要とする人もいます。

549 **head** [héd] 理解
Most of the critic's writing is a little over my head.
ほとんどの批評家の文書は私には少し理解できません。

550 **information** [infərméiʃən] 情報
For information on flights and schedules, press 1 now.
フライトと時刻表の情報には、1を押してください。

551 **interest** [íntərəst] 　　　　　関心
All of us in personnel have read your résumé with a great deal of interest.
人事課の私たちみんなはとても関心をもってあなたの履歴書を読みました。

552 **link** [líŋk] 　　　　　関連
A University of California study has found a direct link between asthma and smog.
カリフォルニア大学の調査で、ぜんそくとスモッグの間の直接の関連が分かりました。

553 **luck** [lʌ́k] 　　　　　幸運
We wish you the best of luck in your search for a teaching position.
教員の職を探すことがうまくいきますように。

554 **manual** [mǽnjuəl] 　　　　　マニュアル、説明書
Do you have some sort of instruction manual I could read?
私が読める何らかの取扱いマニュアルを持っていますか。

555 **message** [mésiʤ] 　　　　　メッセージ
I send and receive 20 or 30 e-mail messages every day.
私は毎日20か30のEメールのメッセージを送り、受けとります。

556 **mistake** [mistéik] 　　　　　誤り、ミス
I found six spelling mistakes in this short letter.
この短い手紙に6つのスペリングの誤りを見つけました。

557 **record** [rékərd] 　　　　　記録
The veteran pitcher has a record of 229 wins and 143 losses.
ベテランの投手は229勝143敗の記録を持っています。

558 **result** [rizʌ́lt] 　　　　　結果
As a result of the lack of public transportation, most people drive to work every day.
公共輸送機関の不足の結果として、たいていの人は毎日車で働きに行きます。

559 **score** [skɔ́ːr] 　　　　　点数
Our students' test scores in science and math are not what they once were.

生徒たちの理科と数学のテストの点は、かつてほどではありません。

560 **sign** [sáin]　　　　　　　掲示
May I put up this "Obama for President" sign in your front lawn?
前の芝地にこの「大統領にオバマを」の掲示をかかげてもよろしいですか。

561 **speech** [spíːtʃ]　　　　　　スピーチ
It's a club whose members learn to give effective speeches.
それはメンバーが効果的なスピーチをすることを学ぶクラブです。

562 **temperature** [témpərətʃər]　温度
The forecast says that the temperature will reach 35°C this afternoon.
予報では温度は今日の午後35°に達するでしょう。

563 **theme** [θíːm]　　　　　　テーマ
The novel's main theme is love in all its varieties.
小説の主なテーマはあらゆる形の愛です。

564 **tip** [típ]　　　　　　　　秘訣
Thanks to your tip, my bowling average has improved by 50 points.
あなたがくれた秘訣のおかげで、ボーリング・アベレージが50点上がりました。

565 **waste** [wéist]　　　　　　無駄
Commuting back and forth to work just seems like a waste of time.
仕事で行ったり来たり通勤することは、ただ時間の無駄のように思えます。

566 **weather** [wéðər]　　　　　天候
Due to the unseasonably warm weather, the cherry blossoms are already in full bloom.
季節はずれの暖かい天候のため、桜の花はすでに満開です。

7 情報（Level 2）

Disc 2
9

567 **anniversary** [æ̀nəvə́ːrsəri]　記念日
New York City recently celebrated the 100th anniversary of the

opening of its subway system.
ニューヨーク市は最近、地下鉄システム開通100周年記念日を祝いました。

568 **announcement** [ənáunsmənt]　　アナウンス、お知らせ
I apologize for interrupting your classes, but I have an important announcement to make.
授業を妨げてすみませんが、重要なアナウンスがあります。

569 **appearance** [əpíərəns]　　出席
The group has had to cancel tonight's appearance due to inclement weather.
そのグループは荒れ模様の天気のため、今夜の出演を中止しなければなりませんでした。

570 **back issues**　　バックナンバー
Does the library have back issues of *Time* magazine?
図書館は雑誌『タイム』のバックナンバーがありますか。

571 **boiling point**　　沸点
On the Celsius scale, the boiling point is 100 degrees, and the freezing point zero degrees.
摂氏の目盛りでは沸点は100度で、氷点は０度です。

572 **business** [bíznis]　　事柄、関心事
Mind your own business. / I'm afraid that's none of your business.
私のことに口を出さないでください。／あなたには関係ありません。

573 **Celsius** [sélsiəs]　　摂氏
The Celsius scale is named for the Swedish astronomer, Anders Celsius.
摂氏目盛りはスウェーデンの天文学者、アンデルス・セルシウスにちなんで名づけられています。

574 **character** [kǽrəktər]　　人格
Believing that Santa knows if they have been "good" or "bad" helps children develop moral character.
「良かった」か「悪かった」かをサンタが知っていると信じることは、子供の道徳的人格を育てる手助けになります。

575 **conclusion** [kənklú:ʒən] 結論
We have reached the conclusion that your manuscript is not publishable.
あなたの原稿は出版できないという結論にいたりました。

576 **consideration** [kənsìdəréiʃən] 考慮
Each employee's proposal and suggestion deserve careful consideration.
各社員の提案と提言は慎重に考慮するに値します。

577 **contribution** [kɑ̀ntribjú:ʃən] 貢献
I would like a job where I can make a contribution to society.
社会に貢献できる仕事が欲しいのですが。

578 **demographic** [dèməgrǽfik] 購買層
This layout projects the right image for our target demographic.
このレイアウトはターゲットの購買層の正しいイメージを投影しています。

579 **documentary** [dɑ̀kjuméntəri] ドキュメンタリー、記録映画
Did you happen to catch that documentary about AIDS on BBC last night?
昨夜BBCのエイズについてのドキュメンタリーをたまたま見ましたか。

580 **earned run average** （投手の）防御率
Nelson's 1.73 earned run average was the lowest in both leagues.
ネルソンの1.73の防御率は両リーグで最も低かったです。

581 **emotional uplift** 感情の高揚
The new "pet" robot responds to stroking, giving patients an emotional uplift and lowering stress levels.
新しい「ペット」のロボットはなでることに応え、患者に感情の高揚を与え、ストレスを下げます。

582 **exterior** [ikstíəriər] 外観
Plans to improve the hotel's exterior have been delayed because of budget problems.
ホテルの外観を改造する計画は、予算の問題で遅れています。

583 **Eye of Providence** 　　　神の目
The eye on the pyramid on the U.S. dollar is called the "Eye of Providence."
アメリカのドル紙幣にあるピラミッドの目は「神の目」と呼ばれます。

584 **Fahrenheit** [fǽrənhàit] 　　　華氏
On the Fahrenheit scale, water boils at 212 degrees and water freezes at 32 degrees.
華氏目盛りでは、水は212度で沸騰し、32度で凍ります。

585 **figure** [fígjər] 　　　数字
Despite these alarming figures, over 50 million Americans still smoke.
これらの驚くべき数字にもかかわらず、5千万以上のアメリカ人がまだタバコを吸っています。

586 **fine** [fáin] 　　　罰金
Do you charge fines for overdue books?
返却期限を過ぎた本に罰金を課しますか。

587 **flier / flyer** [fláiər] 　　　ビラ、チラシ
When the restaurant isn't busy, I have to stand on the corner and pass out fliers.
レストランが忙しくないとき、街角に立ってチラシを配らなければなりません。

588 **harassment** [hərǽsmənt] 　　　セクハラ、いやがらせ
If I were you, I'd report him to your manager for harassment.
もし私があなたなら、彼をセクハラで経営者に報告するでしょう。

589 **instructions** [instrʌ́kʃənz] 　　　使用説明書
Instructions should be clear and concise so that even a child can follow them.
使用説明書は子供でも解るように明快で簡潔であるべきです。

590 **intensive care** 　　　集中治療
Patients in intensive care have their vital signs checked continuously.
集中治療の患者は絶えず生命徴候を検査してもらいます。

591 **last minute notice** 土壇場での通知、ぎりぎりの通知
We sincerely apologize for the last minute notice and inconvenience.
土壇場での通知と不便をかけましたことに心からお詫びいたします。

592 **looked-up word** 調べられた単語
One dictionary publisher released its list of the most frequently looked-up words of the year.
ある辞書出版社が一年間で最もよく調べられた単語リストを公表しました。

593 **lost** [lɔ(:)st] 迷子の、いなくなった
The young girl is offering a $10 reward for her lost kitten.
若い女性が迷子の子猫に10ドルの報酬を申し出ています。

594 **misunderstanding** [mìsʌndərstǽndiŋ] 誤解
Let's speak frankly so that there will be no misunderstanding between us.
私たちの間に誤解がないように率直に話しましょう。

595 **nominal fee** 手数料
We'll deliver your order to your home for a nominal fee of only $5.00.
ほんの5ドルの手数料で注文品を家まで配達いたします。

596 **penalty** [pénəlti] 罰金
There are severe penalties for companies who breach environmental laws.
環境保護法を破った会社には厳しい罰金があります。

597 **personal journal** 個人的な日記
A "blog" is a Website that is like an online personal journal.
「ブログ」はオンライン上の個人的な日記のようなウェブサイトです。

598 **presentation** [prèzəntéiʃən] プレゼンテーション、発表
I think your topic is too broad for a five-minute presentation.
あなたのトピックは5分のプレゼンテーションにはあまりにも広すぎると思います。

599 **regards** [rigá:rdz] よろしくとのあいさつ

"Would you give my regards to all the staff there?"
"I'll make a point of it".
「そこのスタッフの皆さんによろしくお伝えくださいますか」
「必ずそうします」

600 **renewal** [rinjúːəl]　　　再開発、リニューアル
The city has undertaken a mammoth downtown renewal project.
その都市はダウンタウン再開発巨大プロジェクトに着手しています。

601 **resolution** [rèzəlúːʃən]　　決心
Have you made your New Year's resolutions yet?
もう新年の決心をしましたか。

602 **review** [rivjúː]　　　批評、書評
All the movie's reviews have been good so far.
今のところ、すべての映画批評は良いです。

603 **satisfaction** [sæ̀tisfǽkʃən]　満足
The CEO expressed satisfaction with the results of the PR campaign.
最高経営責任者はPRキャンペーンの結果に満足感を表しました。

604 **saw** [sɔ́ː]　　　ことわざ
An old saw says that "No news is good news."
古いことわざは「便りのないのは良い便り」と言います。

605 **sense** [séns]　　　意味、道理
Buying a home makes a lot more sense than renting.
家を買うことは借りることよりも、ずっと道理にかなっています。

606 **statement** [stéitmənt]　　説明
The President will make a statement to the press shortly.
大統領はまもなく報道陣に説明をするでしょう。

607 **statistics** [stətístiks]　　統計
According to the latest statistics, each year some 440,000 Americans die from smoking-related causes.
最新の統計によると、毎年約44万人のアメリカ人が喫煙と関係のある原因で死にます。

608 **wage** [wéidʒ] 賃金

"Do we get paid extra for working on a national holiday?"
"Yes, one and a half times your regular wage."
「国民の祝祭日に働くと余分にお金がもらえますか」
「ええ、通常の賃金の1.5倍です」

＜文法のまとめ２＞

分詞

現在分詞（-ing）、過去分詞（-ed）は形容詞として名詞を修飾

名詞の前

1. 現在分詞〔自動詞〕で現在の状態「～している」
   a crying child（泣いている子供）, a running dog（走っている犬）

2. 過去分詞〔他動詞〕で受身の意味「～された」
   a broken computer（故障したコンピューター）
   an excited crowd（興奮した群衆）

3. 過去分詞〔自動詞〕で完了「たった今～した」
   a departed train（たった今出た列車）

名詞の後：関係代名詞が省略

4. 現在分詞
   The girl singing (=who is singing) is Jessica's daughter.
   （歌っているのはジェシカの娘です）

5. 過去分詞
   Do you remember the sculpture exhibited (=that was exhibited) at the art museum?
   （美術館で展示されていた彫刻を覚えていますか）

分詞構文：分詞が動詞と接続詞の働き

6. 時
   Signing a contract, you must read its terms carefully.
   (=When you sign)
   （契約書に署名するときは、契約条件を読まなければなりません）

7. 原因・理由
   The weather being nice, we decided to go hiking.
   (=As the weather was)
   （天気が良かったので、ハイキングに行くことに決めました）

8. 条件
   Going straight, you'll come to the branch office.
   (=If you go)
   (真っ直ぐ行くと、その支社にたどり着きます)

9. 譲歩
   Living within ten minutes of each, we seldom get together.
   (=Though we live)
   (それぞれ10分以内に住んでいるけれど、私たちはめったに会いません)

10. 付帯状況
    She picked up the goods, putting them on the shelf.
    (=and put)
    (彼女は商品を手にとって、棚に置きました)

11. 分詞構文の否定：not, never を分詞の前
    Not knowing how to handle the current situation, Mike asked the boss.
    (=Because Mike did not know how to handle the situation, he asked the boss)
    (マイクは現在の状態をどう処理していいのかわからなかったので、上司に尋ねました)

12. 分詞構文の完了形：having + 過去分詞
    Having worked in the accounting department for 30 years, I know all our clients.
    (=As I have worked in the accounting department for 30 years, I know all our clients.)
    (30年間会計課で働いたので、すべての顧客を知っています)

to 不定詞（1）

1. 名詞的用法：主語、補語、目的語になる「～すること」
   My dream is to write a novel.
   (私の夢は小説を書くことです)
   I want to study political science.
   (政治学を学びたいです)
   ✕ I don't mind to smoke.　　◯ I don't mind smoking.

2. 形容詞的用法：名詞を後ろから修飾「～すべき」
   There is something to drink in the fridge.
   (冷蔵庫に何か飲み物があります)

3. 副詞的用法：動詞を後ろから修飾。目的「するために」 理由「〜して」
   Emily goes to medical school to be a doctor.
   （エミリーは医者になるために医学部へ行っています）
   Anyway, I'm glad to hear you are doing well.
   （とにかく、あなたがうまく行っているのを聞いてうれしいです）

4. 不定詞の否定形：to の前に not, never をつける。
   My boss advised her not to be late for the meeting.
   （上司は彼女に会合に遅れないように忠告しました）

5. 不定詞＋前置詞：talk with, live in などで名詞を修飾する場合は前置詞をつける。
   My father bought a condominium for us to live in.
   （父は私たちが住むためのマンションを購入しました）

to 不定詞（2）

1. 原形不定詞：to をつけない不定詞
   知覚動詞・使役動詞＋O（目的語）＋原形不定詞の形
   知覚動詞：feel, hear, see
   I saw her go into the conference center yesterday.
   （昨日彼女が会議場へ入って行くのを見ました）

2. 受動態では to 不定詞
   She was seen to go into the conference center yesterday.
   （昨日彼女は会議場へ入っていくのが見られました）

3. 使役動詞：have, let, make
   Liz had her husband carry the suitcase.
   （リズは息子にスーツケースを運ばせました）

4. 完了不定詞
   述語動詞の時より以前のことを表す場合は to have ＋過去分詞
   Michael seems to have been free on that day.
   (＝It seems that Michael was free on that day.)
   （その日、マイケルは暇だったようです）

5. to 不定詞を含む慣用表現
   can afford to「〜する余裕がある」enough to「〜するのに十分」fail to「〜できない」get [come] to「〜するようになる」have only to do「〜さえすればよい」in order to (＝so as to)「〜するために」in order not to (＝so as not to)「〜しないために」so … as to〜「〜するほど

…」too ... to「あまり…なので〜できない」

6. 独立不定詞：1つの意味を表す。
needless to say「言うまでもなく」not to mention「〜は言うに及ばず」so to speak「いわば」strange to say「奇妙なことに」to be frank (with you)「率直に言うと」to be honest「正直に言うと」to be sure「確かに」to begin with「まず第一に」to make matters worse「さらに悪いことに」to say nothing of「〜は言うにおよばず」to tell the truth「実を言うと」

動名詞 (1)

1. 動詞の原形に -ing：主語、補語、目的語、前置詞の目的語になり、「すること」の意味
Emily is fond of reading detective stories.
（エミリーは推理小説を読むことが好きです）

2. 動名詞の完了形
述語動詞より以前の時を表すときは having + 過去分詞「〜したこと」
He is ashamed of having done what he did.
（彼は自分がしたことを恥ずかしく思います）

3. 動名詞の受動態：being + 過去分詞「〜されること」
Everyone likes being praised once in a while.
（みんな時々ほめられることが好きです）

4. 過去の受身を表すとき：having been + 過去分詞「〜されたこと」
I'm proud of having been elected to committee chairman.
（委員会の議長に選ばれたことを誇りに思います）

5. 動名詞の否定形：not [never] + 動名詞「〜がないこと」
Julia always complains of not having enough income.
（ジュリアはいつも十分な収入がないことに不満を言います）

動名詞 (2)

1. 動名詞の意味上の主語：代名詞［名詞］の所有格［目的格］
He never dreamed of his advertising firm going bankrupt.
（彼の広告会社が倒産することを夢にも思いませんでした）

2. 動名詞を目的語にとる動詞：
admit「認める」avoid「避ける」deny「否定する」enjoy「楽しむ」practice「実行する」escape「逃れる」give up「やめる」finish「終える」

go on「続ける」mind「気にかける」put off「延期する」suggest「提案する」

3. 不定詞を目的語にとる動詞：
agree「同意する」arrange「手配する」ask「尋ねる」care「したいと思う」choose「選ぶ」decide「決める」desire「望む」expect「つもりである」hope「望む」plan「計画する」pretend「ふりをする」promise「約束する」propose「申し出る」refuse「断る」mean「つもりである」want「欲する」wish「願う」

4. 動名詞も不定詞も目的語にとる動詞
意味が変わらない：
begin「始める」continue「続ける」fear「恐れる」like「好む」start「始まる」
意味が異なる：
forget　　（-ing:〜したことを忘れる　to:〜するのを忘れる）
remember（-ing:〜したことを覚えている　to: 忘れずに〜する）
stop　　　（-ing:〜するのをやめる　　to:〜するために立ち止まる）
try　　　　（-ing: 試しに〜をしてみる　to:〜しようと試みる）
I remember sending email to him.
（彼にEメールを送ったことを覚えています）・・〈すでに送った〉
I remember to send email to him.
（彼にEメールを忘れずに送ります）・・・・・〈これから送る〉

5. 動名詞の慣用表現
be worth -ing「〜する価値がある」
cannot help -ing「〜しないわけにはいかない」
feel like -ing「〜したい気がする」
It is no use -ing「〜してもむだである」
make a point of -ing「〜することにしている」
mind -ing「〜することをいやがる」
not ... without -ing「…すれば必ず〜する」
of one's own -ing「自分で〜した」
on -ing「〜するとすぐに」
prevent [keep] ... from -ing「…に〜させない」
There is no -ing「〜できない」
worth -ing「〜する価値がある」

形容詞　副詞

形容詞（Level 1）　Disc 2　10

609 **available** [əvéiləbl]　手に入る
Almost all the information you need is available online these days.
近ごろ、あなたが必要とするほとんどすべての情報はオンラインで手に入ります。

610 **dangerous** [déindʒərəs]　危険な
It is dangerous to swim in the ocean when the tide is going out.
潮が引くとき海で泳ぐのは危険です。

611 **due** [djúː]　予定の
New CDs are due back in two days.
新しいCDは2日以内に返却予定です。

612 **empty** [émpti]　空の、がらんとした
The bed of the truck is empty.
トラックの荷台は空です。

613 **expensive** [ikspénsiv]　高価な
Organic fruits and vegetables are quite expensive.
有機栽培の果物と野菜は、かなり高価です。

614 **finest** [fáinəst]　とてもすばらしい
The handcrafted cabinet is made of the finest wood.
手作業でこしらえたキャビネットはとてもすばらしい木材で作られています。

615 **formal** [fɔ́ːrməl]　フォーマルな、正式の
This dinner party is quite formal, so wear a suit and tie.
夕食パーティーはとてもフォーマルだから、スーツとネクタイをしなさい。

616 **free** [fríː]　無料の
The swimming pool and fitness center are free for hotel guests.
水泳プールとフィットネスセンターは、ホテルの客には無料です。

617 **hourly** [áuərli]　　一時間単位で
Hourly parking is available in the parking garage.
この駐車場では、一時間単位で駐車できます。

618 **interesting** [íntərəstiŋ]　　興味深い
I don't mind being transferred as long as the job is interesting.
仕事が興味深いものである限り、転勤はいやではありません。

619 **latest** [léitist]　　最新の
Do you have Stephen King's latest novel?
スチーブン・キングの最新の小説がありますか。

620 **local** [lóukəl]　　地元の
My sister will probably spend her time going to local galleries and museums.
私の姉はおそらく地元の画廊や博物館へ出かけて時間を過ごすでしょう。

621 **loyal** [lɔ́iəl]　　誠実な、忠実な
One loyal friend is worth a thousand relatives.
1人の誠実な友人は、千人の親類の値打ちがあります。

622 **natural** [nǽtʃərəl]　　あたりまえの、自然な
A natural act of love and attention like a simple hug can save a baby's life.
ただの抱擁のような自然な愛と配慮の行為が、赤ん坊の命を救うことになります。

623 **noisy** [nɔ́izi]　　騒がしい
The library is too noisy and crowded to study in.
図書館はあまりにも騒がしく、混んでいて勉強できません。

624 **outdoor** [àutdɔ́:r]　　戸外の
Smoking is only permitted in outdoor cafés.
喫煙は戸外のカフェでのみできます。

625 **pale** [péil]　　青ざめた、青白い
When she heard the news, she turned pale and fainted.
その知らせを聞いたとき、彼女は青ざめ、気を失いました。

99

626 **perfect** [pə́ːrfikt]　　　　完璧な
Kickboxing is the perfect way to kick yourself into shape.
キックボクシングはあなた自身を好ましい状態にする完璧な方法です。

627 **powerful** [páuərfəl]　　　　力強い
The concluding novel shows how powerful a writer Rowling has become.
完結編の小説はローリングがどれほど力強い作家になったかを示しています。

628 **proper** [prápər]　　　　適切な
What's proper behavior in one culture is improper in another.
1つの文化で適切な振舞いであるものは、他の文化では不適切です。

629 **quiet** [kwáiət]　　　　静かな
Could you please keep the boys quiet while I'm on the phone?
電話をしている間は少年たちを静かにさせていただけますか。

630 **ready** [rédi]　　　　用意のできた
He is in his pajamas and ready for bed at 9:00 every night.
彼は毎晩9時にパジャマを着て寝る用意ができています。

631 **refreshing** [rifréʃiŋ]　　　　元気を回復させる、爽快にする
Is your sleep not as refreshing as it could be?
あなたの睡眠はそれほどには爽快でないのですか。

632 **regular** [réɡjulər]　　　　レギュラーサイズの、普通の大きさの
"Do you want regular or decaffeinated coffee?"
"Regular's fine."
「レギュラーサイズか、カフェインなしのコーヒーが欲しいですか」
「レギュラーサイズがいいです」

633 **rocky** [ráki]　　　　岩の多い
The soil in this area is too rocky for farming.
この地域の土は、耕すにはあまりにも岩が多いです。

634 **safe** [séif]　　　　安全な
The water in this pond is not safe for drinking.
この池の水は飲むのに安全ではありません。

635 **similar** [símələr] 似ている、類似の
It's a local cheese similar to sharp cheddar.
それは、においの強いチェダーチーズに似ている地元のチーズです。

636 **special** [spéʃəl] 特別な
Today is a special day, children, because we have a famous visitor.
みなさん、有名な訪問者があるので今日は特別な日ですよ。

637 **straight** [stréit] まっすぐな
The road is straight and narrow all the way from Chicago to the Rocky Mountains.
シカゴからロッキー山脈まではずっと道路がまっすぐで狭いです。

638 **strange** [stréindʒ] 未知の、見知らぬ
What in the world is that strange looking animal?
いったい全体その見たことのない動物は何なですか。

639 **terrible** [térəbl] ひどい、激しい
I have this terrible pain running up and down my right leg.
右足に激痛が走っています。

640 **terrific** [tərífik] ものすごい、すてきな
This pate goes well with crackers and makes a terrific appetizer.
このパテはクラッカーとよく合い、ものすごく食欲がでます。

641 **tough** [tʌf] 厳しい、難しい
Many companies are facing tough competition from China.
多くの会社は中国からの厳しい競争に直面しています。

642 **warm** [wɔ:rm] 暖かい
Everyone, please give tonight's guest of honor a warm welcome.
みなさん、今夜の来賓に暖かい歓迎をお願いします。

643 **willing** [wíliŋ] 〜するのをいとわない、喜んで〜する
Are you willing to work nights and weekends?
週末や夜働くことをいといませんか。

644 **wrong** [rɔ́:ŋ] 調子が悪い

Is there sometning wrong with the copy machine?
このコピー機はどこか調子が悪いのですか。

形容詞（Level 2） Disc 2 / 11

645 **apt** [ǽpt]　　　　　　〜しやすい
Children who breathe polluted air are more apt to come down with the illness.
汚染した空気を吸う子供たちは病気にかかりやすいです。

646 **brand new**　　　　　真新しい
I'm pleased to announce that we have a brand new member of our staff.
社員に新しいメンバーが加わることを喜んでお知らせします。

647 **ceramic** [sərǽmik]　　セラミックの、陶製の
The floor is covered with ceramic tile from Italy.
床はイタリア製のセラミックタイルで覆われています。

648 **comparable** [kámpərəbl]　〜と同様の、同等の
Many used DVDs can be bought on sale at prices comparable to the rental charge for new titles.
多くの中古のDVDは新しいタイトルのレンタル料と同等の料金で買うことができます。

649 **competitive** [kəmpétətiv]　競争の
In today's competitive market, customers are looking for quality goods at reasonable prices.
今日の競争市場では、顧客は手ごろな価格で良質の商品を探しています。

650 **complex** [kɑmpléks]　複雑な、込み入った
Gradually, the Chinese language became more precise and at the same time more complex.
だんだん中国語はより正確になると同時に複雑になりました。

651 **confidential** [kànfədénʃəl]　秘密の、マル秘扱いの
The telephone service offers free confidential counseling, round the

102

clock.
電話サービスは24時間、無料で秘密厳守のカウンセリングを提供します。

652 **convenient** [kənvíːniənt] 便利な
Users complain that the new OS isn't as convenient as it could be.
ユーザーは新しいOSがそれほど便利ではないと不満を言います。

653 **conventional** [kənvénʃənəl] ありきたりの
Our MultiMeal 750 is more than just your conventional rice cooker.
マルチミール750はまさにありきたりの炊飯器以上のものです。

654 **defective** [diféktiv] 欠陥のある
Some 50,000 cars have been recalled for defective air bags.
約5万台の車がエアバッグの欠陥で回収されました。

655 **drive-thru / drive-through** [dráivθrùː] ドライブスルーの
There's always a long line at the drive-thru windows.
ドライブスルーの窓口はいつも長い列があります。

656 **estimated** [éstimèitid] おおよその、推定の
The team traded their star centerfielder for an estimated 115 million dollars.
そのチームは推定1億1千5百万ドルでセンターのスター選手をトレードしました。

657 **excellent** [éksələnt] すばらしい、良い
The players all reported to spring training in excellent shape.
選手たちはみんな良い体調にするため春季トレーニングをしました。

658 **fluffy** [flʌfi] ふわふわした
Just feel how soft and fluffy this kitten's fur is.
ちょっとこの子猫の毛がどれほど柔らかくふわふわしているか感じてください。

659 **guaranteed** [gæ̀rəntíːd] 保証した
The security system provides peace of mind and guaranteed satisfaction.
セキュリティー・システムは心の安らぎと保証された満足を与えます。

660 **heavy-duty** [hèvidjúːti] 丈夫な、頑丈な

The kitchen has a heavy-duty dishwasher and garbage compactor.
台所は丈夫な食器洗い機とゴミ処理器があります。

661 **impressive** [imprésiv]　　　印象的な
We found your list of publications very impressive.
あなたの出版物のリストはとても印象的であることが分かりました。

662 **insightful** [ínsàitfəl]　　　洞察に満ちた
Thank you all for your insightful comments on this month's reading club selection.
今月の読書クラブの選集についての洞察に満ちた意見をありがとうございます。

663 **legendary** [lédʒəndèri]　　　伝説的な
Marilyn Monroe's legendary beauty will live forever.
マリリン・モンローの伝説的な美しさは永遠に生き続けるでしょう。

664 **luxury** [lʌ́kʃəri]　　　豪華な
A luxury Mediterranean cruise is a little beyond our means right now.
今豪華な地中海のクルーズは少し身分不相応です。
　　luxury market 高級品市場
　　luxurious [lʌgʒú(ə)riəs]〔形〕贅沢な、高級な

665 **major** [méidʒər]　　　主な
Traffic congestion has become a major problem because of the Lake Washington Bridge closure.
ワシントン湖ブリッジの閉鎖のため、交通渋滞が主な問題になりました。

666 **multi-purpose** [mʌltipə́ːrpəs] 多目的の
It's a new multi-purpose grammar, usage, and spelling program for writers.
それは作家にとって新しい多目的の文法、語法、スペリングのプログラムです。

667 **out of order**　　　故障して
The elevator will be out of order until at least 4 p.m.
エレベーターは少なくとも午後4時まで故障しているでしょう。

668 **overdue** [òuvərdjúː]　　　返却期限を過ぎた、遅れた

Hip-Hop Music and Video has a dollar a day fine for overdue CDs.
ヒップポップミュージック＆ビデオは返却期限を過ぎたCDに1日1ドルの罰金を課します。

669 **practical** [prǽktikəl]　　実用的な、役立つ
Our writers give practical advice on all kinds of consumer issues.
私たちの著者はあらゆる種類の消費者問題に役立つ助言をします。

670 **rambunctious** [ræmbʌ́ŋkʃəs]　　にぎやかな
The teacher told Billy's mom that her son is too loud and rambunctious.
先生はビリーの母に、息子があまりにも大声でにぎやかであると言いました。

671 **reasonable** [ríːzənəbl]　　手ごろな、妥当な
You'd be surprised at how reasonable some of the new models are.
新モデルのいくつかが、どれほど手ごろな値段であるかについて驚くでしょう。

672 **recycled** [rìːsáikld]　　再生された
The magazine is printed on recycled paper.
その雑誌は再生紙に印刷されています。

673 **responsible** [rispánsəbl]　　責任のある
It is still not clear who was responsible for the accident.
誰がその事故の責任者なのか、まだ明らかではありません。

674 **revolutionary** [rèvəlúːʃənèri]　　革新的な、斬新な
Thanks to a revolutionary technology, our carpets are completely stain resistant.
革新的な技術のおかげで、私たちのカーペットは全く汚れがありません。

675 **rewarding** [riwɔ́ːrdiŋ]　　価値ある、満足が得られる
The transportation museum can be a rewarding experience for both parents and children.
交通博物館は両親と子供の両方にとって価値ある経験になります。

676 **scientific** [sàiəntífik]　　科学の、理科の
These results show how poor the state of American scientific education is.

これらの結果はアメリカの理科教育の状態がいかに不十分かを示しています。

677 **strict** [stríkt]　　　　厳しい、厳格な
The drunk-driving laws are much stricter these days.
近ごろ、飲酒運転法はずっと厳しいです。

678 **successive** [səksésiv]　　　連続的な
With each successive book, the author's stories have become deeper and darker.
それぞれの連続本で、その作家の物語はより深くより暗くなってきました。

679 **suspicious** [səspíʃəs]　　　疑わしい、不審な
Report any suspicious behavior to the police immediately.
どんな不審な行動でも、警察にすぐ届けてください。

680 **sympathetic** [simpəθétik]　　親身になって、同情的な
One of our volunteer councelors will come on the line and lend you a sympathetic ear.
ボランティアのカウンセラーの一人が電話に出て、親身になって耳を傾けるでしょう。

681 **top-of-the-line**　　　最高級の、最も高価な
Winners will receive a top-of-the-line digital camera.
勝者は最高級のデジタルカメラを得るでしょう。

682 **traditional** [trdíʃənəl]　　　伝統的な
Now even the traditional Paris café is smoke-free.
今、伝統的なパリのカフェでさえ禁煙です。

683 **troublesome** [trʌ́blsəm]　　　困難な、めんどうな
Their furniture is cheap, but putting it together yourself is quite troublesome.
その家具は安いけれど、自分で組み立てるのはかなり困難です。

684 **trustworthy** [trʌ́stwə̀ːrði]　　信頼できる、当てになる
Today's banking customers want fast, friendly, trustworthy service.
今日、銀行の顧客は速く、親切で、信頼できるサービスを望みます。

685 **unforgettable** [ʌ̀nfəgétəbl]　　忘れられない

A "voluntourism" trip can be an unforgettable experience.
ボランツーリズムの旅行は忘れられない経験になります。

副詞（Level 1）

Disc 2
12

686 **carefully** [kéərfəli]　　　注意深く
Thinking environmentally means thinking more carefully about all the things we buy.
環境のことを考えることは、私たちが買う全てのものについてより注意深く考えることを意味します。

687 **completely** [kəmplí:tli]　　　完全に
The condo has been completely remodeled and made barrier-free.
その分譲マンションは完全に改造されバリアフリーになっています。

688 **freshly** [fréʃli]　　　新しく
All the units are freshly painted before we rent them out.
すべての部屋は、賃貸しする前に新しく塗装されました。

689 **immediately** [imí:diətli]　　　すぐに
Your bank has asked you to destroy your credit card immediately.
銀行はあなたのクレジットカードをすぐに破棄するように求めました。

690 **indoors** [indɔ́:rz]　　　屋内に、家に
A day like this is a good day to stay indoors all day.
こんな日は、終日家に閉じこもっているのに良い日です。

691 **lately** [léitli]　　　最近
I've been under a lot of stress at work lately.
最近仕事で多くのストレスがあります。

692 **occasionally** [əkéiʒənəli]　　　ときどき
I like to take a day off occasionally and spend some time alone.
ときどき休日を取って一人で過ごすのが好きです。

693 **quietly** [kwáiətli]　　　静かに

107

The pupils are quietly reading while their teacher is grading papers at her desk.
生徒たちは先生が机に向かってレポートの採点をしている間、静かに読書をしています。

694 **slightly** [sláitli]　　　少し、わずかに
This coffee has a slightly richer flavor than our regular blend.
このコーヒーは当店のレギュラー・ブレンドコーヒーよりも少し豊かな風味があります。

695 **slowly** [slóuli]　　　ゆっくりと
It's very important that you start out exercising slowly.
ゆっくりと運動を始めることがとても大切です。

696 **specially** [spéʃəli]　　　特別に
This is a specially equipped bus for wheelchair passengers.
これは車椅子の乗客のための特別な装備のあるバスです。

697 **throughout** [θru:áut]　　　すっかり、全く
There's new wall-to-wall carpet throughout the apartment.
アパートにはすっかり床一面に敷きつめた新しいカーペットがあります。

副詞 (Level 2)

Disc 2
13

698 **after all**　　　結局
My wife and I have decided to move after all.
妻と私は結局、引っ越すことに決めました。

699 **at least**　　　少なくとも
You must practice your golf swing at least 30 minutes a day.
少なくとも1日30分ゴルフのスイングを練習しなけれなりません。

700 **at the latest**　　　遅くとも
I should be home by 7:00 at the latest.
遅くとも7時には家にいるはずです。

701 **at the moment**　　　今のところ
The night manager is not here at the moment.

夜の管理者は今のところここにいません。

702 **automatically** [ɔ̀:təmǽtikəli] 自動的に
Just point and click, and your spelling is checked and corrected automatically.
ただ指さし、クリックすると、スペリングは自動的にチェックされ訂正されます。

703 **barely** [béərli] かろうじて、ほとんど〜ない
My arthritis is so bad at times I can barely walk.
関節炎は時々あまりにもひどいので、かろうじて歩けるぐらいです。

704 **casually** [kǽʒuəli] くだけて、カジュアルに
On Fridays, all the employees dress casually in jeans and polo shirts.
金曜日は、社員は全員ジーンズやポロシャツでカジュアルな服装をします。

705 **drastically** [drǽstikəli] 徹底的に、思い切って
Today's consumers are being forced to drastically cut back on living expenses.
今日の消費者は生活費を徹底的に削減せざるをえません。

706 **even then** それでもなお
I stayed up all night, and even then I had a hard time finishing the report.
徹夜しましたが、それでもなお報告書を仕上げるのに苦労しました。

707 **for good** 永久に、これを最後に
"Have you really given up hunting for good?"
"Yes. I've even given away all my guns and bullets."
「本当に狩をするのを永久に止めたのですか」
「はい、銃も弾丸もすべて手放すことさえしました」

708 **for the first time** 初めて
The number of people out of work fell to under four million for the first time.
失業者数は初めて4百万以下に下がりました。

709 **frankly speaking** 率直に言って
Frankly speaking, I'm getting sick of dealing with arrogant authors.

率直に言って、傲慢な著者を扱うのが嫌になっています。

710 **from now on**　　　　今後
Try to be more careful from now on.
今後、もっと注意するようにしなさい。

711 **more often than not**　　たいてい
You're late more often than not these days. What's up?
君は最近たいてい遅刻します。どうしたのですか。

712 **not once**　　　　一度たりとも
Not once have we regretted our decision to become vegetarians.
一度たりともベジタリアンになる決心を後悔したことはありません。

713 **once and for all**　　きっぱりと
The new drug will help smokers give up the habit once and for all.
その新しい薬はきっぱりと喫煙者に習慣を止めさせる手助けをするでしょう。

714 **online** [ὰnláin]　　　　オンラインで
You can get those shoes a lot cheaper if you buy them online.
オンラインで買うなら、ずっと安くそれらの靴を買うことができます。

715 **practically** [prǽktikəli]　　ほとんど、実際には
I spend practicallly every spare minute surfing the Web.
空き時間はほとんどいつもウェブをサーフして過ごします。

716 **simultaneously** [sàiməltéiniəsli]　　同時に
The human brain is not capable of handling several tasks simultaneously.
人間の脳は同時にいくつかの仕事を扱うことはできません。

717 **some other time**　　いつか
Bob called while you were out and said he'd call again some other time.
あなたが留守中にボブが電話をしてきて、いつかまた電話すると言いました。

718 **strictly** [stríktli]　　厳格に、固く
Online gambling and shopping while on the job are strictly taboo.

仕事中のオンラインでのギャンブルや買い物は固く禁じられています。

719 **succinctly** [səksíŋktli]　　簡潔に
He stated it most succinctly when he said, "We are all ready for change."
彼は「変化の用意ができた」と言ったとき、最も簡潔に述べました。

720 **surprisingly** [sərpráiziŋli]　驚いたことに、意外にも
"Was your annual bonus as big as you expected it to be?"
"Surprisingly, it was even bigger."
「毎年恒例のボーナスは予想していたほどの多さでしたか」
「驚いたことにずっと多かったです」

721 **this time**　　　　　　　今度は
This time, be sure to include the latest survey results in your report.
今度は、報告書に最新の調査結果を必ず含めてください。

＜文法のまとめ３＞

時制：現在、過去、未来、進行形、現在完了形

現在時制

1. 現在の習慣・状態
   John sometimes goes to New York on business.
   （ジョンは時々仕事でニューヨークへ行きます）

2. 一般的真理
   The early bird catches the worm.
   （早起きは三文の得）《ことわざ》

3. 未来の代用
   時や条件を表す副詞節（when, if）では、未来のことでも現在時制
   If it is fine tomorrow, I'll mow the lawn.
   （明日晴れなら、芝生を刈るでしょう）

過去時制

4. 過去の動作・状態や過去の習慣
   I signed up for your service two weeks ago.
   （２週間前にあなたのサービスを申し込みました）

未来時制

5. 未来のこと（単純未来）
   It will be warm this weekend.
   （今週の週末は暖かくなるでしょう）

6. 話し手の意思（意志未来）
   I will do my best to be a good parent.
   （良い親になるために最善を尽くすつもりです）

7. be about to, be going to, be to：
   The parade is about to start.
   （パレードが始まろうとしています）

進行形

8. 現在進行形：動作・出来事が現在進行中
   The company is planning to relocate its headquarters.
   (その会社は本社の移転を計画しています)

9. 過去進行形：動作・出来事が過去の時点で進行中
   He was working hard to gain financial independence.
   (彼は財政的に独立するために一生懸命に働いていました)

10. 進行形にしない動詞：
    状態を表す動詞 (resemble, exist)、知覚・感覚動詞 (like, see, know)
    ○ They resemble each other. (彼らはお互いに似ています)
    × The are resembling each other.

現在完了形

have [has] + 過去分詞で、過去の出来事と関連した現在の状態

11. 完了・結果：just, already, now, yet がよく用いられる。
    I have just finished my course in tourism.
    (観光事業のコースをちょうど終了しました)

12. 経験：ever, never, often, once, before がよく用いられる。
    Have you ever read any of his novels?
    (彼の小説のどれかを読んだことがありますか)

13. 継続：for, since, How long などがよく用いられる。
    Chris has been ill since last week.
    (クリスは先週から病気です)

14. 現在までの動作の継続：現在完了進行形 (have [has] + been + -ing)
    My uncle has been taking a walk in the park every day for many years.
    (私の叔父は今までに何年もの間、毎日公園を散歩しています)

    現在完了形は過去を表す語句 (a moment ago, just now, the other day, yesterday, when, etc.) と共に使用しない。
    ○ John left half an hour ago. (ジョンは30分前に出ました)
    × He has left half an hour ago.
    ○ When did your father come back? (あなたの父はいつ戻ったのですか)

× When has your father come back?

受動態

1. be + 過去分詞：「…によって〜される」動作主は by を用いる。
   Mike is respected by all his co-workers.
   （マイクはすべての同僚に尊敬されています）

2. 否定文の受動態：be + not + 過去分詞
   He was not elected president of the United States.
   （彼はアメリカ大統領に選ばれませんでした）

3. 一般の人々：we, you, they, people は受動態では省略
   English is spoken (by people) in New Zealand. (by people は省略)
   （ニュージーランドでは英語が話されます）

4. by 以外の前置詞：動作主で by 以外を用いる動詞
   be absorbed in「〜に没頭している」 be amazed at [about, by]「〜に驚く」 be concerned with「〜に関心がある」 be covered with「〜で覆われている」 be known to「〜に知られている」 be married to「〜と結婚している」 be opposed to「〜に反対する」 be pleased with「〜が気に入っている」 be satisfied with「〜に満足している」 be worried about「〜について心配する」
   We were surprised at the news.
   （私たちはそのニュースに驚きました）
   I am interested in the current economic climate.
   （現在の経済情勢に興味があります）

5. 助動詞のある受動態：助動詞 + be + 過去分詞
   The North Star can be seen at night.
   （北極星は夜に見ることができます）

6. 群動詞の受動態：そのまま１つの他動詞として扱う。
   The man was laughed at by his friends.
   （その男性は友達に笑われました）
   These children are taken care of properly by Jessie.
   （これらの子供たちは、ジェシーによって適切に世話されています）

助動詞

1. 能力・許可、義務・必要、推量・意志など
   can [could] = be able to：「できる」

may [might]：「〜してもよい」「〜かもしれない」
must = have to：「〜しなければならない」過去形は had to, 未来形は will have to
will：「〜だろう」否定形は won't
should：「〜すべきだ」= ought to
Scientists may never be able to predict when an earthquake will occur.
(科学者はいつ地震が発生するかを予測できないのかもしれません)
Employees have to show their ID cards at the entrance.
(従業員は入口で ID カードを見せなくてはなりません)

2. suggest [propose, request] + that ... ： that 節内の動詞は原形
I suggested that he get [should get] down to business.
(彼は本気で仕事にとりかかるべきだと私は提案しました)

3. 助動詞 + have + 過去分詞
cannot have + 過去分詞 「〜したはずがない」
may have + 過去分詞 「〜したかもしれない」
must have + 過去分詞 「〜したにちがいない」

4. 後悔：過去に実行されなかったり、実行された行為に対する後悔
should have + 過去分詞 「〜すべきだったのに（しなかった）」
need not have + 過去分詞 「〜する必要がなかったのに（してしまった）」

5. 助動詞を含む慣用表現
cannot help -ing 「せざるをえない」　had better 「〜する方がよい」
may well 「〜するのももっともだ」　would rather 〜 than ... 「···するよりは〜した方がよい」

◆ ビジネス頻出語句

1. 会社
2. 人材・キャリア
3. オフィスワーク
4. 取引・契約
5. 広告・販売
6. 通信
7. 待遇制度
8. マネー
9. マーケティング
10. 会議・プレゼンテーション
11. 経済状況
12. 通勤・交通

＜文法のまとめ４＞

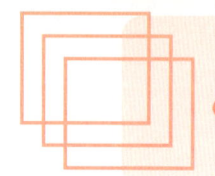

ビジネス語句

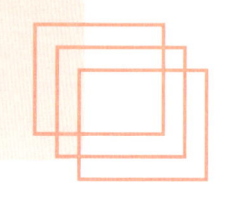

1. 会社
組織・支店・部局

1 **accounting department** 会計課
2 **accounting firm** 会計事務所
3 **affiliate** [əfílièit] 〔名〕支社、系列社
   affiliated [əfílièitid] 〔形〕傘下の、提携している
   affiliated company　関連会社

4 **allied industries** 関連産業
5 **beverage company** 飲料会社
6 **branch** [brǽntʃ] 〔名〕支店
   There were several factors involved in the closing of our branch.
   支店の閉鎖には、いくつかの要因が含まれていました。

7 **company** [kʌ́mpəni] 〔名〕会社
   The company is located in the heart of Birmingham.
   会社はバーミンガムの中心にあります。

8 **conglomerate** [kənglάmərət] 〔名〕複合企業
   international conglomerates　多国籍複合企業

9 **consortium** [kənsɔ́ːrʃiəm] 〔名〕合弁企業
   (類) joint venture　合弁事業

10 **corporation** [kɔ̀ːrpəréiʃən] 〔名〕会社
11 **department** [dipάːrtmənt] 〔名〕部門、部署
12 **division** [divíʒən] 〔名〕部局、課
13 **employment agency** 職業紹介所
14 **enterprise** [éntərpràiz] 〔名〕企業、会社
   a commercial enterprise　営利企業　public enterprises　公営企業

15 **firm** [fə́:rm] 〔名〕会社
a large firm 大企業　a local firm 地元企業

16 **headquarters** [hédkɔ̀:rtərz] 〔名〕本社
(類) head office

17 **institution** [ìnstətjú:ʃən] 〔名〕組織、団体
(類) organization [ɔ̀:rgənizéiʃən]

18 **listed company** 上場企業
19 **manufacturer** [mæ̀njufǽktʃərər] 〔名〕製造会社、メーカー
20 **mom-and-pop** 〔形〕家族経営の
a mom-and-pop store 家族経営店

21 **multinational** [mʌ̀ltinǽʃənəl] 〔形〕多国籍の
22 **parent company** 親会社
23 **personnel** [pɔ̀:rsənél] 〔名〕人事部〔課〕
24 **pharmaceutical company** 製薬会社
He's a biochemist for a pharmaceutical company.
彼は製薬会社の生化学者です。

25 **plant** [plǽnt] 〔名〕工場、プラント
26 **public-service corporation** 公益事業会社
27 **quoted company** 上場企業
28 **real estate company** 不動産会社
(類) property company

29 **section** [sékʃən] 〔名〕課
John and I started working in this section on the same day.
ジョンと私は同じ日にこの課で働き始めました。

30 **sector** [séktər] 〔名〕部門
financial sector 金融部門　manufacturing sector 製造部門

119

service sector サービス部門

31 **securities company** 証券会社
I work for a securities company.
証券会社で働いています。

32 **small business** 中小企業
(類) small and medium companies

33 **subsidiary** [səbsídièri] 〔名〕子会社
(類) branch factory

34 **trading firm** 商社

35 **union** [júːnjən] 〔名〕組合
labor union 労働組合

経営・展開

36 **administration** [ədmìnəstréiʃən] 〔名〕経営、管理

37 **advantage** [ədvǽntidʒ] 〔名〕有利、利点
take advantage of ～を利用する　advantageous〔形〕有利な

38 **alliance** [əláiəns] 〔名〕提携
ally [əlái]〔動〕提携する

39 **bankruptcy** [bǽŋkrʌptsi] 〔名〕破産、倒産
With the economy getting worse, more and more companies are declaring bankruptcy.
経済が悪化するにつれ、ますます多くの会社が倒産を宣告しています。

40 **bureaucracy** [bjuərάkrəsi] 〔名〕官僚主義
bureaucratic [bjùː(ə)rəkrǽtik]〔形〕官僚主義的な、お役所的な

41 **business activities** 事業活動

42 **business community** 実業界、経済界
43 **business management** 企業経営
（類）company management

44 **collaborate** [kəlǽbərèit] 〔動〕協力する、コラボレーションする
collaboration [kəlæbəréiʃən]〔名〕協力、共同
collaborative [kəlǽbərèitiv]〔形〕共同による

45 **commerce** [kámərs] 〔名〕商業
（類）trade

46 **competition** [kàmpətíʃən] 〔名〕競争
compete [kəmpíːt]〔動〕競争する
competitive [kəmpétətiv]〔形〕競争力のある

47 **competitive edge** 競争優位
48 **diversify** [dəvə́ːrsəfài] 〔動〕多角化する
49 **economic unification** 経済統合
50 **establish** [istǽbliʃ] 〔動〕設立する
（類）found [fáund]〔動〕設立する

51 **expansion** [ikspǽnʃən] 〔名〕拡大、拡張
The topic was the planned expansion of the warehouse.
トピックは部品庫の計画的な拡張でした。

52 **franchise** [frǽntʃaiz] 〔名〕（独占）営業権、販売権
franchiser [frǽntʃaizər]〔名〕（独占営業権を与える）親会社

53 **go bankrupt** 倒産する
（類）go bust, go out of business

54 **go into business** 事業を始める
（類）set up a business

55 **incorporate** [inkɔ́ːrpərèiət] 〔動〕会社にする、法人化する
incorporated 法人の（Inc. と略して社名の後につける）

56 **industry** [índəstri] 〔名〕産業

57 **management** [mǽnidʒmənt] 〔名〕経営、管理
manage [mǽnidʒ]〔動〕(会社) を経営する、管理する
management skills 経営能力

58 **merger** [mɔ́ːrdʒər] 〔名〕合併 〔動〕合併する
mergers and acquisitions 合併買収《略 M&R》

59 **monopoly** [mənɑ́pəli] 〔名〕独占
have a monopoly on ～を独占する

60 **open for business** 営業して、営業中で

61 **restructure** [rìːstrʌ́ktʃər] 〔動〕再編する
restructuring [rìːstrʌ́ktʃəriŋ]〔名〕再編成

62 **shut down** 営業を停止する、閉鎖する
shutdown〔名〕操業停止

63 **strategy** [strǽtədʒi] 〔名〕戦略、計画
strategic〔形〕戦略的な

64 **tactics** [tǽktiks] 〔名〕戦術
consider tactics 策を練る

65 **takeover** [téikòuvər] 〔名〕買収、乗っ取り
a hostile takeover 敵対的買収
takeover bid（買収のための）株式公開買い付け

2. 人材・キャリア
幹部・役員

66 **boss** [bɔ́(:)s]　　〔名〕上司、上役
上司のことなので、社長、部長、主任も含む。

67 **branch director** [brǽntʃdəréktər]　支店長
Our long-term branch director suddenly resigned.
長年の支店長が突然辞任しました。
(類) branch manager

68 **business partner**　　共同経営者

69 **chairperson** [tʃéəpə̀ːsn]　　〔名〕会長
chairman、chairwoman の性差別をなくすために生まれた語

70 **Chief Executive Officer (=CEO)** 最高経営責任者
We greatly appreciate your CEO's understanding of our position.
私たちの地位について最高経営責任者のご理解にとても感謝しています。

71 **collaborator** [kəlǽbərèitər]　　〔名〕協力者
72 **controller** [kəntróulər]　　〔名〕経理部長
73 **employer** [implɔ́iər]　　〔名〕雇用主
(反) employee [implɔ́iíː] 〔名〕社員、従業員

74 **executive** [igzékjutiv]　　〔名〕経営幹部、管理職者
75 **financial director**　　財務部長
The financial director proposed that spending be limited to $30,000.
財務部長は出費を3万ドルに制限することを提案しました。

76 **manager** [mǽnidʒər]　　〔名〕経営者、部[局]長
The manager asked for me personally.
部長が個人的に私に頼みました。

77 **managing director**　　常務取締役

78 **mid-level executive** 　　　　中堅管理職者
　　The government has decided to recognize overwork as the cause of the suicide of a mid-level executive.
　　政府は中堅管理職者が自殺した原因を過労と認定することを決めました。

79 **personnel manager** 　　　　人事部長
　　We are looking for a personnel manager.
　　人事部長を探しています。

80 **personnel department** 　　　人事課、人事部
　　Ben worked in the personnel department last year.
　　ベンは昨年、人事課で働きました。

81 **president** [prézidənt] 　　　〔名〕社長

82 **sales manager** 　　　　　　販売部長
　　a general manager 総支配人

83 **senior management** 　　　　最高経営幹部
　　(類) top management

84 **supervisor** [súːpəvàizər] 　〔名〕監督[管理]者、上司

85 **vice president** 　　　　　　副社長
　　As the president has been hospitalized, the vice president is to make a speech instead.
　　社長は入院しているので、代わりに副社長がスピーチをすることになっています。

社員・職種

86 **accountant** [əkáuntənt] 　　〔名〕会計士、会計係
　　We need to make sure the accountant avoids making any more mistakes.
　　会計士がこれ以上ミスをしないようにする必要があります。

87 **appraiser** [əpréizər] 　　　〔名〕鑑定人
　　Expert antique appraisers will be on hand each Sunday of the show.

専門の骨董品鑑定人が日曜日の展示会にはその場にいるでしょう。

88 **auto mechanics**　　　　　自動車修理工
We are tired of receiving service from auto mechanics and other so-called service companies.
自動車修理工と他のいわゆるサービス会社から、ひどいサービスを受けるのがいやになっています。

89 **bookkeeper** [búkkìːpər]　　〔名〕簿記係
90 **businessperson** [bíznispə̀ːrsən]　〔名〕実業家
　(類) businesspeople [bíznispìːpl]

91 **clerk** [kláːrk]　　　　　　〔名〕事務職員
92 **co-worker** [kóuwə̀ːrkər]　　〔名〕同僚
Thank you for not forgetting to offer a kind word to your co-workers.
同僚に親切な言葉をかけることを忘れなくてありがとうございます。
　(類) colleague [káliːg]

93 **distributor** [distríbjutər]　　〔名〕配達者
94 **electrician** [ilektríʃən]　　　〔名〕電気技師
95 **entrepreneur** [à:ntrəprənə́ːr]　〔名〕起業家
Robert is not nearly as good an entrepreneur as you.
ロバートは絶対あなたほど優れた起業家ではありません。

96 **plumber** [plʌ́mər]　　　　　〔名〕配管工
97 **real estate agent**　　　　　不動産業者
A real estate agent is going to show you several possible apartments.
不動産業者は、いくつかの可能なアパートを案内してくれるでしょう。

98 **receptionist** [risépʃənist]　〔名〕受付［案内］係
99 **staff** [stǽf]　　　　　　〔名〕社員、職員、スタッフ
sales staff 販売員、セールスマン

100 **stockbroker** [stáːkbròukər]　〔名〕株式仲買人

125

Are you really a stockbroker?
あなたは本当に株式仲買人ですか。

101 **subordinate** [səbɔ́ːrdənət] 〔名〕部下

昇進・異動

102 **competence** [kámpətəns] 〔名〕能力
103 **competitor** [kəmpétətər] 〔名〕競争者
104 **corporate ladder** 昇格の階段
105 **demotion** [dimóuʃən] 〔名〕降格
　demote [dimóut] 〔動〕降格する、左遷する

106 **hierarchy** [háiərɑ̀ːrki] 〔名〕序列
107 **performance** [pərfɔ́ːrməns] 〔名〕業績、実績
108 **personnel transfer** 人事異動
109 **position** [pəzíʃən] 〔名〕地位
110 **promote** [prəmóut] 〔動〕昇進させる
　promotion [prəmóuʃən] 〔名〕昇格

111 **relocate** [rìːloukéit] 〔動〕配置転換する
　relocation [rìːloukéiʃən] 〔名〕配置転換

112 **replacement** [ripléismənt] 〔名〕後任者
113 **resign** [rizáin] 〔動〕辞任する
　resignation [rèzignéiʃən] 〔名〕辞任、退職

114 **seniority** [siːnjɔ́ːrəti] 〔名〕年功序列
115 **transfer** [trǽnsfəːr] 〔名〕異動

採用・資格

116 **addition** [ədíʃən] 〔名〕追加、加わった人

The latest addition to our company is a man who will surely make it to the top in the near future.
会社に最近加わった人は近い将来、必ず会社のトップになる人です。

117 **applicant** [ǽplikənt] 〔名〕応募者
apply for ～に応募する

118 **application** [æpləkéiʃən] 〔名〕申し込み
119 **background** [bǽkgràund] 〔名〕経歴
120 **candidate** [kǽndidèit] 〔名〕候補者
121 **career** [kəríər] 〔名〕仕事、キャリア
Why not turn your talents into an exciting new career?
わくわくする新しい仕事にあなたの才能を向けたらどうですか。

122 **CV** [sí:ví:] 〔名〕履歴書
curriculum vitae の略

123 **employment** [implɔ́imənt] 〔名〕雇用、職、採用
After one year of employment, employees are eligible for one week's paid vacation.
1年の雇用後、社員は1週間の有給休暇の資格があります。

124 **field** [fí:ld] 〔名〕分野、領域
More opportunities exist in this rewarding field than ever before.
多くの機会が以前よりも、このやりがいのある分野にあります。

125 **flair** [fléər] 〔名〕才能、センス、コツ
Do you have a flair for writing clear, concise English?
はっきりと、正確な英語を書く才能がありますか。

126 **hire** [háiər] 〔動〕採用する
127 **human resources** 人材、人的資源
128 **interview** [íntərvjù:] 〔名〕面接

129 **job opening** 求人、就職口

130 **opportunity** [ɑ́pərtjúːnəti] 〔名〕機会、見込み
We will do our best to find the employment opportunities that best suit you.
あなた方に最も相応しい雇用機会を見つけるため最善を尽くします。

131 **qualification** [kwɑ́ləfikéiʃən] 〔名〕資格

132 **qualified** [kwɑ́ləfàid] 〔形〕資格のある
(類) eligible [élidʒəbl]

133 **reference** [réfərəns] 〔名〕推薦状

134 **top-notch** [tɑ́ːpnɑ́ːtʃ] 〔形〕最高級の、一流の
You have the makings of a top-notch editor.
あなたは一流の編集者の資質があります。

135 **typographical** [tàipəgrǽfikəl] 〔形〕印刷（上）の
Do you have a nose for finding typographical errors?
印刷上の誤りを発見する能力がありますか。

136 **vacancy** [véikənsi] 〔名〕欠員

労働・条件

137 **allocate** [ǽləkèit] 〔動〕割り当てる
(類) assign [əsáin]

138 **appoint** [əpɔ́int] 〔動〕任命する

139 **business hours** 勤務時間
(類) working hours

140 **collaboration** [kəlæ̀bəréiʃən] 〔名〕協力

141 **designate** [dézignèit] 〔動〕指名する

142 **dismiss** [dismís] 〔動〕解雇する

(類) fire [fáiər], lay off

143 **downsize** [dáunsàiz]　〔動〕人員削減をする、縮小する
downsizing [dáunsàiziŋ]〔名〕人員削減、リストラ

144 **during working hours**　就業〔営業〕時間中に
(反) outside working hours 就業〔営業〕時間外に

145 **full-time** [fùltáim]　〔形〕常勤の、フルタイムの
part-time 非常勤の、パートタイムの

146 **job-hop** [dʒáːbhàːp]　〔動〕転勤する
(類) switch jobs

147 **lead the way**　先頭に立つ、導いている
Job increases in the steel and auto-making industries led the way to an economic recovery.
鉄鋼と自動車産業の仕事の増加は経済の回復を導いています。

148 **manual** [mǽnjuəl]　〔形〕肉体労働の
(類) blue-collar

149 **meritocratic** [mèritəkrǽtik]　〔形〕実力主義の
meritocracy [mèritákrəsi]〔名〕実力主義

150 **minimum wage**　最低賃金
151 **periodic pay raise**　定期昇給
152 **promising** [prɑ́ˈməsiŋ]　〔形〕有望な
153 **rat race**　出世競争、生存競争
We gave up the fast-paced, rat race life of London.
私たちはロンドンの速いペースの出世競争をあきらめました。

154 **temporary** [témpərèri]　〔形〕一時的な

155 **tenure** [ténjər] 〔名〕在任期間、任期

156 **unemployment** [ʌ̀nimplɔ́imənt] 〔名〕失業、失業率
For three consecutive months, unemployment has remained below 5.3%.
3ヶ月連続して失業率は5.3%以下のままです。

157 **wage in kind** 現物給与
158 **wage differential** 賃金格差
159 **wage increase** 賃上げ
160 **wage reduction** 賃金カット
161 **welfare facilities** 厚生施設
162 **work condition** 労働条件
This case marks the beginning of a movement to improve severe work conditions.
この事例は厳しい労働条件を改善するための、新たな動きの始まりを示します。

163 **work flexible hours** フレックス制で働く、自由勤務時間制で働く
Working flexible hours allows employees more freedom.
フレックス制で働くことは、社員により多くの自由を与えます。

164 **work overtime** 残業をする
165 **workforce** [wə́:rkfɔ̀:rs] 〔名〕労働力、労働人口
The number of women entering the workforce showed significant increases last year.
昨年、労働人口に入っている女性の数は、かなりの増加を示しました。

166 **workweek** 週間労働時間

3. オフィスワーク
業務

167 **account for** 〜を説明する
168 **assignment** [əsáinmənt] 〔名〕仕事、任務、課題

169	**available** [əvéiləbl]	〔動〕	入手できる
170	**bulletin** [búlətin]	〔名〕	掲示
171	**bundle** [bʌndl]	〔動〕	束ねる 〔名〕束

a bundle of letters 手紙の束

172 **business card** 　　　名刺
　　　（類）name tag 名札

173 **business day** 　　　営業日
174 **call it a day** 　　　仕事を終える、切り上げる
175 **chore** [tʃɔːr] 　〔名〕雑用
176 **company brochure** 　会社紹介パンフレット
177 **correct** [kərékt] 　〔動〕訂正する
178 **distribute** [distríbjəːt] 　〔動〕配る
179 **divisional system** 　事業部制
180 **document** [dάkjumənt] 　〔名〕書類、文書

create a document 文書ファイルを作成する
save a ducument 文書を保存する

181 **draft** [drǽft] 　〔名〕草案 〔動〕下書きを書く

a final draft 最終稿、最終草案

182 **dress code** 　服装規則
183 **enclose** [inklóuz] 　〔名〕同封物 〔動〕同封する
　　　（類）attach [ətǽtʃ] （Eメールにファイル）を添付する

184 **in charge of** 　管理して、担当の
185 **launch** [lɔ́ːntʃ] 　〔動〕始める 〔名〕開始
186 **manageable** [mǽniʤəbl] 　〔形〕扱いやすい、簡単にできる

Learn to make your overcrowded schedule more manageable and less stressful.
過密スケジュールをより簡単にし、ストレスを減らすようにしてください。

187 **memorandum** [mèmərǽndəm] 〔名〕社内メモ、回覧

188 **merit system** 能力主義

189 **night shift** 夜勤
Beth has never worked the night shift in her life before.
ベスは以前一度も夜勤をしたことがありません。
（反）a day shift 日勤

190 **notify** [nóutəfài] 〔動〕知らせる

191 **office work** 事務、オフィスワーク

192 **on schedule** 予定通り

193 **paperwork** [péipəwə:rk] 〔名〕ペーパーワーク、書類作業
We'll teach you the techniques you need to help you handle your paperwork more efficiently.
ペーパーワークをより能率的にするために必要な技術を教えます。

194 **permission** [pərmíʃən] 〔名〕許可、承認

195 **preserve** [prizə́:v] 〔動〕保存する、保管する

196 **proofread** [prú:fri:d] 〔動〕校正する

197 **publicize** [pʌ́bləsàiz] 〔動〕公表する

198 **put in charge** あてがう
I put one of the stock people in charge of the delivery.
配達に予備の1人をあてがいました。

199 **quota** [kwóutə] 割当量、ノルマ
sales quota 販売ノルマ
fill a quota ノルマを果たす

200 **routine** [ru:tí:n] 〔名〕日課

201 **run** [rʌn] 〔動〕経営する
well-run 経営状態の良い
badly-run 経営状態の悪い

202 **sort out** 整理する

203	**stack** [stǽk]	〔名〕(書類の)山　〔動〕山積みする	
	(類) pile [páil]		
204	**turn around**	業績を改善する	
205	**turn in**	提出する	
	(類) hand in		
206	**work on**	取り組む	

財務会計

207	**accounting** [ɑkáuntiŋ]	会計
208	**accounts receivable**	売掛金
209	**appraise** [əpréiz]	〔動〕見積もる
210	**audit** [ɔ́:dət]	〔動〕会計監査をする
211	**auditor** [ɔ́:dətər]	〔名〕監査人
212	**average** [ǽvəridʒ]	〔名〕平均
213	**balance sheet**	バランスシート、貸借対照表
214	**borrow**	〔動〕借りる
	(反) lend 〔動〕貸す	

215 **budget** [bʌ́dʒit]　　〔名〕予算
budget deficit 財政赤字　under budget 予算内で
on a budget 予算通り　over budget 予算超過で

216 **calculation** [kælkjuléiʃən]　〔名〕計算
Please correct errors in calculation, if any, and let me know.
もし計算ミスがあれば直して、私に知らせてください。

217 **capital** [kǽpətl]　　〔名〕資金
capital assets 資本資産

218 **close the books**　　決算する

219 **cost** [kɔ́:st] 〔名〕経費 〔動〕費用がかかる
220 **debt** [dét] 〔名〕負債、借金
221 **default** [difɔ́:lt] 〔名〕債務不履行
222 **depreciation** [dipri:ʃiéiʃən] 〔名〕減価償却
assets depreciation 資産償却

223 **earning** [ə́:rniŋ] 〔名〕収益
224 **expenditure** [ikspéndiʧər] 〔名〕経費, 支出
annual expenditure 歳出
（類）expense [ikspéns] 費用
（反）income [ínkʌm] 収入

225 **finance** [fáinæns] 〔名〕財務、財源
finance company 金融会社

226 **financial** [fənǽnʃəl] 〔形〕財務の、経済的な
When experiencing financial problems, the first step is to try to cut expenses.
経済的な問題を経験するときは、最初のステップは経費を削減する努力です。

227 **fiscal year** 会計年度、営業年度
228 **fixed assets** 固定資産
current assets 流動資産　hidden assets 含み資産
watered assets 水増し資産

229 **fund** [fʌ́nd] 〔名〕資金 〔動〕資金を出す
fund manager 資金運用担当者

230 **gain** [géin] 〔名〕利益
capital gains 資本利得　financial gain 財政利益

231 **gross margin** 総利益
232 **income** [ínkʌm] 〔名〕収入

134

income statement 損益計算書　income distribution 所得分布

233 **investment** [invéstmənt]　〔名〕投資
234 **invoicing** [ínvɔisiŋ]　〔名〕請求
　(類) billing [bíliŋ]

235 **mark up**　値上げする
　(反) mark down 値下げする

236 **net** [nét]　〔名〕純益
　net profit 純利益

237 **net sales**　正味売上高、純売上高
238 **operating profit**　営業利益
　operating expence 営業経費　operating income 営業収入

239 **ordinary income**　経常利益
　current account 経常収支　current expenditure 経常支出

240 **principal** [prínsəpəl]　〔名〕元金、元本
　pricipal payment 元金返済

241 **profit** [práfit]　〔名〕利益　〔動〕利益を得る
　(反) loss [lɔ́:s] 〔名〕損失
　small profits and quick returns 薄利多売
　profit increase 増益　profit decrease 減益

242 **profit margin**　利ざや
　Rising raw materials costs have seriously cut into our profit margin.
　原材料の高騰が厳しく利ざやに食い込みました。

243 **profitable** [práfətəbl]　〔形〕儲かる、利益の上がる
　(類) lucrative [lú:krətiv]

135

244 **quarter** [kwɔ́ːrtər] 〔名〕4 半期
the last fiscal quarter 会計年度の最終 4 半期

245 **rate of return** 収益率
246 **retained profit** 利益剰余金
（類）retained earnings

247 **retrench** [ritréntʃ] 〔動〕（経費）を削減する、節約する
（類）economize [ikánəmàiz]
retrenchment [ritréntʃmənt] 〔名〕削減、節約

248 **revenue** [révənjùː] 〔名〕収入、収益
（類）return [ritə́ːrn]
generate revenue 収益を上げる

249 **sales** [séilz] 〔名〕売り上げ
250 **taxation at sources** 源泉徴収
251 **turnover** [tə́ːrnòuvər] 〔名〕売上高、回転率
annual turnover 年間売上高

事務用品

252 **cardboard** [káːrdbɔ̀ːrd] ボール紙、厚紙
a cardboard box 段ボール箱

253 **drawer** [drɔ́ːr] 〔名〕引き出し
a desk drawer 机の引き出し

254 **equipment** [ikwípmənt] 〔名〕備品、用品、設備
office equipment 事務備品

255 **file cabinet** ファイルキャビネット、書類棚
（類）filing cabilt

256 **letter pads** 便せん

257 **maintenance** [méintənəns] 〔名〕管理、保守
routine maintenace 定期整備 maintenance costs 維持管理費

258 **memo pads** メモ用紙

259 **office machinery** 事務機器

260 **office supplies** 事務用品

261 **out of** ～がなくて
This printer isn't broken. It's just out of paper.
このプリンターは故障していません。ただ紙がないだけです。

262 **out of stock** 品切れで
（反）in stock 在庫があって

263 **paper clip** クリップ

264 **Post-it** [póustit] 〔名〕付箋、ポストイット

265 **repair** [ripéər] 〔名〕修理
repair service 修理サービス

266 **ruler** [rú:lər] 〔名〕定規

267 **short of** 不足して

268 **stapler** [stéiplər] 〔名〕ホッチキス
staple [stéipl] 〔動〕留める

269 **stationery** [stéiʃənèri] 〔名〕文房具

4. 取引・契約
交渉

270 **access** [ækses] 〔名〕アクセス、入手

271 **appointment** [əpɔ́intmənt] 〔名〕予約
Would you kindly call us for an appointment at your earliest

convenience?
できるだけ早く都合のつくときに、予約の電話をしていただけますか。

272 **bid** [bíd] 〔動〕値をつける 〔名〕付け値、入札
the highest bidder 最高入札者

273 **bottom line** （売買の）最低許容額、ぎりぎりの線

274 **compromise** [kάmprəmàiz] 〔動〕妥協する 〔名〕妥協
reach a compromise 妥協に至る

275 **concede** [kənsíːd] 〔動〕譲歩する、しぶしぶ認める

276 **confirm** [kənfə́ːrm] 〔動〕確認する
confirmation [kɑ̀nfərméiʃən] 〔名〕確認、承認

277 **conform** [kənfɔ́ːrm] 〔動〕従う
conformance [kənfɔ́ːrməns] 〔名〕順応、一致

278 **deadline** [dédlàin] 〔名〕締め切り
meet a deadline 締め切りに間に合わせる

279 **decision-making** 〔形〕意思決定の

280 **describe** [diskráib] 〔動〕詳しく述べる

281 **e-commerce** [íːkὰmərs] 〔名〕電子商取引、Eコマース
electronic commerce の略で、インターネットを通じて物品の売買や決済を行うことを言う。

282 **fulfill** [fulfíl] 〔動〕遂行する、実行する
fulfillment [fulfílmənt] 〔名〕実行

283 **haggle** [hǽgl] 〔動〕値切る
haggling [hǽgliŋ] 〔名〕値切り

284 **licensor** [láisənsər] 〔名〕許諾者

licensee [làisənsíː] 〔名〕被許諾者

285 **negotiate** [nigóuʃièit] 〔動〕交渉する
negotiation [nigòuʃiéiʃən] 〔名〕交渉
negotiable [nigóuʃiəbl] 〔形〕交渉の余地のある

286 **offend** [əfénd] 〔動〕違反する
offense [əféns] 〔名〕違反

287 **propose** [prəpóuz] 〔動〕提案する
proposal [prəpóuzəl] 〔名〕提案

288 **quality** [kwάləti] 〔名〕質、品質
The two models are quite different in both quality and price.
２つのモデルは品質も価格も全然違います。
of good qualities 質の良い

289 **quantity** [kwάntəti] 〔名〕数量
in large quantities 多量に

290 **quote** [kwóut] 〔動〕見積る
(類) estimate
quotation [kwoutéiʃən] 〔名〕見積り、見積書

291 **reconcile** [rékənsàil] 〔動〕まとめる、調停する
reconciliation [rèkənsìliéiʃən] 〔名〕提案調停、和解

292 **solvent** [sάlvənt] 〔形〕支払い能力のある
(反) insolvent [insάlvənt] 支払い不能の

293 **transaction** [trænsǽkʃən] 〔名〕取引
transact [trænsǽkt] 〔動〕取引を行う

契約

294 **agreement** [əgríːmənt] 〔名〕契約
sign an agreement 契約を結ぶ

295 **close the deal** 取引をまとめる
296 **come to terms** 合意する、交渉がまとまる
297 **completion** [kəmplíʃən] 〔名〕契約成立、完成
298 **contract** [kántrækt] 〔名〕契約
Your expenses for the last two months have exceeded the amount agreed upon in your contract.
ここ2ヶ月の経費は、契約で同意した金額を超えています。

299 **firm** [fə́ːrm] 〔形〕確定的な、決定された
a firm contract 確定契約　a firm oder 確定注文

300 **modify** [mádəfài] 〔動〕変更する、修正する
modification [màdəfikéiʃən] 〔名〕変更、修正

301 **perform** [pərfɔ́ːrm] 〔動〕履行する、実行する
perform a contract 契約を果たす

302 **signature** [sígnətʃər] 〔名〕署名
303 **take effect** 実施する、実行する
304 **tentative** [téntətiv] 〔形〕一時的な、仮の
a tentative agreement 仮の合意

305 **term** [tə́ːrm] 〔名〕契約期間
a fixed term （取引の）有期期間

306 **terminate** [tə́ːrmənèit] 〔動〕終了する

140

国際取引

307 **capital flight** 資本流出
308 **customs** [kʌ́stəmz] 〔名〕税関
309 **duties** [djúːtiz] 〔名〕関税、税
310 **forex (=foreign exhange)** 〔名〕外国為替
311 **money order** 為替、郵便為替
312 **outsourcing** [áutsɔ̀ːrsiŋ] 〔名〕(業務の)外部委託
313 **tariff** [tǽrif] 〔名〕関税
　　tariffs on imported goods 輸入品の関税

314 **trade** [tréid] 〔名〕貿易
　　trade balance 貿易収入　trade negotiations 通商交渉
　　foreign trade 外国貿易

315 **trade surplus** 貿易黒字
　　(反) trade deficit 貿易赤字

履行条件

316 **acceptable** [əkséptəbl] 〔形〕受け入れられる
　　acceptance [əkséptəns] 〔名〕受諾、容認

317 **apply** [əplái] 〔動〕適応する
　　application [æ̀plikéiʃən] 〔名〕適用

318 **appreciate** [əpríːʃièit] 〔動〕値が上がる
　　(反) depreciate [dipríːʃièit] 値が下がる

319 **comply with** 順守する

320 **cooperate** [kouápərèit] 〔動〕協力する
　　cooperation [kouápəréiʃən] 〔名〕協力、協調

321 **exclusive** [iksklú:siv] 〔形〕独占の
an exclusive right 独占権

322 **grant** [grǽnt] 〔動〕（権利）を与える、認める
323 **intellectual property rights** 知的所有権
324 **liability** [làiəbíləti] 〔名〕責任
liable [láiəbl]〔形〕責任がある　limited liability 有限責任

325 **maximize** [mǽksəmàiz] 〔動〕最大限にする
（反）minimize [mínəmàiz] 最小限にする

326 **obligation** [àbləgéiʃən] 〔名〕義務、責任
327 **patent** [pǽtənt] 〔名〕特許
328 **restrict** [ristríkt] 〔動〕制限する、規制する
restriction〔名〕制限、規制

329 **royalty** [rɔ́iəlti] 〔名〕著作権使用料
330 **terms** [tə́ːrmz] 〔名〕条件
on favorable terms 好条件で

5. 広告・販売
広告

331 **advertising** [ǽdvərtàiziŋ] 〔名〕広告
advertise [ǽdvərtàiz] 広告する

332 **advertising agency** 広告代理店
This advertising agency was founded by four enterprising young women in the sixties.
この広告代理店は1960年代に、4人の意欲的な若い女性によって設立されました。
agency commission 広告手数料

333 **at no charge** 無料で

334 **banner ad** 大見出しの広告
banner advertising バーナー広告

335 **be in need of** 〜を必要とする
When you are in need of home repairs, make sure you visit our website.
家の修理を必要とするときは、必ず私たちのウェブサイトにアクセスしてください。

336 **brochure** [brouʃúər] 〔名〕パンフレット
The brochure explains how the new video game rating system works.
パンフレットは新しいビデオゲームの格づけシステムがどのように役立つかを説明します。

337 **call-in talk show** 視聴者参加番組
I like to listen to radio call-in talk shows when I drive to and from work.
仕事の行き帰りにラジオの視聴者参加番組を聞くのが好きです。

338 **catalogue** [kǽtəlɔ(ː)g] 〔名〕カタログ
339 **circular** [sə́ːrkjulər] 〔名〕広告、案内状、回覧状
340 **classified** [klǽsəfàid] 〔名〕分類広告
classified ads （新聞の）項目別広告（欄）

341 **expiration date** 有効期限が切れる日
342 **eye-catching** [áikætʃiŋ] 〔形〕人目を引く
The advertisement was so eye-catching that I was tempted to buy the bag.
その広告はとても人目を引くので、私はバッグを買いたくなりました。

343 **fad** [fæd] 〔名〕一時的な流行、ブーム
344 **freebie** [fríːbi] 〔名〕試供品、無料サンプル
345 **gimmick** [gímik] 〔名〕（宣伝の）企画
346 **homemaker** [hóummèikər] 〔名〕主婦〔夫〕、家事をする人

This advertisement is intendend for housewives and homemakers.
この広告は主婦や家事をする人を意図して作られています。

347 **magnify** [mǽgnəfài] 〔動〕誇張する
348 **opinion poll** 世論調査
349 **pop-up ad** ポップアップ広告
350 **public relations (=PR)** 広告、広報
351 **public relations department** 広報部
The public relations department is in charge of protecting the company image.
広報部は会社のイメージを守ることを担当しています。

352 **put an ad** 広告を載せる
353 **reasonably-priced** [ríːzənəbli práist] 〔形〕手ごろな値段の
We offer visitors to our site a list of dependable, reasonably-priced service people.
私たちのウェブサイトにアクセスしてくれる人に、手ごろな値段の修理係リストを提供いたします。

354 **reputable** [répjutəbl] 〔形〕評判の良い
Can you recommend a reputable health maintenance organization in the area?
この地域の評判の良い健康管理組織を推薦してくれますか。

355 **trademark** [tréidmὰːrk] 〔名〕商標
356 **trial** [tráiəl] 〔形〕試用の
One of our free 1-month trial plasma TVs was bought back — a day late.
無料で1ヶ月試用のプラズマテレビ1台が、1日遅れで返却されました。

357 **tyranny of advertising** 広告の暴虐行為
Is there nowhere we can go to get away from the tyranny of advertising these days?
最近は広告の暴虐行為から逃れるために行けるところがないのでしょうか。

販売

358 **clearance sale** 在庫一掃セール、クリアランスセール
359 **cold call** 売り込み電話
360 **coupon** [kúːpɑn] 〔名〕割引券、クーポン
 (類) voucher [váutʃər]

361 **customer** [kʌ́stəmər] 〔名〕顧客
Mr. Baker, who is one of our most faithful customers, knows all our staff by name.
最も忠実な客の1人であるベーカーさんは、社員の名前をすべて知っています。

362 **discount** [dískaunt] 〔名〕割引 〔動〕割引する
discount price 割引料金

363 **initial payment** 頭金
364 **inventory adjustment** 在庫調整
365 **limited-time offer** 期限限定（奉仕）
366 **loyalty card** 会員カード
367 **mail order** 通信販売、通販
It has become popular to shop on the Internet and through mail order catalogs.
インターネットや通販のカタログで買い物をすることが人気になってきました。

368 **mark down** 値下げする
369 **merchandize** [máːrtʃəndàiz] 〔動〕販売を促進する 〔名〕商品
370 **on sale** セールで
I bought this coat yesterday, which happened to be on sale at 50% off.
昨日このコートを買ったのですが、それはたまたまセールで50％オフでした。

371 **outlet** [áutlet] 〔名〕直売店
372 **profit ratio** 利益率

373 **release** [rilíːs]　〔動〕発売する、公表する
　(類) launch [lɔ́ːntʃ] 売り出す、市場に出す

374 **retail** [ríːteil]　〔名〕小売
　retailer [ríːteilər] 小売商人

375 **sales forecast**　販売予測
376 **sales network**　販売網
377 **sales promotion**　販売促進
378 **sales representative**　販売員、セールスマン
379 **sponsor a booth**　（展示用）ブースを出す
Over 1,000 dealers of European antiques will sponsor booths showing off their goods.
ヨーロッパの骨董品の1,000以上の業者が、商品を展示するためにブースを出すでしょう。

380 **stationery department**　文房具売り場
Mary in the stationery department didn't show up, and didn't call in either.
メアリーは文房具売り場に現れなかったし、電話もかけてきませんでした。

381 **tag price**　定価
382 **telemarketing** [téləmáːrkəteiŋ]　〔名〕電話販売
383 **toll-free dial**　フリーダイアル
384 **wholesale** [hóulsèil]　〔名〕卸売り

注文・商品

385 **bargain** [báːrgən]　〔名〕お買い得品
　bargain price 特価　loss leader おとり商品
　price leader 目玉商品

386 **best before date**　（食品の）賞味期限
387 **budget price**　安い値段

388 **cash cow** 　　　　　　　　　儲かる事業、ドル箱商品

389 **collectible** [kəléktbl] 　　　〔名〕収集品

390 **confidence** [kánfədəns] 　　〔名〕自信
Our CEO expressed complete confidence in and satisfaction with this new product.
最高経営責任者はこの新しい製品に、完全な自信と満足を表明しました。

391 **design** [dizáin] 　　　　　　〔名〕デザイン
My boyfriend bought me a bag with a design from West Africa.
ボーイフレンドは西アフリカ製のデザインのハンドバッグを私に買ってくれました。

392 **exchange** [ikstʃéindʒ] 　　　〔動〕交換する、両替する

393 **item** [áitəm] 　　　　　　　〔名〕品目、項目
Some catalogs sell items that we can't find in regular stores.
カタログには通常の店で見つけられない品目を売っているのもあります。

394 **list price** 　　　　　　　　表示価格

395 **on the shelves** 　　　　　　店頭に並んで

396 **past sell-by date** 　　　　　賞味期限切れ

397 **place an order** 　　　　　　注文をする
We have been assured that they will be placing an order for 200 computers.
彼らは200台のコンピューターを注文すると確信しています。

398 **procure** [prəkjúər] 　　　　〔動〕確保する、入手する

399 **purchase order** 　　　　　　注文書

400 **reusable** [ri:jú:zəbl] 　　　〔形〕再使用できる
Shoppers who bring reusable shopping bags with them will receive a 5 % discount on all food items.
再利用できる買い物袋を持ってくる買い物客は、すべての食品を5％割引してもらえるでしょう。

401 **shortage** [ʃɔ́:rtidʒ] 　　　　〔名〕不足

402 **stock** [sták]　　　　　　　　〔名〕在庫品
　　in stock 在庫があって
　　out of stock 品切れで、在庫切れで

403 **subscription** [səbskrípʃən]　　〔名〕定期購読
　　When does our subscription to *Newsweek* magagine run out?
　　雑誌『ニューズウィーク』の定期購読は、いつ期限が切れますか。

404 **that was that**　　　　　　　それで終わり
　　Mark was late for work once too often, and that was that.
　　マークは仕事に遅刻しすぎて、とうとうそれで終わりになりました。
　　　once too often「度を越して、やりすぎて（とうとう）」

405 **unit** [júːnit]　　　　　　　　〔名〕単位
　　unit price 単価

請求・支払

406 **bill** [bíl]　　　　　　　　　〔名〕請求書
　　We did indeed overcharge you $32.87 on your gas bill, for which we apologize.
　　ガスの請求書で、確かに32ドル87セントを過剰請求したことをおわびします。

407 **cash on deliverly (=COD)**　　代引き（代金と引き換え渡し）
408 **cash substitute**　　　　　　現金の代用
409 **cashier** [kæʃíər]　　　　　　〔名〕レジ
　　I was surprised to see that cashiers in the U.K. sit down on the job.
　　イギリスのレジ係が座って仕事をしているのを見て驚きました。

410 **charge** [tʃάːrdʒ]　　　　　　〔動〕支払う、請求する
　　Short on cash, she charged a new outfit on her credit card.
　　現金部不足のため、彼女は新しい服をクレジットカードで支払いました。

411 **checkout** [tʃékàut]　　　　　〔名〕支払い、勘定
　　checkout counter〔名〕レジ

148

412 **claim** [kléim] 〔動〕請求する 〔名〕請求
413 **credit to** 振り込む
The overcharged amount will be credited to your October account.
超過請求されたお金は11月の口座に振り込まれるでしょう。

414 **credit voucher** 商品券
415 **installment payment** 分割払い
416 **overcharge** [òuvərtʃɑ́:rdʒ] 〔動〕過剰請求する
I am sick of being overcharged for poor and shoddy work.
へたで雑な仕事に過剰請求され、うんざりしています。

物流・運送

417 **box up** 箱に入れる
I boxed the returned camera up and put it back on the shelf.
返品されたカメラを箱に入れ、棚に戻しました。

418 **cargo** [kɑ́:rgou] 〔名〕貨物、船荷
419 **code sharing** コードシェアリング、共同運行
420 **courier** [kə́:riər] 〔名〕宅配業者
421 **delivery** [dilívəri] 〔名〕配達
deliver [dilívər] 〔動〕配達する
on delivery 配達の際に、現物と引き換えで

422 **distribuition** [dìstribjú:ʃən] 〔名〕流通
423 **export** [ikspɔ́:rt] 〔動〕輸出する
export [ékspɔ:rt] 〔名〕輸出

424 **forwarder** [fɔ́:rwərdər] 〔名〕輸送業者
425 **freight** [fréit] 〔名〕貨物輸送
426 **hub** [hʌ́b] 〔名〕ハブ、拠点
427 **import** [impɔ́:rt] 〔動〕輸入する
import [ímpɔ:rt] 〔名〕輸入

428 **inventory** [ínvəntɔ̀:ri]　　〔名〕在庫、在庫目録
　(類) stock [sták]

429 **invoice** [ínvɔis]　　〔名〕送り状
430 **loading** [lóudiŋ]　　〔名〕最大積載量
431 **logistics** [loudʒístiks]　　〔名〕物流（管理システム）
432 **manifest** [mǽnəfèst]　　〔名〕積荷目録、送り状
433 **pack** [pǽk]　　〔動〕梱包する　〔名〕荷造り
434 **package deal**　　一括取引
435 **shipment** [ʃípmənt]　　〔名〕発送、積荷、発送品
436 **shipping** [ʃípiŋ]　　〔名〕輸送、運送
　shipping and handling costs 運送手数料

437 **surface transport**　　陸上輸送
　air transport 空輸

438 **tracking number**　　追跡番号
439 **transportation** [trænspərtéiʃən]　　〔名〕輸送
　transport [trænspɔ́:rt] 〔動〕輸送する

440 **vessel** [vésəl]　　〔名〕船、飛行機
441 **warehouse** [wéərhàus]　　〔名〕倉庫
　(類) storehouse

6. 通信
コンピューター

442 **break down**　　故障する
443 **compatible** [kəmpǽtəbl]　　〔形〕互換性がある、相いれる
　My new computer is not compatible with this old printer.
　新しいコンピューターは、この古いプリンターと互換性がありません。

150

444 **customize** [kʌ́stəmàiz] 〔動〕カスタマイズする、好みの仕様にする

445 **do well** うまくいく
I am confident you will do very well in your new career.
あなたが新しい仕事でとてもうまくいくことを確信しています。

446 **exit** [égzət] 〔動〕終了する

447 **glare-free screen** スクリーンフィルター
You can install a glare-free screen on your computer to reduce eye strain.
目の疲れを減らすため、コンピューターにスクリーンフィルターを取り付けることができます。

448 **icon** [áikɑn] 〔名〕アイコン

449 **initialize** [iníʃəlàiz] 〔動〕初期化する

450 **justify** [dʒʌ́stəfài] 〔動〕調整する

451 **monitor** [mɑ́nətər] 〔名〕モニター
After only an hour or two of sitting at my monitor, my eyes begin to smart and water.
モニターに座ってほんの1、2時間後に、目がずきずきし、涙がでます。

452 **optimization** [ɑ́ptəməzéiʃən] 〔名〕最適化

453 **peripheral** [pərífərəl] 〔名〕周辺機器

454 **plug** [plʌ́g] 〔名〕(パソコンの)コネクター、プラグ

455 **reflect** [riflékt] 〔動〕反射する
Make sure that sunlight does not reflect directly on the monitor screen.
日光がモニタースクリーンに直接反射しないようにしてください。

456 **remote processing** 遠隔処理

457 **sign up for** ユーザー登録をする
More and more people are signing up for E-dating services to look for their ideal companion.
ますます多くの人が理想的な相手を探すために、Eデート・サービスにユーザー登録しています。

458 **start up** 電源を入れる
shut down 電源を切る

459 **tech-nerd** [téknɚːrd] 〔名〕コンピューターマニア
460 **technology** [teknálədʒi] 〔名〕技術
Innovation in technology is advancing at an increasingly rapid pace.
技術革新は、ますますな急激なペースで進んでいます。

461 **trash bin** ゴミ箱
462 **update** [ʌpdéit] 〔動〕最新にする
463 **user** [júːzɚr] 〔名〕ユーザー、使用者
Your complaint is the most common among computer users.
あなたの苦情はコンピューター・ユーザーの間で最も一般的です。

464 **user authentication** ユーザー確認

インターネット

465 **access charge** 接続料金
466 **be bound to** きっと〜する
If you are looking for information on current or classic films, you are bound to find it here.
現代映画または古典映画に関する情報を探しているなら、きっとここで見つけられます。

467 **blog** [blág] 〔名〕ブログ、日記
468 **bookmark** [búkmàːrk] 〔名〕ブックマーク、お気に入り
469 **broadband** [brɔ́ːdbæ̀nd] 〔名〕ブロードバンド
broadband connection ブロードバンド接続

470 **browse** [bráuz] 〔動〕ブラウズする、閲覧する
471 **fiber optics** 光ファイバー
472 **go on line** 接続する
go off line 接続を切る

473 **herald** [hérəld] 〔動〕到来を告げる
The Internet is heralding a kind of democratization of the news.
インターネットはニュースの一種の民主化の到来を告げています。

474 **hit** [hít] 〔動〕ヒットする

475 **optical communication** 光通信

476 **retrieval system** 検索システム
Have you got used to using the new data retrieval system yet?
あなたはもう新しいデータの検索システムを使うことに慣れましたか。

477 **retrieve** [ritríːv] 〔動〕検索する

478 **search engine** サーチエンジン

479 **server** [sə́ːrvər] サーバー

480 **site** [sáit] 〔名〕サイト
（類）website ウェブサイト
visit a site サイトを訪れる

481 **subscriber** [səbskráibər] 〔名〕加入者

482 **train in** 身につける
She is thoroughly trained in all aspects of hospital management.
彼女は病院経営のあらゆる側面をすっかり身につけています。

483 **transmission rate** 通信速度

484 **up-to-date** 最新の
Check out our website to keep up-to-date with what's new in our company.
絶えず会社の最新情報を入手するために、私たちのウェブサイトをチェックしてください。

セキュリティー

485 **anti-viral software** 〔コンピューター〕ウイルス駆除ソフトウェア
Computer users can help protect themselves against computer viruses by installing anti-viral software.
コンピューター・ユーザーはウイルス駆除ソフトウェアをインストールすることで、コン

ピューターウィルスを防ぐ手立てができます。

486 **hacker** [hǽkər]　　　　　　　〔名〕ハッカー
We were all relieved to hear that the hacker had finally been arrested.
ハッカーがついに逮捕されたということを聞いて、みんな安心しました。

487 **infection** [infékʃən]　　　　　〔名〕感染
infect [infékt]〔動〕感染する

488 **keep an eye on**　　　　　　　～を監視する
This system allows you to use your office Internet connection to keep an eye on your home.
このシステムは家を監視するために、会社のインターネット接続が使えます。

489 **risk management**　　　　　　危機管理
490 **safe and sound**　　　　　　　無事で
Just access your password-protected website to make sure everything is safe and sound.
すべてが無事であることを確かめるために、パスワードで保護されたウェブサイトにアクセスしてください。

491 **secure** [sikjúər]　　　　　　　〔形〕安全な

メール

492 **attach** [ətǽtʃ]　　　　　　　〔名〕添付　〔動〕添付する
To send a document, just click there where it says "attach."
書類を送るには「添付」と書いてあるところをクリックしてください。

493 **attachment** [ətǽtʃmənt]　　　〔名〕添付書類
494 **chat online**　　　　　　　　オンライン上でチャットする
Of course, when you chat online, you won't be able to tell your new friend's age.
もちろんオンライン上でチャットするとき、新しい友人の年齢がわからないでしょう。

495 **chat room** チャットルーム
Meeting people in chat rooms is one of the main advantages of the Internet.
チャットルームで人々に出会うことは、インターネットの主な利点の一つです。

496 **controversial issue** 論争的な問題
Being able to discuss controversial issues anonymously can make for some interesting conversations.
匿名で論争的な問題を議論できることは、いくつかの興味深い会話を可能にします。

497 **correspond with** 〜と通信する

498 **delete** [dilíːt] 〔動〕削除する
deletion〔名〕削除、消去

499 **domain** [douméin] 〔名〕ドメイン、住所表示

500 **easy-to-use** 〔形〕使いやすい
Our latest cellphone model includes an easy-to-use voice mail system.
最新の携帯電話のモデルは使いやすい音声メール・システムを含んでいます。

501 **e-mail** [íːmèil] 〔名〕Eメール
Do you know how to send a document along with an e-mail?
書類をEメールで送る方法を知っていますか。

502 **forward** [fɔ́ːrwərd] 〔動〕送信する、転送する

503 **incoming** [ínkʌmiŋ] 〔形〕着信の
(反) outgoing 送信の

504 **receive confirmation** 受信確認

505 **regarding** [rigáːrdiŋ] 〔前〕〜に関して

506 **reply** [riplái] 〔動〕返信する 〔名〕返信

507 **save** [séiv] 〔動〕保存する
storage [stɔ́ːridʒ]〔名〕保存

508 **spam** [spǽm] 〔名〕スパム、迷惑メール
509 **subject** [sʌ́bdʒekt] 〔名〕件名
subject line 件名欄

510 **wireless** [wáiərləs] 〔形〕ワイヤレスの
Our technicians will equip your home with tiny wireless cameras.
私たちの技術者が小さなワイヤレスカメラを家に備え付けます。

ソフト

511 **copyright** [kápiràit] 〔名〕著作権
512 **fraudulent use** 不正使用
513 **fulfillment** [fulfílmənt] 〔名〕履行、遂行
fulfill [fulfíl] 〔動〕満たす

514 **guidelines** [gáidlàinz] 〔名〕ガイドライン、指針
515 **illegal copy** 違法コピー
516 **index** [índeks] 〔名〕索引
517 **install** [instɔ́ːl] 〔動〕インストールする
installation [instəléiʃən] 〔名〕インストール
reinstall 〔動〕再インストールする

518 **piracy** [páiərəsi] 〔名〕著作権侵害
The government must take steps to deal harshly with online piracy.
政府はオンライン上の著作権侵害を厳しく取り締まるための手段をとらねばなりません。

519 **renewal** [rinjúːəl] 〔名〕更新
520 **upgrade** [ʌ́pgrèid] 〔動〕アップグレードする、性能を高める

パソコン利用と姿勢

521 **discomfort** [diskʌ́mfərt] 〔名〕不快感
The longer you work at your keyboard, the more discomfort you will feel in your wrists and forearms.

キーボードで長く仕事をすればするほど、ますます手首と前腕に不快感を感じるでしょう。

522 **excessive repetition** 　　過度の繰り返し
It is best to vary your activities to avoid excessive repetition.
過度の繰り返しを避けるために、活動を変えることが一番良いです。

523 **frequently** [frí:kwəntli] 　　〔副〕頻繁に

524 **right angle** 　　直角
When you work at your monitor, sit with your back straight so your knees, hips and elbows form right angles.
モニターを見て仕事をするときは、ひざ、ヒップ、ひじが直角になるように背筋を伸ばして座ってください。

525 **stiffen up** 　　こわばる、硬くなる
After a couple of hours or so, my neck stiffens up and I start to get a headache.
2、3時間ほどすると、首がこわばり、頭痛が始まります。

526 **strain** [stréin] 　　〔名〕（身体の）変調、痛み
Jogging puts a lot of stress and strain on the knees.
ジョギングはひざに多くのストレスと痛みを与えます。

527 **tension** [ténʃən] 　　〔名〕緊張
There are several things you can do to relieve tension caused by overwork.
働きすぎて起こる緊張を和らげるためにできることがいくつかあります。

電話

528 **answering machine** 　　留守番電話
529 **area code** 　　市外番号
530 **call back** 　　折り返し電話する、電話をかけ直す
Just leave your name and number and I'll call back later.
名前と電話番号を残してください。そうすれば後で折返し電話します。

531 **call in sick** 病気の電話をする
532 **call-waiting telephone** キャッチホン
533 **cellular phone** 携帯電話
　（類）cellphone, mobile phone 携帯電話

534 **conference call** 電話による会議
　Conference calls have greatly reduced our transportation costs.
　電話会議は交通費を大幅に減らしました。

535 **connect** [kənékt] 〔動〕つなぐ
　connection [kənékʃən]〔名〕接続

536 **extension** [iksténʃən] 内線
537 **get in touch with** ～に連絡をとる
538 **hang up** （電話を）切る
　I'll hang up now and listen to your comments.
　いま電話を切り、あなたの意見を聞きます。

539 **hold on** （電話を）切らずに待つ
540 **international call** 国際電話
541 **leave a message** メッセージを残す
542 **local call** 市内電話
543 **on hold** 待たせておいて、保留状態で
　Put her on hold.
　彼女を待たせておいて。

544 **PBX (=private branch exchange)** 構内交換電話
　You get all the features of an expensive PBX system at a fraction of the cost.
　ごくわずかの費用で高価な構内交換電話システムの特徴のすべてを得られます。

545 **telecommunication** [tèləkəmjùːnikéiʃən]〔名〕通信
546 **wrong number** 間違い電話

郵便・ファックス・宅配

547 **attention** [əténʃən] 〔名〕宛先
548 **by snail mail** 普通郵便で
549 **collect on delivery** 着払いする
550 **confidential** [kɑ̀nfədénʃəl] 〔名〕親展
551 **deliver** [dilívər] 〔動〕配達する
delivery [dilívəri] 〔名〕配達
delivery charge 配達料金

552 **express** [iksprés] 〔名〕速達 〔副〕速達で 〔形〕速達の
553 **fax** [fæks] 〔名〕ファックス 〔動〕ファックスする
554 **fragile** [frǽdʒəl] 〔形〕壊れやすい
Fragile: Handle with Care 壊れ物につき取り扱い注意 (荷物の表示)

555 **package** [pǽkidʒ] 〔名〕小包
556 **PO Box** 私書箱
557 **postage** [póustidʒ] 〔名〕郵便料金
558 **registered** [rédʒistərd] 〔形〕書留の
559 **remittance** [rimítəns] 〔名〕送金
560 **ZIP code** 郵便番号

7. 待遇制度
給与・手当

561 **allowance** [əláuəns] 〔名〕手当
housing allowance 住宅手当 travel allowance 通勤手当

562 **basic pay** 基本給
(類) basic salary

563 **be entitled to** 〜する権利がある

564 **benefit** [bénəfit] 〔名〕手当、給付
benefit package 福利厚生（給付や手当を組み合わせた全体を指す）

565 **by the week** 週給で
In this company all the employees are paid by the week.
この会社ではすべての従業員は週給をもらいます。

566 **compensation** [kὰmpənséiʃən] 給料、報酬
unemployment compensation 失業手当

567 **emergency leave** 緊急の休み
Emergency leaves are granted on a case-by-case basis.
緊急の休みはケースバイケースで認められます。

568 **hourly pay** 時間給
（類）hourly payroll

569 **leave** [líːv] 〔名〕休暇
Mr. Owen has taken an extended leave of absence to get his MBA.
オウエンさんは経営学修士を取るため長期休暇をとっています。

570 **overtime compensation** 残業手当

571 **overtime pay** 超過勤務手当
Strikers are demanding that overtime pay be restored.
ストライキ参加者は超過勤務手当が復活することを要求しています。

572 **paid leave** 有給休暇
（類）paid holiday
on leave 休暇で

573 **paid vacation** 有給休暇
We can't take a paid vacation until we have worked here for at least a year.

少なくとも1年間ここで働くまでは有給休暇をとれません。

574 **pay increase** 　　　　　　　昇給
　(類) pay raise　(反) pay cut 給与カット、減給

575 **paycheck** [péitʃèk] 　　　　〔名〕給料
　(類) payroll [péiròul]
　weekly paycheck 週給

576 **perk** [pə́ːrk] 　　　　　　　〔名〕臨時収入、特典
　(類) perquisite [pə́ːrkwəzit]

577 **raise** [réiz] 　　　　　　　〔名〕昇給

578 **retirement** [ritáiərmənt] 　〔名〕退職
　retire [ritáiər] 〔動〕退職する
　take early retirement 早期退職する
　compulsory retirement 定年退職

579 **retirement benefits** 　　　退職金
　New employees qualify for retirement benefits once they complete their probation period.
　新入社員はいったん試用期間を終えると退職金の資格を得ます。
　(類) retirement allowance

580 **reward** [riwɔ́ːrd] 　　　　　〔名〕報酬

581 **salary** [sǽləri] 　　　　　　〔名〕給料
　(類) wage [wéidʒ]　pay [péi]
　annual salary 年棒　monthly salary 月給　weekly salary 週給

582 **security** [sikjúərəti] 　　　〔名〕保障、安心
　job security 雇用の保障

583 **sick leave** 　　　　　　　　病気休暇
　Full-time, permanent employees receive 10 days' annual sick leave.
　フルタイムの終身雇用の社員は年に10日の病気休暇をとれます。

161

584 **sick pay**　　　　　　　　　　　病気手当
　　maternity pay 出産手当

585 **spouse** [spáus]　　　　　　　〔名〕配偶者
586 **tax** [tǽks]　　　　　　　　　〔名〕税
　　tax break 特別減税　tax cut 減税

587 **workers' compensation**　　　労働者災害補償金
　　Workers' compensation is paid to those who are injured on the job.
　　労働者災害補償金は仕事で怪我をした人に支払われます。

保険・年金

588 **certificate** [sərtífikət]　　　〔名〕保険証、証明書
589 **coverage** [kʌ́vəridʒ]　　　　〔名〕保険金額
590 **dependent** [dipéndənt]　　　〔名〕扶養家族
591 **health insurance**　　　　　　健康保険
　　Does the new employee health insurance plan include coverage for psychological disorders?
　　新入社員用健康保険プランは精神障害の補償を含みます。

592 **insurance** [inʃúərəns]　　　　〔名〕保険
　　insurance premium 〔名〕保険料

593 **insurer** [inʃúərər]　　　　　　〔名〕保険会社
　　insured [inʃúərd] 〔名〕保険契約者

594 **medical benefits**　　　　　　医療給付制度
595 **medical insurance**　　　　　医療保険
596 **pension** [pénʃən]　　　　　　〔名〕年金
　　retirement pension 退職年金

597 **policy** [páləsi]　　　　　　　〔名〕証書、契約

598 **premium** [príːmiəm] 〔名〕保険料
599 **recipient** [risípiənt] 〔名〕(保険)受取人
600 **social security** 社会保障制度
(類) the welfare state

601 **welfare** [wélfèəɾ] 〔名〕福祉
welfare payment 福祉給付金

602 **welfare-to-work** 〔名〕再就職支援政策

8. マネー
銀行

603 **account** [əkáunt] 〔名〕口座
I paid fifteen hundred dollars into my daughter's account to cover this term's tuition.
今学期の授業料を補うため娘の口座に1,500ドルを振り込みました。

604 **amount** [əmáunt] 〔名〕金額
the full amount 全額

605 **ATM card** キャッシュカード

606 **balance** [bǽləns] 〔名〕残高
Could you check and see what my savings account balance is?
普通預金口座の残高をチェックしてくれますか。

607 **banking service** 銀行業務サービス
Call our automated phone banking service to check your balances 24-7.
いつでも残高を確認するため銀行の自動電話サービスに電話してください。
24-7「いつでも」(twenty-four hours a day, seven days a week より)

608 **check** [tʃék] 〔名〕小切手
Alex wrote a check for a large amount of money, but it bounced.

アレックスは高額の小切手を書いたが、不渡りになりました。

609 **checking account** 　　　　当座預金口座
Mike opened a checking account at Gopher State National Bank.
マイクはゴーファーステート国立銀行で当座預金口座を開きました。

610 **city bank** 　　　　都市銀行

611 **click** [klík] 　　　　〔動〕クリックする
I clicked the "My Document" icon, but it wouldn't open.
「マイドキュメント」をクリックしたが、どうしても開きませんでした。

612 **commercial bank** 　　　　商業銀行

613 **credit** [krédit] 　　　　〔動〕入金する　〔名〕信用貸し

614 **credit card** 　　　　クレジットカード
Credit cards are convenient, but they can also lead to financial ruin.
クレジットカードは便利ですが、財政破綻にもつながります。

615 **deposit** [dipázit] 　　　　〔動〕預ける　〔名〕預金
Smart savers deposit at least half their bonus into their savings account.
利口な貯蓄家はボーナスの少なくとも半分を普通預金口座に預けます。
deposit rate 預金利率
deposit box 貸金庫

616 **income tax** 　　　　所得税
property tax 固定資産税

617 **interest** [íntərəst] 　　　　〔名〕利子、利息
Our "preferred customer" checking account pays three times the interest of a regular account.
「お得意様」当座預金口座は、普通の口座の3倍の利息がつきます。

618 **interest rate** 　　　　利子率
619 **official bank rate** 　　　　公定歩合

620 **passbook** [pǽsbuk] 〔名〕預金通帳
621 **PIN (=personal identification number)** 暗証番号
622 **reimbursement** [rìːimbə́ːrsmənt] 〔名〕払い戻し、払い戻し金
　　reimburse [rìːimbə́ːrs] 〔動〕払い戻す

623 **savings account** 普通預金口座
624 **statement** [stéitmənt] 〔名〕取引明細書
625 **telegraphic transfer** 電子送金
626 **time deposit** 定期預金
627 **transfer** [trænsfə́ːr] 〔動〕送金する　〔名〕送金
　　（類）remit [rimít]

628 **withdraw** [wiðdrɔ́ː] 〔名〕（預金）を引き出す
　　withdrawal [wiðdrɔ́ːəl] 〔名〕引き出し（額）

金融

629 **capital gain** キャピタルゲイン、資産売却益
630 **collapse** [kəlǽps] 〔名〕崩壊　〔動〕崩壊する
631 **consultant** [kənsʌ́lt(ə)nt] 〔名〕コンサルタント
632 **currency** [kə́ːrənsi] 〔名〕通貨
　　currency exchange 通貨の両替

633 **currency in circulation** 流通貨幣
634 **deregulation** [dìːrègjəléiʃ(ə)n] 〔名〕規制緩和
635 **exchange rate** 為替相場
　　（類）currency rate 為替レート
　　exchange gain 為替差益
　　exchange loss 為替差損

636 **financial institution** 金融機関
　　financial services 金融サービス

637 **financial policy** 金融政策
  (類) monetary policy
  appreciation of the yen 円高
  depreciation of the yen 円安

638 **financing** [finǽnsiŋ] 〔名〕（金融機関からの）融資金
639 **fiscal deficit** 財政赤字
640 **fluctuate** [fĺʌktʃuéit] 〔動〕（価格が）変動する、上下する
  fluctuation [flʌktʃuéiʃən] 〔名〕変動

641 **foreign currency reserves** 外貨準備高
642 **loan** [lóun] 〔名〕ローン
643 **make ends meet** 帳尻を合わせる
644 **money supply** 通貨供給量
645 **pay off** 清算する
646 **payer** [péiər] 〔名〕支払人
  (反) payee [peií:] 〔名〕受取人

647 **payment** [péimənt] 〔名〕支払い、払い込み
  payment in advance 前払い　payment on account 内払い

648 **rate** [réit] 〔名〕金利、料金
649 **refund** [rifʌ́nd] 〔名〕返金、払戻金
  refundable [rifʌ́ndəbl] 〔形〕払い戻し可能な

650 **reminder** [rimáindər] 〔名〕延滞通知、催促状
651 **skyrocket** [skáirɑ̀kit] 〔動〕（金額が）急上昇する、急騰する
652 **valid** [vǽlid] 〔形〕有効な
  (反) invalid [ínvəlid] 〔形〕無効な

投資

653 **asset** [ǽset] 〔名〕資産、財産
The company's remaining assets are being liquidated to pay off its creditors.
会社の残っている資産は債権者に完済するため清算されています。

654 **bidding price** 入札価格

655 **bond** [bánd] 〔名〕債権
government bonds 国債　deficit financing bowk 赤字国債

656 **broker** [bróukər] 〔名〕株式仲買人

657 **commodities** [kəmádətiz] 〔名〕商品、生産物
agricultural commodities 農産物

658 **consecutive** [kənsékjutiv] 〔形〕連続した

659 **creditor** [kréditər] 〔名〕債権者

660 **dividend** [dívədènd] 〔名〕配当、配当金
pay a dividend 配当がつく

661 **insider dealing** インサイダー取引（違法行為）

662 **invest** [invést] 〔動〕投資する
investment [invéstmənt] 〔名〕投資、出資
investment in stock 株式投資

663 **IPO(=initial public offering)** 新規株式公開

664 **mutual funds** 投資信託

665 **non-performing loans** 不良債権

666 **proceed** [prəsíːd] 〔名〕収益、もうけ
Proceeds from the auction will be donated to several local charities.
オークションの収益はいくつかの現地の慈善団体に寄付されるでしょう。

667 **rebound** [ribáund] 〔動〕（価格が）反発する、回復する

（類）recover [rikʌ́vər]

668 **securities investment** 　　証券投資

669 **shareholder** [ʃéərhòuldər] 　〔名〕株主
　share [ʃéər]〔名〕株

670 **stock** [stάk] 　〔名〕株式
　（類）securities [sikjúərətiz] 　share [ʃéər]
　stock certificate 株券
　over-the-counter stock 店頭株
　active stock 人気株　growth stock 成長株
　listed stock 上場株

671 **stock exchange** 　　証券取引所

672 **stock market** 　　株式市場

673 **stockholder's equity** 　　株主資本

674 **yield** [jíːld] 　〔名〕利回り
　investmet with high yields 高利回りの投資

9. マーケティング
市場

675 **affordable** [əfɔ́ːrdəbl] 　〔形〕手ごろな（価格の）

676 **authentic** [ɔːθéntik] 　〔形〕本物の

677 **brand** [brǽnd] 　〔名〕銘柄、商標

678 **business condition** 　　景気

679 **consumer** [kənsúːmər] 　〔名〕消費者

680 **exhibition** [èksəbíʃən] 　〔名〕展示会
　exhibit [igzíbit]〔動〕展示する

681 **generic** [dʒənérik] 　〔形〕ノーブランドの、無印の
　（反）branded [brǽndid]〔形〕有名ブランドの

168

682	**high-profile** [hàipróufail]	〔形〕	人目を引く
683	**market share**		市場占有率
684	**marketing** [máːrkitiŋ]	〔名〕	マーケティング
685	**niche** [nítʃ]	〔名〕	すき間、ニッチ

niche market ニッチ市場、すき間市場
niche marketing ニッチ戦略

686	**promotion** [prəmóuʃən]	〔名〕	販売促進

promotional [prəmóuʃənəl] 〔形〕販売促進の

687	**questionnaire** [kwèstʃənéər]	〔名〕	アンケート

fill out a questionnaire アンケート用紙に記入する

688	**recognition** [rèkəgníʃən]	〔名〕	認識

recognize [rékəgnàiz] 〔動〕認識する

689	**respondent** [rispá(ː)ndənt]	〔名〕	回答者
690	**session** [séʃən]	〔名〕	セッション、説明会
691	**survey** [sərvéi]	〔名〕	調査
692	**target** [táːrgit]	〔動〕標的にする	〔名〕標的

target market 標的市場

生産

693	**assembly** [əsémbli]	〔名〕	組み立て、組立品

assemble [əsémbl] 〔動〕組み立てる   assembly line 流れ作業

694	**commercialize** [kəmə́ːrʃəlàiz]	〔動〕	商品化する

commercial [kəmə́ːrʃəl] 〔形〕商売になる、商業の

695	**component** [kəmpóunənt]	〔名〕	部品
696	**cost price**		原価
697	**expenses** [ikspénsiz]	〔名〕	経費

Several unforeseen factors have made it impossible for the branch to meet its expenses.
いくつかの不測の要因で支店が経費を満たすことが不可能になりました。

698 **gadget** [gǽdʒit] 〔名〕器具
699 **in progress** 進行中の
700 **innovation** [ìnəvéiʃən] イノベーション、革新
701 **inspect** [inspékt] 〔動〕検査する、念入りに調べる
inspection [inspékʃən] 〔名〕検査

702 **manufacturing** [mæ̀njufǽktʃəriŋ] 〔名〕生産
manufacture 生産する
manufacturer メーカー、製造業者

703 **operation** [àpəréiʃən] 〔名〕業務、営業、経営
be in operation 経営されている

704 **output** [áutpùt] 〔名〕生産高、生産物、商品
set up output 生産を増加する

705 **product** [prádʌkt] 〔名〕製品
Compared with similar products, this one is of significantly higher quality.
似た製品と比べて、これはかなり高品質です。

706 **productivity** [pròudʌktívəti] 〔名〕生産力
Productivity naturally suffered and sales slumped as a result of strained employee-employer relations.
こじれた労使関係の結果として、生産力は当然落ち、売り上げは急に落ち込みました。

707 **raw material** 原材料
708 **spare** [spéər] 〔形〕予備の
709 **specifications** [spèsifikéiʃənz] 〔名〕スペック、仕様書

710 **state-of-the-art** 〔形〕最先端の
(類) cutting-edge [kʌ́tiŋédʒ] 〔形〕最先端の

711 **subcontract** [sʌ̀bká(:)ntrækt] 〔名〕下請け（契約）
subcontractor 下請け業者

712 **supplier** [səpláiər] 〔名〕供給者、納入業者
713 **vendor** [véndər] 〔名〕販売業者、売り手

顧客サービス

714 **apology** [əpálədʒi] 〔名〕わび、謝罪
Please accept our sincere apologies and thank you for your patience.
心からお詫びいたします。ご辛抱いただきありがとうございました。

715 **call center** テレホンセンター
716 **cause** [kɔ́:z] 〔動〕引き起こす
717 **compensate** [kámpənsèit] 〔動〕補償する
compensation [kàmpənséiʃən] 〔名〕賠償金、補償金

718 **complaint** [kəmpléint] 〔名〕苦情
complain [kəmpléin] 〔動〕苦情を言う

719 **customer service** 顧客サービス業務
720 **damage** [dǽmidʒ] 〔名〕損害、破損
721 **defective** [diféktiv] 〔名〕不良品、欠陥
defective merchandise 欠陥商品

722 **dissatisfied** [díssætisfàid] 〔形〕不満足な
723 **flaw** [flɔ́:] 〔名〕不備、欠陥
(類) imperfection [impərfékʃən] 不備　defect [dí:fekt] 傷、欠陥

724 **guarantee** [gærəntíː]　〔名〕保証　〔動〕保証する
a money-back guarantee 返金保証
be under quarantee 保証期間中で

725 **inconvenient** [ìnkənvíːniənt]　〔名〕不便
726 **misuse** [mìsjúːs]　〔名〕不正利用
727 **replace** [ripléis]　〔動〕交換する
728 **valued client** [vǽljuːd kláiənt]　大切な顧客

10. 会議・プレゼンテーション
会議

729 **attend** [əténd]　〔動〕出席する
730 **board member**　委員会のメンバー
All the board members were present with the exception of Sam Johnson.
サム・ジョンソンを除き、すべての委員会のメンバーが出席しました。

731 **board of directors**　取締役会、重役会
732 **business meeting**　仕事の打ち合わせ
733 **ceremony** [sérəmòuni]　〔名〕儀式
734 **chair** [tʃéər]　〔動〕議長をする
735 **conference** [kánfərəns]　〔名〕会議
736 **debate** [dibéit]　〔名〕ディベート　〔動〕討論する
737 **enrolment** [inróulmənt]　〔名〕登録、登録者数
738 **hold a meeting**　会議を開く
739 **participant** [pɑːrtísəpənt]　〔名〕参加者
740 **show up**　現れる
Mary is not at all punctual, and rarely shows up on time.
メアリーはぜんぜん時間を守らず、時間通りに現れることはめったにありません。

172

会議進行

741 **agenda** [ədʒéndə] 〔名〕議事、議題
The next item on the agenda was the budget for the annual Founder's Day Celebration.
議題の次の項目は、毎年恒例の創立記念祝賀会の予算でした。

742 **argument** [ɑ́ːrɡjumənt] 〔名〕議論

743 **call to order** 開会を宣言する
The meeting began at 10:00 a.m. sharp, called to order by the Chairman.
会議は10時きっかりにはじまり、議長によって開会が宣言されました。

744 **disclosure** [disklóuʒər] 〔名〕情報公開

745 **dispute** [dispjúːt] 〔名〕争議

746 **handout** [hǽndàut] 〔名〕配布資料
hand out 配る、配布する

747 **minutes** [mínits] 〔名〕議事録
The minutes of the meeting were recorded by Margaret, secretary to the Chairman.
会議の議事録は議長の秘書のマーガレットが記録しました。

748 **outline** [áutlàin] 〔動〕概略を述べる 〔名〕概要、要点
outline a proposal 提案の概略を述べる

749 **take the minutes** 議事録をとる

プレゼン心構え

750 **absorb** [æbsɔ́ːrb] 〔動〕吸収する、飲み込む、理解させる
When you make an important point, pause to allow the audience to absorb what you are saying.
重要な意見を述べるとき、言っていることを理解してもらうために一息入れなさい。

751 **all-important** [ɔ́:limpɔ́:rtənt] 〔形〕きわめて重要な、必須の
To give a successful dinner party, preparation is all-important.
夕食会を成功させるためには、準備がきわめて重要です。

752 **anecdote** [ǽnikdòut] 〔名〕逸話、秘話
His memoirs are filled with fascinating anecdotes about his years in Hollywood.
彼の自叙伝はハリウッドの年月についての魅惑的な秘話で一杯です。

753 **appropriate** [əpróupriət] 〔形〕適切な、ふさわしい
When dealing with clients from other cultures, you must try to use the appropriate gestures and facial expressions.
文化の異なる顧客に対応するとき、適切なジェスチャーと表情をするようにしなければなりません。

754 **audience** [ɔ́:diəns] 〔名〕聴衆
The audience responded with a standing ovation.
聴衆はスタンディングオベーションで応えました。

755 **beforehand** [bifɔ́:rhænd] 〔副〕前もって、あらかじめ
Always make sure you are familiar with your products' features beforehand.
前もっていつも必ず製品の特徴に精通しておきなさい。

756 **eye contact** アイコンタクト、視線を合わせること
To gain a client's trust, you must maintain eye contact and listen carefully.
顧客の信頼を得るために、視線を合わせ、注意深く聞くようにしなければなりません。

757 **give a speech** スピーチをする
I'm too nervous and shy to give a speech in front of so many people.
あまりにも神経質で恥ずかしがりやなので、そんなに多くの人の前でスピーチをすることができません。

758 **glance** [glǽns] 〔動〕ちらりと見る、さっと見る
Never read your speech; just glance at your notes from time to time.

決してスピーチ（原稿）を読んではいけません、ときどきメモを見るようにしなさい。

759 **impress** [imprés] 〔動〕印象を与える、感動させる
I was very impressed by the way you handled yourself during the trial.
裁判中のあなたの振舞い方にとても感動しました。

760 **monotonous** [mənátənəs] 〔形〕単調な、一本調子の、退屈な
Keep your speech from becoming monotonous by varying your tone of voice.
声の調子を変えることで、スピーチが単調にならないようにしなさい。

761 **on behalf of** （人）のために、代表して
On behalf of all the children, thank you so much for visiting us in class today.
すべての子供たちを代表して、今日は教室に来ていただき心から感謝します。

762 **optimistic** [ὰptəmístik] 〔形〕楽天的な、のんきな
I remain optimistic that one day we shall overcome all our environmental problems.
すべての環境問題を、いつか克服できるだろうと楽天的な気持ちでいます。

763 **organize** [ɔ́ːrɡənàiz] 〔動〕まとめる、整理する
We can help you organize your office for maximum efficiency.
最高の能率にするため、あなたのオフィスをまとめる手助けができます。

764 **podium** [póudiəm] 〔名〕演壇
Walk up to the podium with confidence.
自信を持って演壇に上がりなさい。

765 **poise** [pɔ́iz] 〔名〕落ち着き、落ち着いた態度
You will be judged not only on your beauty, but also on your poise and talent.
あなたの美しさだけでなく、落ち着いた態度と才能でも判断されるでしょう。

766 **pronunciation** [prənʌnsiéiʃən]　　〔名〕発音
Speak slowly so that your pronunciation is clear and easy to understand.
発音がはっきりと理解しやすいようにゆっくりと話しなさい。

767 **proof** [prúːf]　　〔名〕証拠、証明
You will need solid proof to back up such serious accusations.
このような重大な告訴を支援するには、確固たる証拠が必要でしょう。

768 **quotation** [kwoutéiʃən]　　〔名〕引用、引用文〔語句〕
I like to put quotations from famous men and women in my diary.
有名な男女の引用語句を日記に書くのが好きです。

769 **refer to**　　参照する
770 **rehearse** [rihə́ːrs]　　〔動〕リハーサルをする、繰り返し練習する
Would you help me rehearse my lines for tomorrow night's play?
明日の夜の劇のセリフをリハーサルするのを手伝っていただけますか。

771 **self-confidence** [sèlfkɑ́nfədəns]　〔名〕自信
772 **self-improvement** [sèlfimprúːvmənt]〔名〕自己改善
773 **shoulder-width**　　肩幅の、肩の幅まで
Stand straight with your feet shoulder-width apart, look up at your audience, and start singing.
足を肩幅に開いて背すじをのばして立ち、顔を上げて聴衆を見つめ、歌い始めなさい。

774 **table** [téibl]　　〔名〕表

スピーチ・ことば

775 **after-dinner speech**　　（食後の）テーブルスピーチ
Do you know who is going to deliver tonight's after-dinner speech?
今夜のテーブルスピーチをするのは誰だか知っていますか。

776 **all but**　　ほとんど
Poverty in Africa is a situation that at times seems all but hopeless.

アフリカの貧困は時々ほとんど希望のない状態です。

777 **as a result** 結果として

778 **cross-cultural** [krɔ̀:skʌ́ltʃərəl] 〔形〕異文化の

779 **expression** [ikspréʃən] 〔名〕表現

780 **instruction** [instrʌ́kʃən] 〔名〕指示
The assembly instructions were poorly written and difficult to follow.
集会の指示は下手に書かれ、理解するのが困難でした。

781 **objective** [əbdʒéktiv] 〔名〕目標

782 **proficiency** [prəfíʃənsi] 〔名〕熟達
proficient [prəfíʃənt]〔形〕熟達した、堪能な

783 **sexist remark** 性差別発言
The announcer was let go for making sexist remarks on the air.
そのアナウンサーは放送で性差別発言をして解雇されました。

784 **skill** [skíl] 〔名〕能力
skillful [skílfəl]〔形〕巧みな、上手な

785 **specific purpose** 特定の目的

786 **summarize** [sʌ́məràiz] 〔動〕要約する
summary [sʌ́məri]〔名〕要約、概要

提案

787 **accountability** [əkàuntəbíləti] 〔名〕説明義務
accountable [əkáuntəbl]〔形〕説明の責任がある

788 **approval** [əprúːvəl] 〔名〕賛成、承認
(反) objection [əbdʒékʃən]〔名〕反対意見、異議

789 **motion** [móuʃən] 〔名〕動議、提案

790 **second** [sékənd]　　　　　〔動〕支持する
Susan seconded the motion.
スーザンがその動議を支持しました。

791 **speak my piece**　　　　　自分の意見を言う
Thanks for letting me speak my piece.
自分の意見を述べさせてくれてありがとうございました。

792 **suggestion** [səɡdʒéstʃən]　　〔名〕提案
（類）proposal [prəpóuzəl]

11. 経済状況
産業

793 **aerospace** [éərəspèis]　　　〔名〕航空宇宙
an aerospace industry 航空宇宙産業

794 **amusement** [əmjú:zmənt]　　〔名〕娯楽、楽しみ
（類）entertainment [èntərtéinmənt] 〔名〕催し物、ショー

795 **chemical** [kémikəl]　　　　〔名〕化学物質
796 **civil engineering**　　　　　土木工学
797 **construction** [kənstrʌ́kʃən]　〔名〕建設
under construction 工事中で　a construction site 工事現場

798 **cosmetics** [kɑzmétiks]　　　〔名〕化粧品
799 **deindustrialization**　　　　産業の空洞化
800 **fishery** [fíʃəri]　　　　　　〔名〕水産業
801 **industrial** [indʌ́striəl]　　　〔形〕産業の、工業の
industrial develpoment 産業振興
industry [índəstri] 〔名〕産業　industrial waste 産業廃棄物

802 **local industry**　　　　　　地場産業

803 **machinery** [məʃíːnəri] 〔名〕機械
804 **material** [mətíəriəl] 〔名〕素材
raw material 原材料

805 **mechanic** [məkǽnik] 〔名〕機械工
806 **mine** [máin] 〔名〕炭鉱
807 **petroleum** [pətróuliəm] 〔名〕石油、原油
petroleum products 石油製品

808 **pharmaceutical** [fɑ̀ːrməsúːtikəl] 〔形〕医薬品の
pharmaceutical products 医薬品

809 **publish** [pʌ́bliʃ] 〔動〕出版する
publisher [pʌ́bliʃər] 〔名〕出版社 publishing [pʌ́bliʃiŋ] 〔名〕出版

810 **safeguard** [séifgɑ̀ːrd] 〔名〕予防措置

811 **textile** [tékstail] 〔名〕織物
the woollen textile industry 毛織物産業

812 **trade imbalance** 貿易不均衡
813 **venture** [véntʃər] 〔名〕ベンチャー事業
venture business ベンチャービジネス

科学・技術

814 **achievement** [ətʃíːvmənt] 〔名〕達成
815 **analyze** [ǽnəlàiz] 〔名〕分析
816 **apparatus** [æ̀pərǽtəs] 〔名〕器具
817 **astronomy** [əstrá(ː)nəmi] 〔名〕天文学
818 **atomic number** 原子番号
Each element has a number, called an atomic number.
それぞれの元素は原子番号と呼ばれる番号があります。

819 **biologist** [baiάlədʒist]　〔名〕生物学者
biology [baiάlədʒi]〔名〕生物学　biological [bàiəlάdʒikəl]〔形〕生物の

820 **capacity** [kəpǽsəti]　〔名〕収容能力
821 **chemist** [kémist]　〔名〕化学者
822 **conductor** [kəndʌ́ktər]　〔名〕伝導体
823 **data** [déitə]　〔名〕データ
824 **element** [éləmənt]　〔名〕元素
There are 92 different elements that occur naturally.
自然に発生する92の異なる元素があります。

825 **energy** [énərdʒi]　〔名〕エネルギー
The ancient Greek word for "work," *energia*, gave the word "energy" to the English Language.
古代のギリシア語で「仕事」を意味するenergiaが、英語に「エネルギー」という語をもたらしました。

826 **evolution** [èvəlú:ʃən]　〔名〕進化
Evolution is being carried out through natural selection.
進化は自然淘汰によってなされています。

827 **experiment** [ikspérəmənt]　〔名〕実験
You must conduct some experiments to prove your hypothesis.
あなたは仮説を証明するためにいくつかの実験をしなければなりません。

828 **fertilizer** [fə́:rtəlàizər]　〔名〕化学肥料
829 **fuel** [fjú:əl]　〔名〕燃料
fossil fuel 化石燃料（石油、天然ガスなど）
fuel efficiency 燃料効率

830 **genetically modified foods**　遺伝子組み換え食品
Are there any genetically modified foods in that can of soup?
そのスープの缶詰には遺伝子組み換え食品がありますか。
additional free foods 無添加食品

preserved foods 保存食
processed foods 調理済み食品

831 **hypothesis** [haipάθəsis] 〔名〕仮説

832 **integrated circuit** 集積回路

833 **laboratory** [lǽbərətɔ̀:ri] 〔名〕実験室
The drugs are artificial — created by scientists in the laboratory.
その薬は実験室で科学者によって作られた人工的なものです。

834 **medium** [mí:diəm] 〔名〕媒体、媒介（物）

835 **molecule** [mάləkjù:l] 〔名〕分子

836 **optical** [άptikəl] 〔形〕光学の
optical instruments 光学機器　optical fiber 光ファイバー
optical disk 光ディスク

837 **organism** [ɔ́:rgənìzm] 〔名〕生物、生体組織
Some believe that man is too complex an organism to have evolved in the way Darwin says.
人間はダーウィンの言う方法で進化したとするには、あまりにも複雑な生物であると信じる人もいます。

838 **oxygen** [άksidʒən] 〔名〕酸素
Oxygen's symbol is O, hydrogen's is H, and K stands for potassium.
酸素の記号は O、水素の記号は H、K はカリウムを表します。

839 **paleontologist** [pèiliɑntάlədʒist] 〔名〕古生物学者

840 **radiation** [rèidiéiʃən] 〔名〕放射能

841 **researcher** [risə́:rtʃər] 〔名〕研究員

842 **semiconductor** [sèmikəndʌ́ktər] 〔名〕半導体

843 **separate branch** 独立した分野
Mathematics is not really a science but a separate branch of learning on its own.
数学は実は科学ではなく、それ自体学問の独立した分野です。

844 **simulator** [símjulèitər]　　〔名〕模擬実験装置

845 **sophisticated** [səfístəkèitid]　　〔形〕最先端の
The university bought some sophisticated new equipment for the physics department.
大学は物理学科に最先端の新しい設備を購入しました。

846 **synthetic** [sinθétik]　　〔形〕合成の
synthetic chemistry 合成化学　synthetic fiber 合成繊維

847 **theory** [θíːəri]　　〔名〕理論
The Big Bang theory states that the universe began with an explosion.
ビッグバン理論は宇宙が爆発で始まったということを述べています。

848 **ultrasonic** [ʌ̀ltrəsánik]　　〔形〕超音波の

849 **up-to-the-minute**　　〔形〕最新の
（類）cutting edge 最先端

850 **validity** [vəlídəti]　　〔名〕妥当性、正当性
validity check 妥当性検査

景況感

851 **booming** [búːmiŋ]　　〔形〕好況の
brisk （商売が）活発な　bull 強気の　bull market 強気市場、上げ相場

852 **business is slow**　　商売が不調である、景気が悪い
（反）business is brisk 商売が繁盛する、景気が良い

853 **capital investment**　　設備投資

854 **consumption tax**　　消費税
income tax 所得税　corporation tax 法人税
inheritance tax 相続税　resident tax 住民税

855 **CPI(=consumer price index)**　消費者物価指数
856 **cut taxes**　減税する
　(類) raise taxes 増税する

857 **declare** [dikléər]　〔動〕宣言する、発表する
Without government assistance, we will be forced to declare bankruptcy.
政府の援助がなければ、倒産を宣言しなければならないでしょう。

858 **demand** [dimǽnd]　〔名〕需要
　(反) supply [səplái] 供給

859 **depression** [dipréʃən]　〔名〕不況、不景気
　(類) bust [bʌ́st]

860 **economic** [èkənámik]　〔形〕経済の
The latest housing industry figures indicate that the economic picture is brightening.
最新の住宅産業の数字は経済の情況が明るいことを示しています。

861 **fiscal policy**　財政政策
862 **fundamentals** [fʌ̀ndəmént(ə)lz]　〔名〕（経済の）基礎、基本
863 **growth rate**　成長率
864 **potential** [pəténʃəl]　〔形〕潜在的な　〔名〕潜在能力
potential buyer 潜在購買者

865 **privatize** [práivətàiz]　〔動〕民営化する
privatization [pràivətizéiʃən]〔名〕民営化

866 **public works**　公共事業
867 **recession** [rìséʃən]　〔名〕景気後退、不況
868 **recovery** [rikʌ́vəri]　〔名〕景気回復
　(類) upturn [ʌ́ptəːrnz]〔名〕景気回復

869 **robust** [roubʌ́st] 〔形〕（経済状態が）活気のある
870 **silver lining** [láiniŋ] 明るい希望
The silver lining in the gas price increase is reduced air pollution from auto emissions.
ガソリン価格の値上げの明るい希望は、車の排ガスによる大気汚染の減少です。

871 **sluggish** [slʌ́giʃ] 〔形〕不況の
dull（商売が）不振な　bear 弱気の　bear market 弱気市場

872 **stimulus package** 景気刺激策
873 **turnaround** [tə́ːnəráund] 〔名〕売り上げの向上、好転
turn around（経済が）好転する

874 **uncertainty** [ʌnsə́ːtənti] 〔名〕先行き不安
875 **unemployment rate** 失業率
（類）jobless rate 失業率
（反）employment rate 雇用率、就業率

876 **vicious circle** 悪循環
877 **walkout** [wɔ́ːkàut] 〔名〕ストライキ

12. 通勤・交通
通勤

878 **carpool** [káːrpùːl] 〔動〕車の相乗りをする
879 **commute** [kəmjúːt] 〔動〕通勤する
commute time 通勤時間

880 **commuter** [kəmjúːtər] 〔名〕通勤者
Several commuters were injured when a car smashed into a jam-packed bus yesterday.
昨日、車がすし詰めのバスに衝突したとき、何人かの通勤客が怪我をしました。

184

881 **commuter train** 通勤電車
882 **commuting by bike** 自転車通勤
883 **flexible** [fléksəbl] 〔形〕フレックスに、柔軟な
Our employees can avoid the rush hours if we make our office hours more flexible.
勤務時間をより柔軟にするなら、社員はラッシュアワーを避けることができます。

884 **mass transit** 都市交通網
885 **pedestrian** [pədéstriən] 〔名〕歩行者
886 **telecommuting** [tèlikəmjúːtiŋ] 〔名〕在宅勤務

道路

887 **bus stop** バス停
The bus stops are equipped with devices that show when the next bus will arrive.
バス停は次のバス到着時間を示す装置が備えられています。

888 **crosswalk** [krɔ́ːswɔ̀ːk] 〔名〕横断歩道
《英》pedestrian crossing

889 **dead end** 行き止まり
890 **detour** [díːtuər] 〔名〕迂回、遠回り
take a detour 迂回する

891 **freeway** [fríːwèi] 〔名〕高速道路
（類）expressway [ikspréswei]
《英》motorway

892 **highway** [háiwèi] 〔名〕幹線道路、本通
893 **intersection** [ìntərsékʃən] 〔名〕交差点
894 **lane** [léin] 〔名〕車線
avenue, boulevard 大通り

895 **roundabout** [ráundəbàut]　〔名〕（交差点にある）ローターリー
《米》rotary, traffic circle

896 **shortcut**　近道
take a shortcut 近道をする

897 **toll** [tóul]　〔名〕通行料金
898 **tollbooth**　〔名〕料金所

交通

899 **by noon**　正午までに
I should have this order ready by noon at the latest.
遅くとも正午までにこの注文を用意すべきです。

900 **by way of**　～を通って、～経由で

901 **cab** [kǽb]　〔名〕タクシー
（類）taxicab, taxi
take / get a cab タクシーに乗る

902 **collide** [kəláid]　〔動〕衝突する
collision〔名〕衝突

903 **compartment** [kəmpá:rtmənt]　〔名〕車両

904 **congest** [kəndʒést]　〔動〕混雑する
Although the traffic was very congested, I left early and reached the office on time.
交通はとても混雑していたけれども、早く出て時間通りに会社に着きました。

905 **connection** [kənékʃən]　〔名〕（交通機関の）乗り継ぎ

906 **convenient** [kənvíːnjənt]　〔形〕便利な
The underground is the cheapest and most convenient way to get around the city.
地下鉄は町をあちこち移動するのに一番安くて最も便利な方法です。

907 **convert** [kənvə́ːrt] 〔動〕変わる、切りかわる
The 400-watt motor detaches to convert to a standard pedal bike.
400ワットのモーターは、標準的なペダルでこぐ自転車に切りかわるために取り外せます。

908 **cruise** [krúːz] 〔名〕クルーズ

909 **disrupt** [disrʌ́pt] 〔動〕混乱させる
Service on several bus lines has been disrupted indefinitely due to the chemical spill.
いくつかのバス路線の便は、化学薬品漏れにより無期限に混乱させられました。

910 **heavy traffic** 交通渋滞

911 **hold up** ストップさせる、遅らせる
Traffic was held up for over two hours, as road crews cleared the accident site.
道路整備員が事故現場を片付けていたので、交通は2時間以上にわたってストップしました。

912 **jam** [dʒǽm] 〔動〕混雑する
jammed [dʒǽmd]〔形〕渋滞した

913 **on time** 時間通りに

914 **pack up** [pǽkʌp] まとめる、荷造をする
The easy-to-fold design means you can pack your bike up and take it with you.
容易に折りたためるデザインは、自転車を荷造りし持って行けることを意味します。

915 **reckless driving** 無謀運転

916 **stop** [stáp] 〔名〕停止、止まること、バス停
Don't fall asleep, or you'll miss your stop.
眠ってはいけない、さもないとバス停を見逃すでしょう。

917 **timetable** [táimtèibl] 〔名〕時刻表
a train timetable 列車の時刻表

918 **ticket** [tíkət] 〔名〕チケット、切符

919 **traffic congestion** 交通渋滞
Because of increased traffic congestion, it is becoming difficult for employees to get to work at 9:00 a.m.
交通渋滞の増加のため、従業員が午前9時までに職場に着くことが難しくなってきています。

920 **train schedule** 列車の時刻表

921 **tram** [trǽm] 〔名〕路面電車

922 **transfer** [trǽnsfəːr] 〔名〕乗り換え
transfer [trǽnsfəːr] 〔動〕乗り換える

923 **transportation** [trænspərtéiʃən] 〔名〕輸送、交通機関
University students and faculty were advised to find alternative means of transportation.
大学生と教職員は代替の交通手段を見つけるように勧められました。

924 **trolly car** 市街電車

車関係

925 **automobile** [ɔ́ːtəməbìːl] 〔名〕自動車
automotive [ɔ́ːtəmóutiv] 〔形〕自動車の、自動の

926 **concept car** 試作車・コンセプトカー

927 **driver's license** 運転免許証

928 **flat** [flǽt] 〔形〕パンクした
get a flat tire タイヤがパンクする

929 **hood** [húd] 〔名〕ボンネット

930 **horn** [hɔ́ːrn] 〔名〕クラクション

931 **hybrid** [háibrid] 〔名〕ハイブリッドカー

932 **parking lot** 駐車場

933 **parking ticket** 駐車違反の切符

934 **rearview mirror** バックミラー
バックミラーは和製英語

935 **reserve** [rizə́:rv] 〔動〕取っておく、空けておく
Parking in this lot is reserved for bank customers.
この駐車場の駐車は銀行の顧客のために取っておかれています。

936 **satellite navigation** 衛星ナビゲーション
Thanks to my new satellite navigation system, I'll never get lost again.
衛星ナビゲーションシステムのおかげで、決して二度と迷わないでしょう。

937 **skid** [skíd] 〔動〕スリップする 〔名〕スリップ
938 **speeding** [spí:diŋ] 〔名〕スピード違反
939 **steering wheel** ハンドル
940 **windshield** [wíndʃi:ld] 〔名〕フロントガラス

＜文法のまとめ４＞

冠詞

不定冠詞（a, an）：数えられる名詞の前につける。

1. 初めて話題に上る可算名詞の単数形
   I have a cellphone made in Sweden.
   （スウェーデン製の携帯電話をもっています）

2. １つの：one
   You will have to wait an hour to see the doctor.
   （医者に診てもらうには１時間待たなければならないでしょう）

3. 〜につき：per
   The magazine comes out once a month.
   （その雑誌は１ヶ月に１回出ます）

4. 種類：「〜というもの」
   A dog is a faithful animal.
   （犬というものは忠実な動物です）

5. 同じ：the same
   These business suits are all of a size.
   （これらのスーツはみんな同じサイズです）

6. という人：a [an] + 固有名詞
   I have a Mr. White on the phone.
   （ホワイトさんという人からお電話です）

定冠詞（the）：単数形、複数形につける。特定のものを指す。

7. すでに出た名詞、情況からわかるとき
   I have a cat.　The cat is very cute.
   （ネコを飼っています。そのネコはとてもかわいいです）
   I took a taxi yesterday.　The driver was very kind.
   （昨日タクシーに乗りました。その運転手はとても親切でした）

8. 最上級、序数を修飾
   This is the deepest lake around here.
   （これはここあたりでは一番深い湖です）

9. 唯一のもの：the earth, the east, the moon, the sky, the sun, etc.

10. 新聞、河川、海洋、海峡、半島、船、列車
    the Mississippi「ミシシッピ川」　the Pacific Ocean「太平洋」
11. 総称：単数名詞につけて「〜というもの」
    The computer has changed office work.
    （コンピューターはオフィスの仕事を変えました）
12. 〜のような人々：the ＋ 形容詞（複数扱い）
    the young (=young people)「若い人々」　the poor「貧しい人々」

冠詞の慣用表現

13. 不定冠詞：once in a while「ときどき」　all of a sudden「突然に」　in a sense「ある意味では」　as a rule「概して」　at a loss「途方にくれて」
14. 定冠詞：by the way「ところで」　in the distance「遠くに」　on the way「途中で」　in the long run「長い目で見れば」　on the whole「概して」　on the contrary「反対に」

名詞・代名詞

可算名詞：数えられる名詞

1. 複数・単数の区別（a box / boxes）
2. 数詞がつく（three boxes）
   The store offers a wide selection of boxes and packing supplies.
   （その店は箱と包装用品を幅広くそろえて提供しています）

不可算名詞：数えられない名詞

3. 複数形にしない（× cakes　× furnitures）
4. 不定冠詞をつけない（× an equipment）
5. 数詞は直接つけない（○ three pieces of cake　× three cakes）
   He disposed of his unwanted furniture at a garage sale.
   （彼はガレージセールで不要な家具を処分しました）

不可算名詞の種類

6. 物質名詞：物

beer, bread, butter, coffee, gas, meat, milk, oil, tea, water, etc.
Peter likes to have a cup of coffee and bread and butter for breakfast.
（ピーターは朝食に一杯のコーヒーとバターつきのパンを食べるのが好きです）

7. 抽象名詞：性質、感情、状態
advice, honest, information, love, kindness, knowledge, wisdom, etc.
For further information, please contact the sales department.
（さらなる情報は、営業部に連絡ください）

8. 不可算名詞の量には much, little, a lot of などを使う。
The magazine offers a lot of advice for business people.
（その雑誌は実業家に、たくさんの助言を提供します）

代名詞：同じ名詞の繰り返しを避ける。

9. 人称代名詞：he, she, they, it, etc.

10. 指示代名詞：近いもの this, these, 離れたもの that, those.

11. 不定代名詞：不特定の人や物、数量　another, any, both, each, either, neither, none, one, other, some, the other, etc.
I received an e-mail from her, and read it right away. (it=e-mail)
（彼女からEメールを受け取り、すぐにそれを読みました）
I don't like this sweater.　Show me another.
（このセーターは気に入りません。他のを見せてください）
I have two computers; one is new and the other is old.
（2台のコンピューターを持っています。1つは新しく、もう1つは古いです）

12. 疑問代名詞：who, which, what

13. it の特別用法：天候、時間、曜日、季節、距離、明暗など
Is it still raining?　　　（まだ雨が降っていますか）
It is 60 miles to Chicago.　（シカゴまで60マイルです）
It is a quarter to 9 in the morning.　（午前9時15分前です）

関係詞（1）：関係代名詞

1. who：先行詞が「人」の場合
which：先行詞が「物・動物」の場合
I received a letter from Jane, which I read immediately.
（ジェーンから手紙を受け取り、すぐにそれを読みました）

2. whose：所有格
   I have a sister whose husband is a college professor.
   （夫が大学教授である姉がいます）

3. that：先行詞が形容詞の最上級、every, all, the only, the same などを伴うとき
   Jim is the staff member that has the relevant experience in sales.
   （ジムは販売に関連した経験を持つ社員です）

4. what：先行詞を含み「～すること」
   What he said was true.（＝ The thing which he said was true.）
   （彼が言ったことは本当です）

関係詞（2）：関係副詞

1. where: place, city, house, town など場所を表す語が先行詞
   This is the office where my father works.
   （これは私の父が働くオフィスです）

2. when: time, day, year など時を表す語が先行詞
   She remembered the time when she first joined the company.
   （彼女は初めて会社へ行ったときを覚えていました）

3. 前置詞 + which：when, where は書き換え可能
   This is the house where she was born.
   (= This is the house in which she was born.)

4. why：理由を表す語を先行詞
   That is the reason why he left the town.
   （それが彼が町を出て行った理由です）

日常生活頻出語句

1. 気象
2. 旅行
3. 環境
4. 健康・医療
5. 映画・DVD
6. 教育・スポーツ
7. マスコミ・メディア
8. 不動産・引越し
9. 社交・パーティー
10. 日常生活

＜文法のまとめ５＞

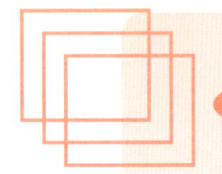

日常生活語句

1. 気象
天気・予報

1 **atmosphere** [ǽtməsfìər] 〔名〕大気
Increased fossil fuel emissions are warming the earth's atmosphere.
化石燃料の排ガスの増加は、地球の大気を暖かくしています。

2 **chance of rain** 降雨確率

3 **clear up** 晴れる
The fog cleared up around noon, allowing planes to land and take off.
霧は正午ごろに晴れて、飛行機の離発着ができるようになりました。

4 **climate** [kláimət] 〔名〕気候

5 **cloudy** [kláudi] 〔形〕曇りの
partly cloudy 所により曇りの　mostly cloudy ほとんど曇りの

6 **cold front** 寒冷前線
warm front 温暖前線

7 **condition** [kəndíʃən] 〔名〕状態
Weather is defined as the condition of the atmosphere at a particular time and place.
天気は特定の時間、場所における大気の状態と定義されます。

8 **controllable** [kəntróuləbl] 〔形〕制御できる
Indoor humidity is controllable with air-conditioners and other appliances.
屋内の湿度はエアコンと他の器具で制御できます。

9 **drizzle** [drízl] 〔名〕霧雨

10 **foggy** [fɔ́:gi] 〔形〕霧の立ちこめた
11 **freeze** [frí:z] 〔動〕冷え込む、凍る
12 **gust** [gʌ́st] 〔名〕突風
13 **heavy rain** 豪雨
14 **high** [hái] 〔名〕最高気温
low [lóu] 〔名〕最低気温

15 **high tide** 満潮
low tide 干潮

16 **high-pressure** [háipréʃər] 〔形〕高気圧の
(反) low-pressure [lóupréʃər] 〔形〕低気圧の

17 **humid** [hjú:mid] 〔形〕湿気のある
18 **humidity** [hju:mídəti] 〔名〕湿気、湿度
Outdoor humidity is at the mercy of ever-changing weather systems.
戸外の湿度は、常に変化する天候の状態次第です。

19 **in a row** 連続で
The temperature rose above 35°C for the sixth day in a row today.
気温は今日で、6日連続35℃以上に上昇しました。

20 **inclement** [inklémənt] 〔形〕荒れ模様の
21 **meteorologist** [mì:tiərálədʒist] 〔名〕気象官、気象学者
Meteorologists say future temperature rises will greatly change global weather patterns.
気象学者は、将来の気温上昇は地球の天気図を大きく変化させるであろうと言っています。

22 **meteorology** [mì:tiərálədʒi] 〔名〕気象学
23 **mild** [máild] 〔形〕穏やかな、温暖な
Last year we had a mild winter, but this year we probably won't.
昨年は穏やかな冬だったが、今年はたぶんそうではないでしょう。

24 **occasional rain** 時々雨
It will be cloudy with occasional rain tomorrow.
明日は曇り時々雨になるでしょう。
（類）intermittent rain 時おり雨

25 **ominous-looking** [ámənəslúkiŋ] 〔形〕不気味な
26 **precipitation** [prisipətéiʃən] 〔名〕降水（量）
There will be a slight chance of precipitation tomorrow due to a trough moving into the area.
明日はその地域へ気圧の谷が移動するため、少し降水が見込まれるでしょう。

27 **shiny** [ʃáini] 〔形〕晴れた、晴天の
28 **shower** [ʃáuər] 〔名〕にわか雨
29 **signal** [sígnəl] 〔名〕兆候、前触れ
30 **snowstorm** [snóustɔːrm] 〔名〕吹雪
31 **thermometer** [θəmámətər] 〔名〕温度計
32 **thunderstorm** [θʌndəstɔːrm] 〔名〕雷雨
Did you hear this morning's thunderstorm?
今朝の雷雨を聞きましたか。

33 **tornado** [tɔːrnéidou] 〔名〕竜巻
Unlike hurricanes, tornadoes don't fall neatly into a specific time of year.
ハリケーンとは違い、竜巻は1年の特定の時期にきちんと発生しません。

34 **visibility** [vìzəbíləti] 〔名〕視界
35 **warning** [wɔːrniŋ] 〔名〕警報、警告
36 **water shortage** 水不足
The area has been suffering from a water shortage since two years ago.
その地域は2年前から水不足で苦しんでいます。

37 **weather report** 天気予報
Yesterday's weather report was completely wrong.

昨日の天気予報は、まったく間違っていました。
(類) weather forecast

38 **wet to the skin / soak through**　　びしょぬれになる
It started to rain heavily and I got wet to the skin.
激しく雨が降り始め、びしょぬれになりました。

39 **windy** [wíndi]　　　　　　　　〔形〕風の強い

地理

40 **area** [éəriə]　　　　　　　　〔名〕地域、区域
On Monday, thunderstorms will head into the area from the Midwest.
月曜日には雷雨が中西部からその地域に向かうでしょう。

41 **continent** [kάntənənt]　　　〔名〕大陸
42 **inland** [ínlənd]　　　　　　〔名〕内陸
43 **peninsula** [pənínsələ]　　　〔名〕半島
44 **region** [ríːdʒən]　　　　　　〔名〕地域、地方
Sunday will bring a rain-free day to the entire region.
日曜日は全地域で雨の降らない日となるでしょう。

45 **tropical** [trάpikəl]　　　　　〔形〕熱帯の

雲の形状

46 **altocumulus** [æ̀ltoukjúːmjuləs]　〔名〕高積雲
Altocumulus clouds are puffy gray blobs that form into rows or waves.
高積雲は列や波を形成する、ふっくらとした灰色のかたまりです。

47 **altostratus** [æ̀ltoustréitəs]　〔名〕高層雲
Altostratus clouds form a smooth blue or gray sheet across the sky.
高層雲は空全体になめらかな青色や灰色の雲を形成します。

48 **cirrocumulus** [siroukjúːmjuləs] 〔名〕巻積雲
Cirrocumulus clouds are called a mackerel sky because they look like the skin of a fish.
巻積雲は魚のうろこに似ているため「鯖（サバ）雲」と呼ばれます。

49 **cirrostratus** [siroustréitəs] 〔名〕巻層雲
Cirrostratus clouds form a thin white veil across the sky, giving it a milky appearance.
巻層雲は空全体に薄くて白いヴェールを形成し、空が乳白色に見えるようになります。

50 **cirrus** [sírəs] 〔名〕巻雲（けんうん）
Cirrus clouds are thin, white, feathery clouds made of ice crystals.
巻雲は氷晶でできた、薄く白い羽毛のような雲です。

51 **cumulonimbus** [kjùːmjəlounímbəs] 〔名〕積乱雲
Cumulonimbus clouds are known as storm clouds because they augur severe storms with thunder and lightening.
積乱雲は雷と稲妻を伴う激しい嵐の前兆となるので、嵐雲として知られています。

52 **cumulus** [kjúːmjuləs] 〔名〕積雲
Cumulus clouds are large, puffy, whitish clouds that resemble a head of cauliflower.
積雲はカリフラワーの頭に似ていて、大きくてふっくらした白っぽい雲です。

53 **feathery** [féðəri] 〔形〕羽毛のような
54 **layer** [léiər] 〔名〕層
55 **nimbostratus** [nìmboustréitəs] 〔名〕乱層雲
Nimbostratus clouds form a thick dark layer, completely blocking out the sun.
乱層雲は完全に太陽を遮断し、厚くて黒い層を形成します。

56 **scale** [skéil] 〔名〕うろこ

2. 旅行
海外旅行

57 **accommodation** [əkɑ̀mədéiʃən]　〔名〕宿泊施設

58 **agency** [éidʒənsi]　〔名〕代理店

59 **alternative** [ɔːltə́ːrnətiv]　〔形〕代替の、代わりの
Since September 11, many Americans are choosing alternative means of travel.
9月11日以来、多くのアメリカ人は代わりの旅の手段を選んでいます。

60 **business trip**　ビジネス旅行、出張

61 **cancel** [kǽnsl]　〔動〕キャンセルする

62 **delicacy** [délikəsi]　〔名〕ごちそう、珍味
There are hundreds of outdoor eating establishments serving local delicacies.
地元のごちそうを出す何百もの戸外で食べる店があります。

63 **disadvantage** [dìsədvǽntidʒ]　〔名〕欠点、デメリット
One of the disadvantages of traveling long-distance by bus is the need to eat along the way.
バスでの長距離旅行の欠点の一つは、途中で食事をとる必要があることです。

64 **dozens of**　何十もの
Major tour companies have added dozens of tours to their schedules.
大手の旅行会社は何十ものツアーをスケジュールに加えました。

65 **embassy** [émbəsi]　〔名〕大使館

66 **itinerary** [aitínərèri]　〔名〕日程表、旅行計画
Our tour itinerary includes stops at Vancouver, Calgary, Toronto and Montreal.
ツアーの日程表は、バンクーバー、カルガリー、トロント、モントリオールに立ち寄ることを含みます。

67 **leave for** 〜へ出発する

68 **lodging** [lάdʒiŋ] 〔名〕宿泊所、宿
Lodging for tour members will be provided in private homes whenever possible.
ツアーメンバーの宿泊所は、可能な限り個人の家にあてがわれるでしょう。

69 **lost and found** 遺失物取扱所
I found my briefcase in the lost and found at Victoria Station.
ヴィクトリア駅の遺失物取扱所でブリーフケースを見つけました。

70 **on business** 仕事で、所用で
I often travel on business, but I rarely have enough time to do the sights.
よく仕事で出かけるが、観光するのに十分な時間はめったにありません。

71 **on foot** 徒歩で
The tour meets at Elliott Bay Cafe and then proceeds from gallery to gallery on foot.
ツアーはエリオット・ベイ・カフェに集合し、それから美術館から美術館へ徒歩で移動します。

72 **on leave** [líːv] 休暇で
73 **one-way** [wʌ̀nwéi] 〔形〕片道の
74 **overseas** [òuvərsíːz] 〔形〕海外の
75 **pastime** [pǽstàim] 〔名〕気晴らし、娯楽
76 **peak months** 最盛期
77 **personal belongings** [bilɔ́ːŋiŋz] 所持品
78 **pickpocket** [píkpàkit] 〔名〕スリ
Hundreds of thieves and pickpockets work the market looking for unsuspecting tourists.
何百人もの泥棒やスリが、疑うことを知らない観光客を探しながら市場で仕事をします。

79 **reception desk** フロント
80 **round-trip** [ráun(d)trìp] 〔形〕往復旅行の

Round-trip fares are usually only slightly higher than one-way fares.
往復旅行の料金は片道料金よりも普通少しだけ高いです。

81 **shot in the arm**　　　　　カンフル剤、刺激剤
The boom in travel to Southeast Asia has come as a shot in the arm for many of Tokyo's struggling travel agencies.
東南アジアへの旅行ブームは、多くの東京の苦労している旅行代理店にとって刺激剤となりました。

82 **souvenir** [sùːvəníər]　　　〔名〕みやげ
The area boasts all sorts of kiosks selling everything from souvenirs to jasmine tea.
その地域はあらゆる種類の売店が、みやげものからジャスミン茶まですべてのものを売っているのを自慢しています。

83 **special fare**　　　　　　特別料金
Some special fares have travel conditions that make them difficult to take advantage of.
特別料金は、利用するのを難しくさせる旅行条件があります。

84 **tourist attraction** [ətrǽkʃən]　観光名所

85 **valuables** [vǽljuəblz]　　〔名〕貴重品
The tour guide recommends that we leave our valuables in the hotel safe.
観光ガイドは貴重品をホテルの金庫に入れておくことを勧めます。

86 **wake-up call**　　　　　モーニングコール

空港

87 **airfare** [éəfèə]　　　　〔名〕航空料金
88 **baggage** [bǽɡidʒ]　　　〔名〕手荷物
If your baggage doesn't show up on the carousel, call the Service Desk.
もし手荷物が回転コンベヤーに出てこないなら、サービスカウンターに電話してください。

89 **baggage claim** [kléim]　　　　手荷物受取書
90 **boarding pass**　　　　　　　　搭乗券
　（類）boarding card

91 **carousel** [kæ̀rəsél]　　　　〔名〕回転コンベヤー
92 **check in**　　　　　　　　　チェックインする
　Passengers are asked to check in at least two hours before flight time.
　乗客はフライト時間の少なくとも2時間前にチェックインするよう求められています。

93 **customs declaration**　　　　税関申告書
　May I see your passport and customs declaration, please?
　どうぞパスポートと税関申告書を見せていただけますか。

94 **damage claim**　　　　ダメージクレーム、損害賠償請求
　All damage claims must be reported within 24 hours of arrival.
　すべてのダメージクレームは到着の24時間以内に届けなければなりません。

95 **disembarkation** [disèmbɑːrkéiʃən]〔名〕入国
　landing card 入国カード

96 **duty-free** [djúːtifríː]　　　〔形〕免税の
97 **expire** [ikspáiər]　　　　　〔動〕期限が切れる
　John's passport has expired, so he can't go anywhere overseas until he gets a new one.
　ジョンのパスポートは期限が切れたので、新しいのを手に入れるまで海外のどこへも行くことができません。

98 **fare** [féər]　　　　　　　　〔名〕運賃
99 **immigration** [ìməgréiʃən]　〔名〕（外国からの）移住
　emigration [èmigréiʃən]（外国への）移住

100 **list** [líst]　　　　　　　　〔動〕記載する、一覧表にする
　Fares listed for New York, Los Angeles and Chicago apply to the

many airports serving those cities.
ニューヨーク、ロサンゼルス、シカゴ行きの料金表は、それらの都市に飛んでいる多くの空港に適用されます。

101 **metal detector** [ditéktər] 　　金属探知器

102 **overnight** [òuvənáit] 　　〔副〕夜通し、一晩中
Passengers planning to stay overnight in Singapore must go through immigration and customs.
シンガポールで一晩中いるつもりの乗客は、入国審査・税関へ進まなければなりません。

103 **passport** [pǽspɔ̀ːrt] 　　〔名〕パスポート

104 **patient** [péiʃənt] 　　〔形〕我慢強い、辛抱強い
What with the long lines at check-in and security, travelers must be more patient than ever.
チェックインやセキュリティーでの長い列やらで、旅行者は今までよりも我慢強くなければなりません。

105 **procedure** [prəsíːdʒər] 　　〔名〕手続き、処置
Airline security procedures are now in line with recent government advisories.
航空の安全手続きは今、最近の政府勧告に従っています。

106 **runway** [rʌ́nwèi] 　　〔名〕滑走路

107 **step up** 　　増す、高める、強化する
Travelers can expect long lines due to stepped up security measures.
旅行者は安全対策を強化するための長い列を予想します。

108 **terminal** [tə́ːrmənəl] 　　〔名〕ターミナル

109 **to be on the safe side** 　　念のために

フライト

110 **aisle** [áil] 　　〔名〕通路
aisle seat [áil síːt] 通路側の席　　window seat 窓側の席

111 **altitude** [ǽltətjùːd] 〔名〕高度

112 **belt** [bélt] 〔名〕（コンベヤー）ベルト
Passengers must empty their pockets, remove their shoes, and place bags and jackets on the belt.
乗客はポケットを空にし、靴を脱ぎ、バッグとジャケットを（コンベヤー）ベルトの上に置かなければなりません。

113 **blanket** [blǽŋkət] 〔名〕毛布

114 **board** [bɔ́ːrd] 〔動〕〜に乗る
Alex must accidentally have boarded the wrong flight in Johannesburg.
アレックスは偶然、ヨハネスバーグで違う便に乗ったにちがいありません。

115 **boarding gate** 搭乗口

116 **bound for** 〜行きの

117 **carry-on luggage** 機内持ち込み手荷物
Airport officials suggest that passengers limit their carry-on luggage to one small bag per person.
機内持ち込み手荷物は、1人につき小さいバッグ1個に制限したらどうかと空港職員は提案しています。

118 **complimentary** [kàmpləméntəri] 〔形〕無料の、サービスの
Non-alcoholic beverages are no longer complimentary in economy class.
非アルコール飲料は、もはやエコノミークラスでは無料ではありません。

119 **crew** [krúː] 〔名〕乗務員

120 **departure** [dipáːrtʃər] 〔名〕出発
（反）arrival [əráivəl] 到着

121 **destination** [dèstənéiʃən] 〔名〕目的地

122 **fasten** [fǽsn] 〔動〕（シートベルトを）締める

123 **flight attendant** 客室乗務員

124 **headset** [hédsèt] 〔名〕ヘッドセット（マイクとヘ

125 **jet lag** 時差ぼけ
126 **takeoff** [teikɔ́:f] 〔名〕離陸
127 **turbulence** [tə́ːrbjuləns] 〔名〕乱気流
128 **upright position** 正しい位置

3. 環境
大気

129 **acid rain** 酸性雨
130 **air pollution** 大気汚染
131 **carbon dioxide** 二酸化炭素、炭酸ガス
132 **disproportionately** [dìsprəpɔ́ːrʃənətli] 〔副〕不釣合いに
Rising atmospheric temperatures disproportionately affect the poorer countries.
大気の気温上昇が、より貧しい国に不釣合いに影響しています。

133 **glacier** [gléʃər] 〔名〕氷河
Melting glaciers indicate that temperatures are increasing faster than expected.
氷河が溶けることは、気温が予想したより速く上昇していることを示します。

134 **global warming** 地球温暖化
Global warming is already responsible for more than 150,000 deaths and 5 million cases of illness each year.
地球温暖化はすでに毎年死者15万人、病気患者500万人以上の原因になっています。

135 **greenhouse gas** 温室効果ガス
greenhouse effect 温室効果

136 **ozone** [óuzoun] 〔名〕オゾン
ozone layer オゾン層　ozone depletion オゾン層破壊

137 **pollution** [pəlúːʃən] 〔名〕汚染
Air pollution in the city has been reduced thanks to restrictions on diesel-burning vehicles.
都市の大気汚染はディーゼル燃焼車の規制のおかげで減少しました。

自然

138 **biosphere** [báiəsfiə] 〔名〕生物圏

139 **cell** [sél] 〔名〕細胞
Unlike other living cells, bacteria lack a nucleus.
他の生きている細胞とは違って、バクテリアには核がありません。

140 **deforestation** [difɔ̀ːristéiʃən] 〔名〕森林破壊

141 **disaster** [dizǽstər] 〔名〕災害

142 **earthquake** [ə́ːrθkweik] 〔名〕地震
The earthquake began with a slow tremble and then struck with a violent jolt.
地震はゆるい揺れで始まり、それから激しい揺れが襲いました。

143 **ecology** [ikálədʒi] 〔名〕生体学、エコロジー

144 **ecosystem** [ékousìstəm] 〔名〕生態系
It is man himself who is upsetting the balance of nature and destroying ecosystems.
自然のバランスを乱し、生態系を破壊しているのは人間自身です。

145 **endangered species** 絶滅危惧種

146 **fossil fuel** 化石燃料

147 **gene** [dʒíːn] 〔名〕遺伝子
Our facial features, body type and maybe even our personalities are encoded in our genes.
私たちの顔の特徴、体形、そしてたぶん個性さえ遺伝子に記号化されます。

148 **habitat** [hǽbitæt] 〔名〕生息地
Once the animals have reached a certain number, they can be returned to their natural habitats.

いったん動物が一定数に到達すると、自然の生息地に帰されます。

149 **living thing** 生物
Bacteria, the simplest living things in nature, are both harmful and helpful to man.
自然界で最も単純な生物であるバクテリアは、人間に有害にもなり役立ちもします。

150 **logging** [lɔ́:giŋ] 〔名〕伐採

151 **national park** 国立公園
It is about time the government did something about creating more national parks.
さらに多くの国立公園を作ることについて、そろそろ政府が何かをするべきときです。

152 **natural resources** 天然資源
The new law aims to keep our natural resources from dwindling further.
その新しい法律は天然資源がさらに減少しないようにすることを目指しています。

153 **organic** [ɔːrɡǽnik] 〔形〕有機の

154 **rain forest** [réin fɔ́:rəst] 熱帯雨林

155 **reproduce** [rìːprədjúːs] 〔動〕増殖する、繁殖する
Many animals in captivity lose their instinct to reproduce.
多くの捕獲動物は繁殖する本能をなくしています。

156 **resource** [ríːsɔːrs] 〔名〕資源

157 **soil** [sɔ́il] 〔名〕土壌

158 **spawn** [spɔ́:n] 〔動〕産卵する
This is a sensitive salmon spawning area, so please refrain from throwing soapy water into the pools.
ここは敏感なサケが産卵する地域であるので、石けん水を川の深みに流すのはご遠慮ください。

159 **substance** [sʌ́bstəns] 〔名〕物質

160 **the polar ice cap** 極地の氷冠

161 **virus** [vάiərəs] 〔名〕ウイルス
The virus that causes AIDS was first discovered in Africa several decades ago.
エイズを引き起こすウイルスは、数十年前アフリカではじめて発見されました。

環境保全

162 **conservation** [kὰnsəvéiʃən] 〔名〕保護
163 **conserve** [kənsə́ːv] 〔動〕保全する
164 **desertification** [dizə̀ːrtəfikéiʃən] 〔名〕砂漠化
Spreading desertification is making more and more of the earth unfit for farming.
広がる砂漠化はますます多くの地球の部分を農耕に適さなくしています。

165 **dispose of** 処理する、処分する
The conference will explore new methods to dispose of toxic waste from electronic products.
会議は電化製品の有害な廃棄物を処理するための新しい方法を調査するでしょう。

166 **environmental** [invàiərənméntl] 〔形〕環境の
Environmental deterioration will be a major issue in the next general election.
環境の悪化は次の総選挙の主な争点になるでしょう。

167 **environmentalist** [invàiərənméntəlist] 〔名〕環境（保護）論者
Environmentalists say that human activity is the real culprit behind melting polar ice caps.
環境論者は人間の活動が、溶ける極地氷冠の背後に隠れた真犯人であると言います。

168 **environment-friendly** [invάiərənmənt fréndli] 〔形〕環境に優しい
169 **lethal impact** 致命的な影響
The high levels of energy consumed by the rich countries are having a lethal impact on people in less fortunate countries.
裕福な国によって消費される高レベルのエネルギーが、あまり裕福でない国の人々に致命的な影響を与えています。

170 **level** [lévəl]　　　　　　　〔名〕水準、レベル
The oceanographic research vessel is going to be testing the bay's water for pollution levels.
海洋学調査船は湾の水の汚濁レベルを調べるでしょう。

171 **protect** [prətékt]　　　　　〔名〕保護する

172 **solar cell**　　　　　　　　太陽電池

173 **supply** [səplái]　　　　　　〔名〕供給、供給量
Climate change will threaten the water supply in many areas.
気候の変化は多くの地域で水の供給を脅かすでしょう。

174 **symbiosis** [sìmbióusis]　　　〔名〕共存

175 **wilderness area**　　　　　　自然保護区域

176 **worldwide** [wə́ːrldwáid]　　〔形〕世界中で

食品

177 **additive** [ǽdətiv]　　　　　〔名〕添加物
We offer a full line of food products that contain no additives or preservatives.
私たちは添加物や保存剤を含んでいない完全な食品を提供します。
additive free foods 無添加食品

178 **assess** [əsés]　　　　　　　〔動〕評価する

179 **chemicals** [kémikəlz]　　　〔名〕化学薬品、化学製品
Our organic goods are raised with special care, using no chemicals.
有機産物は化学薬品を使わずに、特別な世話をして育てられます。

180 **critical** [krítikəl]　　　　　〔形〕極めて重要な

181 **hazardous** [hǽzərdəs]　　　〔形〕危険な

182 **intake** [íntèik]　　　　　　〔名〕摂取

183 **malnutrition** [mæln(j)uːtríʃən]　〔名〕栄養失調
The organization was set up to counter the increasing rates of

211

malaria, malnutrition and diarrhea in Central Africa.
その組織は中央アフリカでマラリア、栄養失調、下痢の増加率を抑制するために設立されました。

ゴミ・リサイクル

184 **bin** [bín] 〔名〕ゴミ箱

185 **burnable** [bə́ːrnəbl] 〔名〕可燃物、可燃性のごみ
burn〔動〕燃える

186 **contaminate** [kəntǽmənèit] 〔動〕汚す、汚染する

187 **cooperation** [kouàpəréiʃən] 〔名〕協力
The proposed law calls for three-way cooperation among consumers, government, and business and industry.
提案された法律は、消費者、政府、ビジネス産業の3者間の協力を求めています。

188 **discharge** [distʃáːrdʒ] 〔動〕放出する、排出する

189 **disposal** [dispóuzəl] 〔名〕処理
The recycling and disposal of used appliances will be carried out by various business and industries.
使い古した器具のリサイクルや処理は、さまざまなビジネスや産業によって行われるでしょう。

190 **emission** [imíʃən] 〔名〕排気ガス、放出
(類) exhaust gas

191 **exhaust** [igzɔ́ːst] 〔動〕排出する

192 **landfill** [lǽn(d)fìl] 〔名〕ゴミ投棄場

193 **litter** [lítər] 〔動〕散らかす 〔名〕ごみ

194 **recyclable** [rìːsáikləbl] 〔形〕リサイクル可能な

195 **recycling** [rìːsáikliŋ] 〔名〕再利用、リサイクル
Remember to take your old computers back to the store for recycling.
リサイクルのために、店へ古いコンピューターを忘れずに持っていってください。

196 **recycling law** リサイクル法

197 **recycling site** リサイクル場
City and local governments are in charge of collecting the trash and transporting it to recycling sites.
市や地方自治体はゴミを集め、それをリサイクル場へ運ぶことを担当します。

198 **responsibility** [rispɑ̀nsəbíləti]　〔名〕責任
Making sure trash is sorted into the proper bins is the responsibility of all the complex's tenants.
確実にゴミを適切なゴミ箱に分類することは、すべての複合テナントの責任です。

199 **sewage** [sú:idʒ]　〔名〕汚水、下水

200 **toxic** [táksik]　〔形〕有害な
toxic waste 有害な廃棄物

201 **waste** [wéist]　〔名〕ゴミ、廃棄物
（類）trash [trǽʃ]〔名〕ゴミ
industrial waste 産業廃棄物　waste collection ゴミ収集

4. 健康・医療
健康

202 **affected** [əféktid]　〔形〕感染した
Animals found to be affected with the disease will be destroyed immediately.
病気に感染したとわかった動物は、すぐに処分されるでしょう。

203 **aggressive** [əgrésiv]　〔形〕攻撃的な
Post-traumatic stress disorder victims suffer from learning difficulties, aggressive behavior, and nervousness.
心的外傷ストレス障害の患者は、学習の困難、攻撃的な振る舞い、神経障害を患います。

204 **beneficial** [bènəfíʃəl]　〔形〕有益な
Yoga is beneficial for young and old alike and can be take up at any

age.
ヨガは若者と老人どちらにも有益であり、何歳でも始められます。

205 **bird flu**　　　　　　　　　鳥インフルエンザ
Thailand has discovered several new cases of bird flu.
タイで鳥インフルエンザのいくつかの新しい事例が発見されました。

206 **body** [bɑ́di]　　　　　　　〔名〕体
ankle [ǽŋkl] 足首　arm [ɑ́ːrm] 腕　back [bǽk] 背中　beard [bíərd] あごひげ　belly [béli] 腹　breast [brést] 胸　cheek [tʃíːk] ほお　elbow [élbou] ひじ　forehead [fɔ́ːrid] ひたい　jaw [dʒɔ́ː] あご　knee [níː] ひざ　limb [lím] 手足　palm [pɑ́ːm] 手のひら　shoulder [ʃóuldər] 肩　thigh [θái] もも　throat [θróut] のど　thumb [θʌ́m] 親指　toe [tóu] つま先　waist [wéist] 腰

207 **carcinogen** [kɑːrsínədʒən]　　〔名〕発がん性物質
208 **clinic** [klínik]　　　　　　　〔名〕診療所
209 **concentration** [kɑ̀nsəntréiʃən]　〔名〕集中、集中力
Solving crossword puzzles helps enhance mental concentration.
クロスワードパズルを解くことは精神的集中力を高めます。

210 **coordination** [kouɔ́ːrd(ə)néiʃən]　〔名〕調整、連動
The early symptoms of muscular dystrophy include poor muscle and hand coordination.
筋ジストロフィーの初期の症状には、ひ弱な筋肉と手の連動が含まれます。

211 **discipline** [dísəplin]　　　　〔名〕訓練法
Yoga is an ancient discipline developed in India over 5000 years ago.
ヨガは5000年以上も前に、インドで発達した古来の訓練法です。

212 **emergency room**　　　　　　緊急処置室
213 **expert** [ékspəːrt]　　　　　〔名〕専門家
Experts fear that the disease might change into a form that could easily be passed from person to person.
専門家はその病気が人から人へ容易にうつる形に変わるかもしれないと恐れています。

214 **healing power** 治癒力
Since ancient times, herbs have been used for their almost magical healing powers.
昔から薬草はほとんど魔法のような治癒力をもつために使われてきました。

215 **health care** 健康管理、保健医療

216 **heredity** [hərédəti] 〔名〕遺伝

217 **hot spring** 温泉
Native Americans have long considered hot springs as sacred ground.
アメリカ先住民は久しく温泉を聖地として考えてきました。

218 **nothing but** ただ〜だけ
For a solid month, the film's director ate nothing but McDonald's fast food to prove its harmful effects.
まる1ヶ月の間、映画監督は有害な影響を証明するために、ただマクドナルドのファーストフードだけを食べました。

219 **out of shape** 体調が悪い
If you are feeling out of shape and run-down, perhaps you need a lifestyle change.
体調が悪く、健康がすぐれないと感じているなら、たぶんライフスタイルを変える必要があるでしょう。

220 **physical** [fízikəl] 〔形〕身体の
The report indicates that children's lack of physical exercise is affecting their intelligence.
報告は、子供の身体の運動不足が知性に影響していることを示しています。

221 **policy** [pάləsi] 〔名〕政策、方針、方策
The fast-food industry's irresponsible policies are affecting people's health.
ファーストフード産業の無責任な方針は、人々の健康に影響を与えています。

222 **pregnant** [prégnənt] 〔形〕妊娠した

If you think you might be pregnant, you need to see a doctor.
妊娠しているかもしれないと思うなら、医者に診断してもらう必要があります。

223 **productive** [prədʌ́ktiv] 〔形〕生産的な
A healthy employee is a happy and productive employee.
健康な従業員は、幸せで生産的な従業員です。

224 **set off** 引き起こす
Officials fear that the virus could set off a global outbreak that would kill millions.
職員は、そのウイルスが何百人も殺す地球規模の発生を引き起こすだろうと心配しています。

225 **supplement** [sʌ́pləmənt] 〔動〕補う、追加する
Bowing to public and government pressure, fast-food chains have begun to supplement their menus with healthier choices.
大衆と政府の圧力に屈して、ファーストフード・チェーンはメニューにより健康的な選択肢を追加し始めました。

226 **take a leave of absence** 休暇をとる
If you apply to take a leave of absence for health reasons, you will need a notice from a certified physician.
健康上の理由で休暇をとることを申し出るのであれば、公認の医師からの通知が必要でしょう。

227 **the World Health Organization** 世界保健機関

228 **throughout** [θruːáut] 〔前〕～を通して、～の間
Physical and emotional problems continue throughout the victim's life, as there is no cure.
身体的情緒障害は治療法がないので、患者の人生を通して続きます。

229 **transmit** [trænsmít] 〔動〕感染させる
There is no hard proof that BSE can be transmitted to humans.
狂牛病が人間に感染するという確固たる証拠はありません。

230 **well-being** [wélbíːiŋ] 〔名〕幸福、福利
Our staff knows how concerned you are about your family's health and well-being.
私たちのスタッフはあなたが家族の健康と幸福について、どれほど関心があるかを知っています。

症状・病気

231 **ache** [éik] 〔動〕痛む 〔名〕痛み
232 **allergic** [əláːrdʒik] 〔形〕アレルギーの
233 **asthma** [ǽzmə] 〔名〕ぜん息
Practitioners say that yoga is beneficial for ailments like asthma, anxiety and stress as well.
医者は、ヨガはまたぜん息、不安、ストレスのような病気に有益であると言います。

234 **bleed** [blíːd] 〔動〕出血する
235 **blood pressure** 血圧
After a month in the diet, his blood pressure and cholesterol levels dropped dramatically.
ダイエットの1ヵ月後、彼の血圧とコレステロール値は著しく下がりました。

236 **cancer** [kǽnsər] 〔名〕癌（がん）
237 **cavity** [kǽvəti] 〔名〕虫歯
238 **cold** [kóuld] 〔名〕風邪
239 **contagious** [kəntéidʒəs] 〔形〕伝染性の
240 **cough** [kɔ́(ː)f] 〔名〕咳 〔動〕咳をする
241 **depression** [dipréʃən] 〔名〕うつ病
His depression came on suddenly, for no apparent reason.
彼のうつ病は、明白な理由がなく突然やってきました。

242 **diabetes** [dàiəbíːtiːz] 〔名〕糖尿病
I'm afraid you have type II diabetes.
あなたは2型の糖尿病であると思います。

217

243 **diarrhea** [dàiərí:ə] 〔名〕下痢
244 **disorder** [disɔ́:rdər] 〔名〕（身体の）不調
245 **disrupt** [disrʌ́pt] 〔動〕混乱させる
Insomnia disrupts the body's natural rhythms, leaving victims confused and disoriented.
不眠症は患者を当惑、混乱させて、身体の自然のリズムを混乱させます。

246 **dizzy** [dízi] 〔形〕めまいがする
One cup of coffee and I feel dizzy and jittery all morning.
私は一杯のコーヒーで朝じゅうめまいがし、いらいらします。
dizziness [dízinəs]〔名〕めまい

247 **fever** [fí:vər] 〔名〕熱
248 **flu** [flú:] 〔名〕インフルエンザ
249 **hangover** [hǽŋòuvə] 〔名〕二日酔い
250 **hypertension** [hàipərténʃən] 〔名〕高血圧
251 **illness** [ílnəs] 〔名〕病気
　（類）disease [dizí:z]

252 **insomnia** [insámniə] 〔名〕不眠症
253 **itchy** [ítʃi] 〔形〕かゆい
254 **nauseous** [nɔ́:ʃəs] 〔形〕吐き気がする
255 **obesity** [oubí:səti] 〔名〕肥満
256 **rash** [rǽʃ] 〔名〕発疹
257 **runny nose** 鼻水
258 **seasonal affective disorder (=SAD)** 〔名〕季節性情緒障害
SAD is a form of depression that occurs during the fall and winter months when the amount of sunlight is limited.
季節性情緒障害は日照量が限られる秋や冬の月に起こる、一種のうつ病です。

259 **sluggish** [slʌ́giʃ] 〔形〕だるい
The patient felt so fatigued and sluggish that he could barely carry out his daily activities.

患者はあまりにも疲労とだるさを感じ、日常の活動をかろうじてできただけでした。

260 **sneeze** [sníːz] 〔名〕くしゃみ 〔動〕くしゃみをする
261 **symptom** [sím(p)təm] 〔名〕兆候、症状
262 **withdrawal** [wiðdrɔ́ːəl] 〔動〕引きこもり
The disorder's most common symptoms are excessive sleeping and social withdrawal.
その病気の最も一般的な症状は、過度の睡眠、社会的な引きこもりです。

医療

263 **abortion** [əbɔ́ːrʃən] 〔名〕妊娠中絶
264 **ambulance** [ǽmbjələns] 〔名〕救急車
265 **antibody** [ǽntibàdi] 〔名〕抗体
266 **checkup** [tʃékʌp] 〔名〕健康診断
267 **cure** [kjúər] 〔名〕治療
268 **diagnosis** [dàiəgnóusis] 〔名〕診断
Thanks to the new test, diagnosis is quick and painless.
新しい検査のおかげで、診断は早く苦痛がありません。

269 **emergency** [imɔ́ːrdʒənsi] 〔名〕緊急
emergency medicine 緊急医療

270 **heal** [híːl] 〔動〕治療する、治す
In the elderly, a broken bone takes far longer to heal, if at all.
お年寄りになると、骨折は治るとしても治すのにはるかに長くかかります。

271 **home care** 在宅介護
272 **hospitalization** [hàspitəlizéiʃən] 〔名〕入院
273 **kidney** [kídni] 〔名〕肝臓
274 **nagging** [nǽgiŋ] 〔形〕絶え間のない
While working on the site, workers developed severe headaches and nagging stomach problems.

その場所で働いている間に、労働者はひどい頭痛と絶え間のない胃の問題が始まりました。

275 **nursing care** 看護、介護
276 **operating room** 手術室
Please prepare the operating room for an emergency appendectomy.
緊急虫垂切除のため手術室を準備してください。

277 **operation** [ὰpəréiʃən] 〔名〕手術
278 **organ** [ɔ́ːrgən] 〔名〕臓器
279 **physician** [fizíʃən] 〔名〕内科医
280 **precaution** [prikɔ́ːʃən] 〔名〕予防措置
281 **psychiatrist** [səkáiətrist] 〔名〕精神科医
A British psychiatrist says that believing in Santa Claus is good for children.
イギリスの精神科医は、サンタクロースを信じることは子供にとって良いと言います。

282 **recommend** [rèkəménd] 〔動〕勧める
For a cold, doctors recommend getting plenty of rest, and drinking lots of fluids.
医者は、風邪には十分な休養をとり、多くの水分をとることを勧めます。

283 **relieve** [rilíːv] 〔動〕和らげる
Treatment with artificial light usually relieves the depression within a few days.
人工的な明かりでの治療は、ふつう数日間でうつ病を和らげます。

284 **round-the-clock** 〔形〕24時間の、昼夜ぶっ通しで
The assisted living center provides round-the-clock nursing care, as well as weekly visits from the doctor.
アシステッド・リビングセンター（老人介護施設）は、医者の毎週の往診だけでなく、24時間の看護を提供します。

285 **scalpel** [skǽlpəl] 〔名〕外科用メス
The surgery requires the most delicate movement of the scalpel.
その手術は外科用メスが最も微妙に動くことを必要とします。

286 **scan** [skǽn] 〔動〕 スキャンする、走査する
More and more people are having their bodies scanned for early detection of health problems.
ますます多くの人が健康問題を早期発見するため、身体をスキャンしてもらっています。

287 **shot** [ʃát] 〔名〕 注射

288 **surgeon** [sə́ːrdʒən] 〔名〕 外科医

289 **surgery** [sə́ːrdʒəri] 〔名〕 手術
Patients are encouraged to get up and walk as soon after their surgery as possible.
患者は手術の後、できるだけ早く起きて、歩くことを奨励されます。

290 **therapy** [θérəpi] 〔名〕 治療法

291 **treat** [tríːt] 〔動〕 治療する
treatment [tríːtmənt] 〔名〕治療

292 **vaccination** [væ̀ksənéiʃən] 〔名〕 予防接種

293 **wheelchair** [hwíːltʃèər] 〔名〕 車椅子

294 **X-ray** [éksrèi] エックス線、レントゲン
Our state-of-the-art diagnostic scanner uses X-rays and computerized digital imaging.
最先端の診断スキャナーは、エックス線とコンピューター処理したデジタル画像を使います。

薬

295 **abuse** [əbjúːz] 〔名〕 濫用

296 **antibiotics** [æ̀ntibaiátiks] 〔名〕 抗生物質

297 **dose** [dóus] 〔名〕 （薬の）服用量
The doctor prescribed too large a dose and I kept dozing off at my desk all day.
医者はあまりにもたくさんの服用量を処方したので、私は終日デスクでうたた寝をしていました。

298 **miracle drug** 奇跡の薬
The race is on among major pharmaceutical companies to come up with a miracle drug for preventing Alzheimer's disease.
アルツハイマー症を防ぐ奇跡の薬を考え出すために、大手の製薬会社の中で競争がなされています。

299 **pharmacy** [fá:rməsi] 〔名〕薬局
300 **pill** [píl] 〔名〕錠剤
301 **prescription** [priskrípʃən] 〔名〕処方箋
302 **side effect** 副作用
Side effects of chemotherapy incude nausea and hairloss.
化学療法の副作用は吐き気と髪がなくなることを含みます。

303 **tablet** [tǽblit] 〔名〕錠剤

禁煙・アルコール

304 **addiction** [ədíkʃən] 〔名〕中毒
305 **alcohol dependency** アルコール依存
306 **confront** [kənfrʌ́nt] 〔動〕直面する、立ち向かう
If you suspect your child is using drugs, confront him/her right away.
子供が麻薬をやっていることを疑うなら、すぐに立ち向かってください。

307 **consequence** [kánsəkwèns] 〔名〕結果
The earlier children learn that every action has its consequences, the better.
子供がすべての行為には結果が伴うことを知るのは、早ければ早いほどよいです。

308 **consumption** [kənsʌ́mpʃən] 〔名〕消費
The best example you can give your child is to be moderate in your own alcohol consumption.
子供に伝える最も良い例は、あなた自身のアルコール消費を適度なものにすることです。

309 **drinking** [dríŋkiŋ] 〔名〕飲酒

In my frank opinion, you have no choice but to stop smoking and drinking.
率直に意見を言うと、あなたはタバコと飲酒を止めるしか選択の道がありません。
　　　have no choice but to 「〜するしか選択の道がない、〜せざるを得ない」

310 **drunk driving / DUI**　　　　　飲酒運転

311 **effect** [ifékt]　　　　　〔名〕影響
The effects of smoking can even extend to your ability to think clearly.
喫煙の影響は、はっきり考える能力に及ぶことさえあります。

312 **indicate** [índikèit]　　　　　〔動〕示す
Be aware of signs that indicate your child may have a problem with alcohol.
子供がアルコールの問題を持っているかもしれないことを示す兆候に気づいてください。

313 **liver function**　　　　　肝機能
The liver function of those taking the painkiller deteriorated to the level of a chronic alcoholic.
鎮痛剤を服用している人の肝機能は慢性的アルコール依存症患者のレベルまで悪くなりました。

314 **lung cancer**　　　　　肺がん
lung [lʌŋ] 〔名〕肺

315 **naive** [nɑːíːv]　　　　　〔形〕無知である
Parents cannot afford to be naive about teenage drinking and peer pressure.
親は十代の飲酒と仲間の圧力に無知でいることはできません。

316 **nicotine-free** [níkətìːn fríː]　　　　　〔形〕ニコチンのない
317 **nicotine patch**　　　　　ニコチンパッチ
318 **no-smoking rule**　　　　　禁煙規則
Since the no-smoking rule went into effect, business has actually increased.

禁煙規則が実施されてから、仕事は実際に増えました。

319 **reasonable** [ríːzənəbl] 〔形〕道理に合った
Set reasonable but firm house rules regarding drinking.
飲酒に関して、道理にかなうが、断固たる家庭のルールを作ってください。

320 **secondhand smoke** 受動喫煙、間接喫煙

321 **smoke-free** [smóuk fríː] 〔形〕禁煙の
The multiplex is a completely smoke-free environment.
シネコンは完全に禁煙の環境です。

322 **smoking-related cause** 喫煙と関係がある原因

323 **syndrome** [síndroum] 〔名〕症候群
Fetal alcohol syndrome, or FAS, is a disease that causes various physical problems in babies.
胎児期アルコール症候群は赤ん坊に様々な身体的な問題を引き起こす病気です。

324 **tolerate** [tálərèit] 〔動〕寛大に扱う、許容する
Surprisingly, some states still tolerate drinking and driving and let drunk drivers off easy.
驚くことに、飲酒と運転に寛大で、飲酒ドライバーを容易に放免する州もあります。

感情・気持

325 **anxious** [ǽŋkʃəs] 〔形〕心配して
326 **bored** [bɔ́ːrd] 〔形〕うんざりした
327 **calm down** 落ち着く
328 **comfortable** [kʌ́mftəbl] 快適な
329 **concern** [kənsə́ːrn] 〔動〕心配する 〔名〕心配
330 **disappointed** [dìsəpɔ́intid] 〔形〕不満足な
　（類）dissatisfied [dìssǽtisfàid]

331 **down in the mouth** 気落ちして
What is Ann looking so down in the mouth about today?

今日、アンは何について気落ちしているのですか。

332 **embarrassed** [imbǽrəst] 〔形〕当惑した

333 **emotion** [imóuʃən] 〔名〕感情、情緒

334 **excuse** [ikskjú:z] 〔名〕言い訳、弁解
Saying you overslept is no excuse for being late.
寝過したと言うことは、遅れたことの言い訳になりません。

335 **gloomy** [glú:mi] 〔形〕ゆううつな

336 **grieve** [grí:v] 〔動〕深く悲しむ

337 **let down** 落ち込ませる

338 **nervous** [nə́:rvəs] 〔形〕緊張した、不安な

339 **pleased** [plí:zd] 〔形〕うれしい

340 **regret** [rigrét] 〔動〕後悔する
Beth regrets staying out so late last night.
ベスは昨夜遅くまで外出していたことを後悔しています。

341 **relax** [rilǽks] 〔動〕くつろがせる

342 **scared** [skéərd] 〔形〕怖がって

343 **serious** [síəriəs] 〔形〕まじめな

344 **sympathy** [símpəθi] 〔名〕同情、共感、思いやり
You might try to show a little sympathy for those less fortunate than yourself.
あなた自身よりも幸せでない人に、少し思いやりを示そうとしてもよいかもしれません。

345 **take it easy** くつろぐ、リラックスする
(類) make yourself at home, feel at home くつろぐ

5. 映画・DVD
映画

346 **acting** [ǽktiŋ] 〔名〕演技
The local community college is offering an acting workshop for adults who are serious about breaking into the movie business.
地元の短期大学は映画界へ入ることに関してまじめな大人に、演技研修会を提供しています。

347 **actor's agent** 俳優の代理人

348 **air** [éər] 〔動〕放送する、放映する
If you missed this award-winning drama series when it aired on TV, now is your chance to catch it on DVD.
テレビで放映されたとき、この賞を取ったドラマシリーズを見逃したなら、今がDVDで見るチャンスです。

349 **animated movie** アニメ映画
Many of today's computer-generated animated movies are as much for adults as for children.
今日のコンピューター処理されたアニメ映画の多くは、子供と同じように大人のためのものでもあります。

350 **audition** [ɔːdíʃən] 〔名〕オーディション

351 **base on** ～に基づかせる
The Sound of Music was originally a stage musical based on a true story.
『サウンド・オブ・ミュージック』は、もともと実際の話に基づいた舞台ミュージカルです。

352 **blockbuster** [blɑ́kbʌ̀stər] 〔名〕大ヒット、大成功

353 **boring** [bɔ́ːriŋ] 〔形〕退屈な
The movie was so slow and boring that I felt like walking out of the theater.
映画はとてもスローで退屈だったので、私は映画館から立ち去りたいと思いました。

354 **celebrity** [səlébrəti] 〔名〕有名人

355 **confidence** [kánfidəns] 〔名〕自信、信頼
Working with an acting teacher helps you develop more confidence in front of the camera.
演技指導の先生と仕事をすることは、カメラの前でより自信をつける手助けになります。

356 **film director** 映画監督

357 **footage** [fútidʒ] 〔名〕（映画の）場面

358 **genre** [ʒá:nrə] 〔名〕ジャンル

359 **highest-grossing** 〔名〕最高総収入、最高収益
The highest-grossing film of all time is still *Titanic*.
空前の最高収益映画はまだ『タイタニック』です。

360 **horror film** ホラー映画
Psychologists say that watching horror films may even be good for us.
心理学者はホラー映画を見ることは私たちにとって良いかもしれないと言います。

361 **lead actor** 主役の俳優
With his good looks and wit, he would make a good lead actor in a romantic comedy.
ハンサムでウィットがあるので、彼はロマンチック・コメディでいい主役を演じるでしょう。

362 **lot** [lát] 〔名〕映画撮影場

363 **megahit** [mégəhit] 〔名〕超ヒット作品

364 **movie critic** 映画批評家

365 **moviegoer** [mú:vigòuər] 〔名〕映画ファン

366 **moviemaker** [mú:vimèikər] 〔名〕映画製作者

367 **nominee** [nàməní:] 〔名〕指名された人

368 **popularity** [pàpjulǽrəti] 〔名〕人気

369 **reputation** [rèpjutéiʃən] 〔名〕評判

370 **shoot the film** 映画を撮影する

The Chinese govenment won't permit them to shoot the film on location in Shanghai.
中国政府は彼らが上海のロケ地で映画を撮影するのを認めないでしょう。

371 **star** [stáːr]　　　　　　　　〔動〕主演する　〔名〕スター、主役

372 **subtitles** [sʌ́btàitlz]　　　　〔名〕字幕、スパーインポーズ
I don't think the subtitles accurately convey what the characters are saying.
字幕は登場人物が言っていることを正確に伝えていないと思います。

373 **talent scout**　　　　　　　　タレントスカウト

374 **unleash** [ʌnlíːʃ]　　　　　　〔動〕爆発させる、発揮する
These techniques and exercises are designed to help you unleash your creativity.
これらの技術と練習は、創造性を発揮する手助けをするようにデザインされています。

映画館・劇場

375 **attendance** [əténdəns]　　　〔名〕入場者、参加者
Attendance at the movies has fallen off because of cable TV, DVDs, and other forms of entertainment.
映画の入場者はケーブルテレビ、DVD、他の形態の娯楽のために減少しました。

376 **auditorium** [ɔ̀ːdətɔ́ːriəm]　　〔名〕観客席、講堂
The auditorium offers stadium-style seating and a state-of-the-art sound system.
講堂はスタジアムスタイルの座席と最先端技術の音響システムを提供します。

377 **box office**　　　　　　　　　チケット売場
Special devices for hearing-impaired patrons are available free of charge at the box office.
難聴のお客のための特別な装置は、チケット売場で無料で利用できます。

378 **box office receipts**　　　　　チケット売上高
United States domestic box office receipts sailed to new heights this past year.

この1年間のアメリカ国内のチケット売上高は、過去最高になりました。

379 **facility** [fəsíləti] 〔名〕施設、設備
This new facility will allow amateur and independent filmmakers to show their work in a real theater.
この新しい設備は、アマチュアや独立した映画製作者が本物の劇場で作品を上映することを可能にするでしょう。

380 **factor in** 〜を計算に入れる

381 **in line** 並んで
Get your movie tickets on-line and you no longer have to wait in line at the box office.
映画のチケットをオンラインで買いなさい。そうすればチケット売り場でもはや並んで待つ必要がありません。

382 **in progress** 上映中、進行中
Cellular phones must be turned off inside the theater and no talking while the movie is in progress.
携帯電話は劇場内では切らなければなりません。そして上映中は話さないでください。

383 **matinee** [mætinéi] 〔名〕昼間興行、マチネ

384 **multiplex cinema** シネコン
The largest multiplex cinema in the city boasts 18 large screens, all showing different films.
その町の最大のシネコンは18のスクリーンを誇り、すべて異なる映画を上映しています。

385 **outside** [àutsáid] 〔形〕外からの
No outside food or drinks are allowed in the theater.
劇場に外からの食物や飲物は許可されません。

386 **popcorn box** ポップコーンの箱
Kindly deposit your popcorn boxes and beverage containers in the trash bins at the rear of the auditorium.
どうかポップコーンの箱、飲み物の容器は、観客席の後ろのゴミ箱に入れてください。

387 **script** [skrípt] 〔名〕脚本、スクリプト
The script for each episode of the series is written by a different scriptwriter.
そのシリーズの1話1話の脚本は、異なる脚本家によって書かれています。

388 **seat** [síːt] 〔動〕着席させる
Ladies and gentlemen, please be seated. The performance is about to begin.
みなさま、ご着席ください。まもなく演奏が始まります。

389 **sharp** [ʃάːrp] 〔副〕きっかりに
Curtains up for tonight's performance of *Tosca* is at eight sharp.
今夜の演目「トスカ」の開演は8時きっかりです。

390 **sneak preview** 特別試写会
Sneak previews give directors and producers a chance to evaluate audience reaction and make last-minute changes to their films.
特別試写会は監督とプロデューサーが観客の反応を評価し、映画を土壇場で変更するチャンスを与えます。

391 **soundproof viewing room** 防音視聴室
There is a special soundproof viewing room in the balcony for patrons with small children.
幼い子供のいるお客様のために、バルコニーに特別防音視聴室があります。

392 **stub** [stʌb] 〔名〕半券
Please retain your ticket stub so that you can re-enter the theater.
劇場へ再入場できるように、切符の半券を持っていてください。

393 **well-known** [wélnóun] 〔形〕よく知られている、有名な
Adams is a well-known local philanthropist who likes to help out struggling young creative artists.
アダムズさんは努力している若い独創的な芸術家に手を貸すのが好きな、有名な地元の慈善家です。

DVD・ゲーム

394 **by all means**　　　　　ぜひとも、必ず
If you didn't get a chance to see the controversial documentary in theaters, then by all means check it out now on DVD.
映画館で論争の的になる記録映画を見る機会がなかったなら、ぜひとも今DVDを借りなさい。

395 **cop** [káp]　　　　　〔名〕警官
The game has been criticized because players score points by killing cops, stealing cars, and breaking into homes.
そのゲームは、プレーヤーが警官を殺し、自動車を盗み、家に押し入ることでポイントを得るので非難されました。

396 **damage** [dǽmidʒ]　　　　　〔名〕損害、傷
Renters will be charged for any damage done to game machines and software.
借りた人はゲーム機やソフトに傷をつけると料金を請求されるでしょう。

397 **explicit** [iksplísit]　　　　　〔形〕あからさまな、露骨な
The game also has some sexually explicit content which parents should be aware of.
そのゲームは親が気づいておくべき露骨な性描写の内容があります。

398 **general public**　　　　　一般の人、一般大衆
The senator proposed a bill aimed at protecting the general public from such negative influences.
上院議員はこのような有害な影響から一般大衆を守ることを目的とした法案を提案しました。

399 **in response to**　　　　　～に応えて、応じて
Video game makers are cooperating in response to the National Institute on the Media and Family's recent attacks.
ビデオゲーム・メーカーは国立メディアと家族研究所の最近の非難に応えて協力しています。

400	**late fee**	遅滞料
401	**movie memorable**	映画の思い出の品
402	**new release**	新発売
403	**premium** [príːmiəm]	割増金
404	**rate** [réit]	〔動〕等級にわける、ランク付けする

The games are rated according to their level of violent and sexual content.
ゲームは暴力と性描写の内容のレベルによってランク付けされています。

405	**rating** [réitiŋ]	〔名〕レベル、等級、格付け

The five ratings for games are similar to those used for movies.
ゲームの5段階のレベルは、映画で使われるレベルに似ています。

406	**rental charge**	レンタル料
407	**restriction** [ristrík∫ən]	〔名〕規制
408	**return** [ritə́ːrn]	〔動〕返す

DVDs and CDs can also be returned at our 24-hour drive-through slot.
DVDとCDは24時間開いているドライブスルーの投入口に返すこともできます。

409	**secondhand** [sékən(d)hǽnd]	〔形〕中古の
410	**selection** [səlék∫ən]	〔名〕品ぞろえ
411	**special offer**	〔名〕特別提供
412	**suitable** [súːtəbl]	〔形〕適した、ふさわしい

A label is attached to the box warning that the game may not be suitable for young children.
そのゲームは幼い子供に適切でないかもしれないということを、警告するラベルが箱に付けられています。

6. 教育・スポーツ
指導

413	**academic** [ækədémik]	〔動〕学問の

414 construct [kənstrʌ́kt]　　　〔動〕建設する
Peace Corps volunteers join with village residents to construct wells and washing facilities.
平和部隊のボランティアは、井戸や洗濯施設を建設するために村の住民といっしょに取り組んでいます。

415 do one's best　　　ベストを尽くす
When life puts challenges in front of you, do your best to get past them and move on.
人生があなたの前に難題を課すとき、乗り切り、進むためにベストを尽くしなさい。

416 education [èdʒəkéiʃən]　　　〔名〕教育

417 encourage [enkə́:ridʒ]　　　〔動〕勇気づける、励ます
The library's staff will encourages your children to become more active and better readers.
図書館の職員は子供たちがより活発で、より良い読者になるように励ますでしょう。

418 enroll [inróul]　　　〔動〕入学する
enrollment [inróulmənt]〔名〕入学、登録

419 evaluate [ivǽljuèit]　　　〔動〕評価する
evaluation [ivæ̀ljuéiʃən]〔名〕評価

420 fundamental [fʌ̀ndəméntl]　　　〔形〕基本的な

421 graduate [grǽdʒuət]　　　〔名〕卒業生　〔動〕卒業する
Thousands of technical school graduates are actively working in the careers they have always dreamed of.
何千もの専門学校の卒業生が、いつも夢見ていた仕事で活発に働いています。

422 instruction [instrʌ́kʃən]　　　〔名〕授業、教育
The citizenship course includes instruction in U.S. history and government as well as English as a second language.
市民権コースは第2言語としての英語だけでなく、米国の歴史と政治の教育を含みます。

423 intelligent design　　　知的デザイン

Intelligent design is being proposed as an alternative to Darwin's theory of evolution.
知的デザインはダーウィンの進化論に代わるものとして提案されています。

424 **librarian** [laibréəriən] 〔名〕図書館員
425 **postgraduate** [pòus(t)grǽdʒuət] 〔名〕大学院生
　（類）a graduate student

426 **principal** [prínsəpəl] 〔名〕学長、校長
427 **professor** [prəfésər] 〔名〕教授
428 **registration** [rèdʒəstréiʃən] 〔名〕登録
　register [rédʒistər]〔動〕登録する

429 **research** [risə́ːrtʃ] 〔名〕研究　〔動〕研究する
430 **scholarship** [skάlərʃip] 〔名〕奨学金
431 **school board** 教育委員会
432 **school phobia** 学校嫌い
433 **semester** [səméstər] 〔名〕学期
　a spring semester 春学期

434 **seminar** [sémənὰːr] 〔名〕セミナー
435 **session** [séʃən] 〔名〕授業
　a morning session 午前中の授業

436 **social issue** 社会問題
437 **stimulate** [stímjulèit] 〔動〕刺激する
　Dewey believed that education stimulate learners' imagination as well as increase their knowledge.
　デューイは、教育は知識を増やすだけでなく、学習者の想像力を刺激すると信じていました。

438 **study abroad** 留学する
　（類）study overseas

439 **suggest** [səgdʒést] 〔動〕提案する
The school board brochure suggests ways to keep your children busy during the long June-September holidays.
教育委員会のパンフレットは、6月から9月の長い休みの間、子供たちを忙しくさせておく方法を提案しています。

440 **tuition** [tjuːíʃən] 〔名〕授業料

441 **tutor** [tjúːtər] 〔名〕チューター、個別導教員
My mother worked as a volunteer English tutor for newly arrived immigrants.
母は新たにやって来た移住者のためにボランティアの英語のチューターとして働きました。

442 **undergraduate** [ʌ̀ndərgrǽdʒuət] 〔名〕大学生

課程

443 **a compulsory subject**　　必修科目
an elective subgect 選択科目

444 **accounting** [əkáuntiŋ] 〔名〕会計学

445 **adult education**　　生涯教育、成人教育
All our adult education classes are held in the evening and on weekends for the convenience of full-time workers.
すべての生涯教育の授業は、正規労働者に便利なように夜と週末に開かれます。

446 **associate (degree)** [əsóuʃièit] 〔名〕準学士号

447 **bachelor's (degree)** [bǽtʃələrz] 〔名〕学士号

448 **business administration**　　経営学

449 **correspondence course**　　通信教育課程
Another exellent way to change careers is through online and correspondence courses.
キャリアを変えるもう1つのすばらしい方法は、オンラインと通信教育課程を通してです。

450 **credit** [krédit] 〔名〕単位

451 **curricula** [kəríkjələ] 〔名〕カリキュラム
Fundamentalists insist that Bible's story of creation should be introduced into our schools' curricula.
原理主義者は、聖書の創造の話は学校カリキュラムに導入されるべきだと主張しています。

452 **degree** [digríː] 〔名〕学位

453 **diploma** [diplóumə] 〔名〕修了証書、卒業証書
(類) sheepskin [ʃíːpskin] 〔名〕修了証書

454 **economics** [èkənámiks] 〔名〕経済学

455 **educational institution** 教育機関
Carter Academy is one of the nation's oldest and most prestigious private educational institutions.
カーター・アカデミーは国で最も古く、最も名門の私立教育機関の1つです。

456 **elementary school** 小学校

457 **faculty** [fǽkəlti] 〔名〕学部

458 **higher education** 高等教育

459 **humanities** [hjuːmǽnətiz] 〔名〕人文科学
Science students must be well-read in the humanities and liberal arts students must have a good kowlege of science.
自然科学の学生は人文科学に精通しなければならないし、教養の学生は十分な自然科学の知識を持たねばなりません。

460 **intensive** [inténsiv] 〔形〕集中的な
intensive course 集中コース

461 **jurisprudence** [dʒùərisprúːdns] 〔名〕法学
(類) law

462 **liberal arts** 一般教養科目

463 **major** [méidʒər] 〔名〕専攻 〔動〕専攻する

464 **master's (degree)** [mǽstərz]　〔名〕修士号

465 **paper** [péipər]　〔名〕レポート
term paper 学期末レポート

466 **psychology** [saikálədʒi]　〔名〕心理学

467 **specialty** [spéʃəlti]　〔名〕専門、専攻

スポーツ・レジャー

468 **backpacking** [bǽkpækiŋ]　〔名〕徒歩旅行

469 **camper** [kǽmpər]　〔名〕キャンプする人
The forest fire was set off by a camper who tossed a burning cigarette into dry brush.
森林火災はキャンプをする人が乾燥した雑木林に火のついたタバコを投げたことで発生しました。

470 **campsite** [kǽmpsàit]　〔名〕キャンプ場

471 **canoeing** [kənúːiŋ]　〔名〕カヌーこぎ
canoeist [kənúːist]〔名〕カヌーをこぐ人

472 **excursion** [ikskə́ːrʒən]　〔名〕小旅行

473 **fitness fad**　フィットネスの流行
Fitness fads come and go, but walking never goes out of fashion.
フィットネスの流行は現れたり消えたりするが、ウォーキングは決して廃れません。

474 **fun** [fʌ́n]　〔名〕楽しさ、おもしろさ
Ballroom dancing is excellent exercise and good fun at the same time.
社交ダンスはすばらしい運動で、同時にとてもおもしろいです。

475 **go fishing**　魚釣りに行く
Once a year we charter a boat and go salmon fishing off the coast of Washington state.
1年に1度、ワシントン州の海岸沖へ、ボートをチャーターしてサーモン釣りに行きます。

476 **hiker** [háikər]　　〔名〕ハイカー、徒歩旅行者
Cellphones have made it much easier to find hikers who get lost in the wilderness.
携帯電話は荒地で迷子になったハイカーを発見することをずいぶん容易にしました。

477 **horseback riding**　　乗馬

478 **kayaking** [káiækiŋ]　　〔名〕カヤックこぎ

479 **leisure** [líːʒər]　　〔名〕余暇、自由時間
leisure activities 余暇活動

480 **match** [mǽtʃ]　　〔名〕試合

481 **no matter what**　　どんなことがあろうとも
It's a new form of recreation that teaches you to meet all challenges and to keep trying no matter what.
それは、あらゆる難題に出くわし、どんなことがあろうとも試み続けることを教える新しい形のレクリエーションです。

482 **obstacle** [ábstəkl]　　〔名〕障害物
The goal of the sport's enthusiasts is to run, jump, or climb over fences, walls and other obstacles.
そのスポーツに熱中している人の目的は、走り、跳び、フェンスや壁やその他の障害物を乗り越えることです。

483 **on account of**　　～のせいで、～のために
On account of the warm weather, ski areas are being forced to close their slopes.
暖かい天候のために、スキー場はゲレンデを閉鎖せざるをえません。

484 **paddle** [pǽdl]　　〔動〕櫂（かい）でこぐ
I was paddling a canoe across the swamp when I saw a crocodile swimming towards me.
沼地でカヌーを櫂でこいでいると、私の方に向かってワニが泳いでくるのが見えました。

485 **participant** [pɑːrtísəpənt]　　〔名〕参加者
Participants in the triathlon must first pass a rigid physical

examination.
トライアスロンの参加者は、まず厳しい身体検査に合格しなければなりません。

486 **provide** [prəváid] 〔動〕与える
Telling each other stories privides people in nursing homes with a great deal of pleasure.
お互いの話をすることは老人ホームの人たちに多くの喜びを与えます。

487 **provisions** [prəvíʒənz] 〔名〕食糧

488 **rafting** [ræftiŋ] 〔名〕ラフティング
raft [ræft]〔名〕ゴムボート、いかだ

489 **run high** 高くなる
Surfers can expect waves to be running high during the early hours of the afternoon tomorrow.
サーファーは、明日は波が午後の早い時間に高くなると期待できます。

490 **trail** [tréil] 〔名〕小道
There's nothing more relaxing than a refreshing hot spring bath after a long day on the trail.
小道で長い1日を過ごした後、温泉でリフレッシュすることほど、リラックスできるものはありません。

491 **waterfall** [wɔ́:tərfɔ̀:l] 〔名〕滝
At this time of year, you can watch the salmon jump over the waterfalls.
1年のこの時期には、サケが滝をジャンプするのを見ることができます。

492 **white-water ride** 急流いかだ下り
This week's program lineup includes a hair-raising, white-water ride down the Snake River with two intrepid teenage adventurers
今週の予定表は、恐れを知らぬ十代の冒険家2人による、スネーク川のぞっとするような急流いかだ下りを含みます。

493 **workout** [wə́:rkàut] 〔名〕トレーニング

These quick-and-easy at-your-desk workouts will help make you look and feel better.
これらの速くて容易な机に向かって行うトレーニングは、見た目も気分も良くなるのに役立つでしょう。

芸術

494 **admission** [ædmíʃən]　〔名〕入会、入場料、承認
495 **ancient** [éinʃənt]　〔形〕古代の
medieval [mìːdíːvəl]〔形〕中世の　contemporary art 現代芸術

496 **artist** [áːrtist]　芸術家、画家
Visitors to the gallery can meet the artist in person between the hours of 7 and 9 p.m.
美術館への入場者は午後7時から9時の間、芸術家に直接会えます。

497 **author** [ɔ́ːθər]　〔名〕著者
498 **award-winning mural**　受賞壁画
499 **civilization** [sìvələzéiʃən]　〔名〕文明
500 **classical** [klǽsikəl]　〔形〕クラシックの
classical music クラシック音楽

501 **era** [íərə]　〔名〕時代
502 **exhibit** [igzíbit]　〔名〕展示品、展示
503 **expert commentary**　専門家の解説
504 **heritage** [hérətidʒ]　〔名〕遺産
505 **instrument** [ínstrəmənt]　〔名〕楽器
506 **intermission** [intərmíʃən]　〔名〕中断、幕間
507 **leading** [líːdiŋ]　〔形〕優れた
The exhibition by one of Denmark's leading young artists should not be missed.
デンマークの優れた若手芸術家の1人による展示会は、見逃すべきではありません。

508	**masterpiece** [mǽstərpiːs]	〔名〕傑作
509	**novel** [nάvəl]	〔名〕小説
510	**prose** [próuz]	〔名〕散文
511	**publication** [pʌblikéiʃən]	〔名〕出版物
512	**remains** [riméinz]	〔名〕遺跡
513	**sculpture** [skʌ́lptʃər]	〔名〕彫刻

statuette [stæ̀tʃuét] 小彫像

| 514 | **tune** [tjúːn] | 〔名〕曲 |
| 515 | **wire sculpture** | 針金彫刻 |

7. マスコミ・メディア
報道

| 516 | **affair** [əféər] | 〔名〕事件、出来事 |
| 517 | **anonymous** [ənάnəməs] | 〔形〕匿名の |

an anonymous donor 匿名の提供者

| 518 | **authority** [əθɔ́ːrəti] | 〔名〕当局 |
| 519 | **breaking news** | ニュース速報 |

(類) news flash

520 **broadcast** [brɔ́ːdkæst]　　〔名〕放送　〔動〕放送する

521 **editorial department**　　編集部
The errors in the article are the fault of our editorial department, and not the fault of the author.
記事の間違いは著者の過失ではなく、編集部の過失です。

522 **exceed** [iksíːd]　　〔動〕超える
The number of U.S. soldiers in the Middle Eastern nation now exceeds 165,000 and is still rising.
中東の国におけるアメリカ兵士の数は今、165,000人を超え、まだ増え続けています。

523 **front page** 第1面

524 **headline** [hédlàin] 〔形〕大見出し、ヘッドライン

525 **human interest stories** 三面記事

526 **inconvenience** [ìnkənvíːnjəns] 〔名〕不便、不都合
The producers of the broadcast apologize to our viewers for our carelessness and for any inconvenience we may have caused you.
その放送番組のプロデューサーは、不注意と不便をおかけしたかもしれないことについて視聴者にお詫びいたします。

527 **investigation** [invèstəgéiʃən] 〔名〕調査
The financial scandal came to light during a *Sunday Times* undercover investigation.
金銭上のスキャンダルがサンデータイムズの内密の調査中に明らかになりました。

528 **newscaster** [njúːzkæ̀stə] 〔名〕ニュースキャスター

529 **op-ed** [ápèd] 〔名〕社説面
Mr. Best's column, which appears weekly on the op-ed page, urged America to withdraw its troops from Iraq.
社説面のページに毎週載るベストさんのコラムは、イラクから軍隊を撤退させることをアメリカに促しました。
op-ed（=opinion-editorial の略）

530 **periodical** [pìəriádikəl] 〔名〕定期刊行物

531 **post** [póust] 〔名〕職、地位
Two history dons were forced to resign their academic posts yesterday for plagiarism.
2人の歴史の大学教員が昨日、盗作で大学の職を辞職せざるを得ませんでした。

532 **press** [prés] 〔名〕記者、報道陣

533 **prevail** [privéil] 〔動〕流布する、広くいきわたる

534 **prime time** ゴールデンアワー

535 **program** [próugræm] 〔名〕番組
（類）show（テレビ、ラジオの）番組

536 **rumor** [rúːmər] 〔名〕うわさ

537 **say-so** [séisòu] 〔名〕決定権
Blogs give their creators the right to have some say-so on issues that are important to them.
ブログは重要な問題に関して決定権をもつ権利を創設者に与える。

538 **source** [sɔ́ːrs] 〔名〕情報源
a reliable source 信頼筋

紛争

539 **ally** [əlái] 〔名〕同盟国

540 **assault** [əsɔ́ːlt] 〔名〕攻撃 〔動〕攻撃する
(類) attack [ətǽk]

541 **bilateral** [bailǽtərəl] 〔形〕2国間の
a bilateral treaty 2国間条約

542 **border** [bɔ́ːrdər] 〔名〕国境

543 **ceasefire** [síːsfáiər] 〔名〕停戦

544 **conflict** [kánflikt] 〔名〕紛争、衝突
an armed conflict 武力衝突

545 **destruction** [distrʌ́kʃən] 〔名〕破壊
weapons of mass destruction 大量破壊兵器

546 **devastate** [dévəstèit] 〔動〕破壊する
The countries devastated by 2003's earthquake and tsunami have not yet fully recovered.
2003年の地震と津波で破壊された国々は、まだ完全に復興していません。

547 **disarmament** [disáːrməmənt] 軍縮

548 **feature** [fíːtʃər] 〔動〕特集する 〔名〕特集
This week's issue features a story on illegal kangaroo hunting in

New South Wales.
今週の問題はニューサウスウェールズでの違法なカンガルー狩猟についての話を特集します。

549 **insurgent** [insə́ːrdʒənt]　　〔名〕武装勢力

550 **military personnel**　　〔名〕兵士
American military personnel are frequent targets of car bombings and suicide attacks.
アメリカの兵士はしばしば自動車爆弾と自爆攻撃のターゲットになります。

551 **military strength**　　兵力
The general argues that the nation's military strength depends on starting up the draft again.
その軍司令官は、国の兵力は徴兵制の再開次第だと主張しています。

552 **peacekeeping** [píːskiːpiŋ]　　〔名〕平和維持

553 **presence** [prézns]　　〔名〕駐留
maintain a military presence 軍隊の駐留を維持する

554 **refugee** [rèfjudʒíː]　　〔名〕難民

555 **rocket attack**　　ロケット攻撃

556 **tactical withdrawal**　　戦略的撤退

557 **territory** [térətɔ̀ːri]　　〔名〕領土

558 **troop** [trúːp]　　〔名〕軍隊

559 **trouble-spot location**　　紛争多発地帯
Each year, many journalists assigned to dangerous, trouble-spot locations lose their lives.
毎年危険な紛争多発地帯へ配属される多くのジャーナリストが命を落とします。

560 **war zone**　　戦闘地域

政治

561 **administration** [ədmìnəstréiʃən]　　〔名〕政権

562 **bureau** [bjúərou] 〔名〕局
563 **cabinet** [kǽbənit] 〔名〕内閣
cabinet reshuffle 内閣改造

564 **campaign** [kæmpéin] 〔名〕活動
565 **citizenship** [sítizənʃip] 〔名〕市民権
Immigrants can apply for American citizenship if they have lived in the U.S. for at least six years.
住者はアメリカに少なくとも6年間住んだら、アメリカの市民権を申請できます。

566 **coalition cabinet** 連立内閣
567 **Congress** [kά:ŋgrəs] 〔名〕議会《米国》
(類) Parliament《英国》the Diet《日本》

568 **debt relief** 債務免除〔軽減〕
Many nations around the globe have already extended debt relief to countries where flooding has destroyed crops and entire villages.
世界中の多くの国が、洪水が穀物と村全体を破壊した国々に、すでに債務免除を申し出ています。

569 **debt repayment** 債務返済
570 **developed nations** 先進国
571 **developing nations** 発展途上国
572 **diplomat** [dípləmæt] 〔名〕外交官
573 **diplomatic break** 国交断絶
574 **diplomatic corps** 外交団
575 **diplomatic privilege** 外交特権
576 **economic climate** 経済情勢
Under the current economic climate, consumers are reluctant to spend money on luxury items.
現在の経済情勢のもとでは、消費者は贅沢な品物にお金を使うことを渋ります。

577 **election** [ilékʃən] 〔名〕選挙

elect [ilékt] 〔動〕選挙する　election district 選挙区
election returns 開票結果　election violation 選挙違反

578 **face** [féis]　〔動〕立ち向かう
579 **follow suit**　先例に従う
As a nation we should follow suit and offer medical technical assistance whenever it is needed.
一国として前例に従い、必要なときに医療や技術の援助を提供するべきです。

580 **government** [gʌ́vərnmənt]　〔名〕政府
581 **governor** [gʌ́vərnər]　〔名〕知事
582 **independence** [ìndipéndəns]　〔名〕独立
583 **issue** [íʃuː]　〔名〕問題
584 **lawmaker** [lɔ́ːmèikər]　〔名〕国会議員
585 **local government**　地方自治
586 **ministry** [mínəstri]　〔名〕省
587 **municipal** [mjuːnísəpəl]　〔形〕市の
588 **nationalize** [nǽʃənəlàiiz]　〔動〕国営化する
589 **official** [əfíʃəl]　〔名〕職員
590 **organized votes**　組織票
591 **pact** [pǽkt]　〔名〕条約、協定
592 **party** [páːrti]　〔名〕党
593 **political climate**　政治情勢
The unstable political climate in the region discourages both short- and long-term investment.
その地域の不安定な政治情勢は、短期と長期のどちらの投資も思いとどまらせます。
political bias 政治的偏見　political contribution 政治献金

594 **politician** [pàlətíʃən]　〔名〕政治家
595 **poll** [póul]　〔名〕世論調査
596 **province** [právins]　〔名〕州、地方

597	**regulate** [régjəlèit]	〔動〕規制する
598	**ruling** [rúːliŋ]	〔名〕与党、政権党
	(反) opposition [əpəzíʃən] 野党	
599	**senator** [sénətər]	〔名〕上院議員
	representative [rèprizéntətiv] 〔名〕下院議員	
600	**solemn duty**	誠意ある義務

It is our solemn duty to uphold the constitution and laws of the nation.
国の憲法や法律を維持することが、私たちの誠意ある義務です。

601	**sovereign** [sávərən]	〔名〕主権
602	**state** [stéit]	〔名〕国家、州
603	**summit conference**	首脳会議
604	**vote** [vóut]	〔動〕投票する

法律

605	**amendment** [əméndmənt]	〔名〕改正
606	**arrest** [ərést]	〔動〕逮捕する
607	**ban** [bǽn]	〔動〕禁止する
608	**client** [kláiənt]	〔名〕依頼人
609	**committee** [kəmíti]	〔名〕委員会
	(類) commission [kəmíʃən]	
610	**Constitution** [kànstətjúːʃən]	〔名〕憲法
611	**copyright** [kápirài t]	〔名〕著作権
612	**corruption** [kərʌ́pʃən]	〔名〕汚職
613	**criminal justice**	刑法
614	**evidence** [évidəns]	〔名〕証拠
615	**federal law**	連邦政府の法律

616 **go into effect** 実施される、発効する
A new state law requiring daily breathalyzer checks for all school bus drivers goes into effect today.
スクールバスのドライバー全員に、毎日の酒気検知器チェックを求める新しい州法が今日実施されます。

617 **guilty** [gílti] 〔形〕有罪の
618 **harass** [hərǽs] 〔動〕～を困らせる

619 **human rights** 基本的人権
620 **illegal** [ilíːɡəl] 〔形〕違法な
Some citizens are suing the government for illegal wiretapping and spying.
違法な盗聴やスパイで政府を訴えている市民もいます。

621 **imprisonment** [imprízn mənt] 〔名〕禁固
622 **jail** [dʒéil] 〔名〕刑務所
623 **judge** [dʒʌdʒ] 〔名〕裁判官、判事
624 **jury** [dʒúəri] 〔名〕陪審（員団）
一定の数の陪審員（juror）からなる。

625 **juvenile** [dʒúːvənáil] 〔形〕未成年の
juvenile delinquency 未成年の犯罪

626 **lawyer** [lɔ́ːjər] 〔名〕弁護士
（類）solicitor [səlísətər]〔名〕事務弁護士

627 **legal** [líːɡəl] 〔形〕法律上の、法的
628 **legislation** [lèdʒisléiʃən] 〔名〕立法、法律
629 **obey** [oubéi] 〔動〕従う
Obeys the law or take the consequences.
法律に従うか、責任をとりなさい。

630	**offense** [əféns]	〔名〕	犯罪、違法行為 《英》offence
631	**petty crimes**		軽犯罪
632	**plaintiff** [pléintif]	〔名〕	原告
	defendant [diféndənt] 〔名〕 被告		
633	**prosecutor** [prάsikjùːtər]	〔名〕	検事、検察官
634	**punishment** [pʌ́niʃmənt]	〔名〕	刑罰

An alternative form of punishment like community service makes more sense than jail in some cases.
社会奉仕のような代替の刑罰形式は、場合によっては刑務所よりも理にかなっています。

635	**resort** [rizɔ́ːrt]	〔動〕	訴える
636	**right** [ráit]	〔名〕	権利
637	**robbery** [rάbəri]	〔名〕	強盗
638	**sentence** [séntəns]	〔動〕 判決を下す 〔名〕判決、刑	

a light sentence 軽い刑　a heavy sentence 重い刑

639	**suit** [súːt]	〔名〕	訴訟

a criminal suit 刑事訴訟　a civil suit 民事訴訟

640	**suspect** [sʌ́spɛkt]	〔名〕	容疑者
641	**treaty** [tríːti]	〔名〕	条約
642	**trial** [tráiəl]	〔名〕	裁判
643	**verdict** [vɔ́ːrdikt]	〔名〕	評決
	(類) judgment [dʒʌ́dʒmənt]		
644	**witness** [wítnis]	〔動〕	目撃する、証言する

8. 不動産・引越し
不動産

645	**apartment** [əpάːrtmənt]	〔名〕	アパート

I found my apartment by looking in the paper.
新聞を見てアパートを見つけました。

646 **basement** [béismənt]　　〔名〕地下室
647 **condominium** [kàndəmíniəm]　　〔名〕分譲マンション
648 **efficiency** [ifíʃənsi]　　〔名〕能率、効率
These new "smart" homes offer maximum energy efficiency.
これらの新しい「しゃれた」家は最大のエネルギー効率を提供します。

649 **estate agent**　　〔名〕不動産（仲介）業者
The estate agent promised to find a house that would satisfy the needs of a large family like ours.
不動産業者は私たちのような大家族のニーズを満たす家を見つけることを約束しました。

650 **function** [fʌ́ŋkʃən]　　〔名〕機能
Every household function is controlled by a central computer.
すべての家庭の機能はセントラル・コンピューターで制御されます。

651 **furniture** [fə́ːrnitʃər]　　〔名〕家具
652 **hall** [hɔ́ːl]　　〔名〕廊下、玄関
653 **household** [háushòuld]　　〔名〕家族、所帯　〔形〕家庭用の
household goods 〔名〕家財

654 **improvement** [imprúːvmənt]　　〔名〕改築、改良
The government subsidizes home improvements that make homes more environment-friendly.
政府は、家をより環境にやさしくするための改築に補助金を支給します。

655 **long-term** [lɔ́(ː)ŋtə́ːrm]　　〔形〕長期の
656 **occupant** [ákjupənt]　　〔名〕入居者
657 **on-site** [ánsàit]　　〔形〕現地の
658 **outskirts** [áutskə̀ːrts]　　〔名〕郊外
659 **premises** [prémisiz]　　〔名〕敷地、土地

Unauthorized solicitors will be removed from the premises.
認可されていない事務弁護士は、その土地から移動させられるでしょう。

660	**property** [prápərti]	〔名〕	資産、不動産、財産
661	**real estate**	〔名〕	不動産

（反）movables [múːvəblz]〔名〕動産

662	**realtor** [ríːəltər]	〔名〕	不動産業者
663	**refurbish** [riːfə́ːrbiʃ]	〔動〕	リフォームする、改装する
664	**renovate** [rénəvèit]	〔動〕	改装する、修理する

renovation [rènəvéiʃən]〔名〕修復

665	**rent** [rént]	〔名〕家賃 〔動〕賃貸する
666	**residence** [rézədəns]	〔名〕 住宅、住宅地
667	**show** [ʃóu]	〔動〕 案内する、見せる

show a person around 人を案内する

668	**sink** [síŋk]	〔名〕	流し
669	**spacious** [spéiʃəs]	〔形〕	広々とした、ゆったりした

The master bedroom is spacious and has a huge walk-in closet to boot.
主寝室は広々とし、その上、大きな押入れがあります。
　　To boot「その上、おまけに」

670	**surrounding** [səráundiŋ]	〔形〕	周囲の
671	**urban** [ə́ːrbən]	〔形〕	都会の

Urban heat islands are downtown areas where the temperature is higher than in the surrounding rural areas.
都会のヒートアイランドは、気温が周りの田舎の地域よりも高いダウンタウンの地域です。

672	**vicinity** [visínəti]	〔名〕	近所、周辺地域

（類）neighborhood

引越し

673 **deliver** [dilívər] 〔動〕配達する
We'll deliver your new furniture to your home or office and assemble it for you on the spot.
あなたの家かオフィスへ家具を配達し、その場で組み立てます。
　　on the spot「その場で、即座に」

674 **do-it-yourself** [dù:itjərsélf] 〔形〕自分でする、自分で運転する
We have a great selection of do-it-yourself moving vans and trucks.
たくさんの自分で運転するバンやトラックを取り揃えています。

675 **estimate** [éstəmèit] 〔名〕見積り 〔動〕見積る
at a rough estimate ざっと見積もって

676 **fee** [fí:] 〔名〕料金
ACE's moving fee includes up to 75 cardboard packing boxes.
ACE社の引越し料金は荷造り用段ボールを最高で75箱まで含んでいます。

677 **move** [mú:v] 〔名〕引越し
Robert lent me his truck for the move.
ロバートは引越しのために私にトラックを貸してくれました。

678 **move into** 引っ越す
Residents cannot move into the new building until the elevators meet government reguóltions.
居住者はエレベーターが政府の規則に合うまでは、新しい建物に引っ越すことができません。

679 **relocate** [rì:loukéit] 〔動〕移転する
They asked me to relocate to Detroit so I was forced to change companies.
彼らは私にデトロイトへ移転することを求めたので、会社を変えざるをえませんでした。

680 **relocation** [rì:loukéiʃən] 〔名〕移転

252

681 **removal company** 引越し会社
682 **settle in** 住む
683 **ship** [ʃíp] 〔動〕（荷物を）送る
684 **storage** [stɔ́:ridʒ] 〔名〕保管
685 **time frame** 〔名〕時間枠
686 **utilities** [ju:tílətiz] 〔名〕水道光熱費
687 **vacate** [véikeit] 〔動〕明け渡す、空ける

契約

688 **damage deposit** 損害保証金
Usually, the damage deposit is returned if there is no major damage to the unit.
普通、ユニットに大きな損傷がないなら、損害保証金は返されます。

689 **down payment** 頭金
I can't afford a big down payment right now.
ちょうど今、大きな頭金を払う余裕がありません。

690 **earnest money** 〔名〕手付け金
691 **have no choice but to** 選択の余地がない、仕方がない
If you continue to break the rules, we will have no choice but to terminate your lease.
規則を破り続けるなら、あなたの賃貸借契約を終わらせるより仕方がないでしょう。

692 **insurance** [inʃúərəns] 〔名〕保険
693 **key money** 権利金、保証金
We don't have to pay key money like Japanese apartment renters.
日本のアパート賃借人のように権利金を払う必要がありません。

694 **mortgage** [mɔ́:rgidʒ] 〔名〕住宅ローン
（類）a house loan, take out a mortgage 住宅ローンを組む

695 **requirement** [rikwáiərmənt] 〔名〕要求

家電

696 **air cleaner** 空気清浄機
697 **air conditioner** エアコン
698 **appliance** [əpláiəns] 〔名〕家電製品
699 **brand name** 商標名
700 **built-in** [bíltin] 〔形〕はめ込み式の、作り付けの
built-in cupboard 作り付けの食器棚

701 **compactor** [kəmpǽktər] 〔名〕(台所の)ゴミ処理器、ゴミ圧縮器
702 **desired** [dizáiərd] 〔形〕望んだ、希望の
Simply turn the temperature control knob on the wall to the desired temperature.
壁の温度調節つまみを希望の温度に回してください。

703 **efficient** [ifíʃənt] 〔形〕効率の良い
704 **electric gadget** 電気器具
(類) electric appliances

705 **fix** [fíks] 〔動〕修理する 〔名〕修理
706 **freezer** [frí:zər] 〔名〕冷凍室
The refrigerator has a large meat compartment, handy vegetable bin, and huge freezer.
冷蔵庫は大きな肉用の冷蔵室、便利な野菜室、大きな冷凍室があります。

707 **high-powered** [háipáuəd] 〔形〕高性能の、強力な
708 **humidifier** [hju:mídifàiər] 〔名〕加湿器
Using a humidifier can help prevent colds and sore throats.
加湿器を使うことは、風邪とのどの痛みを防ぐ手助けになります。

709 **incredibly** [inkrédəbli] 〔副〕信じられないほど、非常に

You can get some incredibly good deals on widescreen TVs during the store's going-out-of-business clearance sale.
店の閉店クリアランスセール中、ワイド画面のテレビで非常にいい買い物ができます。
going-out-of-business「閉店、店じまい」

710 **instructions** [instrʌ́kʃənz]　〔名〕マニュアル、取り扱い説明書
（類）manual [mǽnjuəl]

711 **invent** [invént]　〔動〕開発する、考え出す
The genius who invented this software is no longer living, but his vision lives on.
このソフトを開発した天才はもはや生きていないが、彼のビジョンは生きています。

712 **lawn mower**　芝刈り機

713 **liquid crystal**　液晶
liquid crystal display (=LCD) 液晶ディスプレー

714 **outlet** [áutlèt]　〔名〕（電気の）コンセント

715 **rack** [rǽk]　〔名〕ラック、棚

716 **regularly** [réɡjulərli]　〔副〕規則的に、定期的に
Make sure you empty the dryer's lint filter regularly.
定期的に乾燥機のけば取りフィルターを空にしてください。

717 **removable** [rimúːvəbl]　〔形〕取り外しのできる
The racks, shelves, and drawers are all removable for easy cleaning.
ラック、棚、引き出しは簡単な掃除のためにすべて取り外しができます。

718 **thermos** [θə́ːrməs]　〔名〕魔法びん

719 **timesaver** [táimsèivər]　〔名〕時間節約器

720 **warranty** [wɔ́(ː)rənti]　〔名〕保証（書）
You can extend the warranty to five years for an extra $100.
100ドル追加で、保証を5年延長できます。

721 **washing machine**　洗濯機

9. 社交・パーティー
社交

722 **alumni** [əlʎmnai] 〔名〕同窓会

723 **arrangement** [əréinʤmənt] 〔名〕手配
We'll make arrangements to drive you home if you've had too much to drink.
たくさん飲んだのなら、あなたを家まで車で送らせるよう手配しましょう。

724 **celebrate** [séləbrèit] 〔動〕祝う

725 **ceremony** [sérəmòuni] 〔名〕式典
（類）rite [ráit]〔名〕儀式

726 **commemoration** [kəmèməréiʃən]〔名〕記念、記念の式典
commemorate [kəméməreit]〔動〕記念する

727 **compliment** [kámpləmənt] 〔名〕賛辞 〔名〕お祝いを言う

728 **engagement** [engéiʤmənt] 〔名〕婚約

729 **invite** [inváit] 〔動〕招待する
If everyone we invited shows up, we'll have to move the party onto the patio.
招待したみんなが来るなら、パーティーをテラスへ移動しなけばならないでしょう。

730 **name tag** [tǽg] 名札

731 **participate** [pɑːrtísəpèit] 〔動〕参加する
For some reason, Jill rarely participates in her company's excursions.
何らかの理由で、ジルはめったに会社の小旅行に参加しません。

732 **partner** [pɑ́ːrtnər] 〔名〕パートナー
Of course, this invitation includes your spouse, partner or one other guest.
もちろん、この招待にはあなたの配偶者かパートナー、あるいは他の1人のゲストが含まれています。

733 **reunion** [ri:jú:njən] 〔名〕再会

734 **RSVP** お返事ください
Répondez, s'il vous plait. ≪フランス語≫の略 (= Reply, please.)

■ パーティー

735 **banquet** [bǽŋkwət] 〔名〕祝宴、宴会

736 **beverage** [bévəridʒ] 〔名〕飲料、飲み物
Sales of imported alcoholic beverages have dropped due to consumer concern about possible contamination.
輸入アルコール飲料の売り上げは、汚染の可能性について消費者が心配しているために減少しました。

737 **bride and groom** 花嫁・花婿、新郎新婦

738 **buffet** [bəféi] 〔名〕ビュッフェ、立食

739 **by far** はるかに、とびぬけて
I believe this is by far the best wine for the price.
これはこの値段では、とびぬけて最高のワインだと思います。

740 **catering** [kéitəriŋ] 〔名〕出前サービス

741 **celebration** [sèləbréiʃən] 〔名〕祝うこと、祝賀
Lighting a candle for each child in the family is part of the celebration.
家庭でそれぞれの子供のためにキャンドルに火をつけることは祝賀の一部です。

742 **come-as-you-are party** くだけた仲間だけのパーティー
BBQ バーベキュー

743 **decoration** [dèkəréiʃən] 〔名〕飾りつけ
décor [deíkɔ:r] 室内装飾

744 **favor** [féivər] 〔名〕景品

745 **get under way** 始まる
Before the party gets under way, I would like you all to know how

pleased we are to have you in our new home.
パーティーが始まる前に、新しい家に招待できてどれほどうれしいか、あなたがた全員に知っていただきたいと思います。

746 **guest** [gést]　　　　　　　　〔名〕客、ゲスト
Women dressed in traditional local costumes served wine to the guests.
伝統的な地元の服をきた女性が、ゲストにワインを出しました。

747 **housewarming party**　　　引越し祝いパーティー
farewell party お別れパーティー

748 **invitation** [invitéiʃən]　　　〔名〕招待状
We'd better put a map, showing how to get to our house in the envelopes along with the invitations.
封筒の中に招待状と共に家へ来る来かたを示す地図を入れた方がいいです。

749 **microphone** [máikrəfòun]　　〔名〕マイク
I had the microphone fixed before the party began.
パーティーが始まる前にマイクを修理してもらいました。

750 **notice** [nóutəs]　　　　　　〔名〕お知らせ
Our party planners provide everything you need — at just a few days' notice.
ほんの数日前にお知らせいただけると、パーティーの企画者が、必要なすべてのものを提供いたします。

751 **office party**　　　　　　　　職場パーティー

752 **reception** [risépʃən]　　　　〔名〕披露宴、歓迎会

753 **snack** [snǽk]　　　　　　　〔名〕軽食
Meg was running around the kitchen like a professional chef making snacks for the party.
メグがパーティーのために軽食を作りながら、プロのシェフのように台所で走り回っていました。

258

754 **tableware** [téiblwèə] 〔名〕食器類

755 **toast** [tóust] 〔名〕乾杯 〔動〕乾杯する
drink a doast, offer a toast 乾杯する

756 **trick** [trík] 〔名〕手品

757 **trust** [trʌ́st] 〔動〕任せる
Trust PAT'S PERFECT PARTIES to make your child's birthday a truly unforgettable one.
お子さんの誕生日を本当に忘れられないものにするためパッツ・パーフェクト・パーティーズにお任せください。

758 **wedding shower** 結婚前祝いパーティー
baby shower 出産前祝いパーティー

759 **wrapping paper** 包装紙

食事

760 **a free pint of** 無料の1パイントの〜

761 **appetizer** [ǽpətàizər] 〔名〕前菜（食事の最初の軽い料理・飲み物）
appetite [ǽpətàit] 〔名〕食欲

762 **cafeteria** [kæ̀fətíəriə] 〔名〕食堂

763 **cook** [kuk] 〔動〕食事を作る、料理する
I learned to cook while working as a kitchen helper at a family restaurant.
ファミリーレストランで調理場の助手として働いている間に料理することを学びました。

764 **cuisine** [kwizí:n] 〔名〕料理（法）
The street is lined with a new restaurants serving exotic cuisines from around the world.
その通りは世界中からの異国風の料理を出す新しいレストランが並んでいます。

765 **custom** [kʌ́stəm] 〔名〕習慣

The custom of eating with a fork probably originated 500 years ago in Venice, where touching one's food was considered impolite.
フォークで食べる習慣はおそらく500年前のベニスで始まりました。そこでは人の食べ物に触れるのは無作法と考えられていました。

766 **delicious** [dilíʃəs] 〔形〕おいしい、うまい

767 **eat out** 外食する
Most families are so busy these days that they eat out more often than not.
たいていの家族はこの頃とても忙しいので普通は外食します。
more often than not「普通は、たいていは」

768 **entrée** [á:ntrèi] 〔名〕主要料理、主菜
The list of entrées changes daily, depending on the availability of main course.
主菜のリストはメインコースの利用状況によって毎日変わります。

769 **ingredient** [ingríːdiənt] 〔名〕材料、食材
One bite and I can tell if the ingredients are fresh or not.
一口食べると、食材が新鮮かどうか分かります。

770 **luncheon** [lʌ́ntʃən] 〔名〕昼食、昼食会
luncheonette [lʌ̀ntʃənét]〔名〕軽食堂

771 **nutritious** [nju:tríʃəs] 〔形〕滋養分が多い、栄養になる
Our locally-grown vegetables are naturally safer, tastier and more nutritious.
地元で栽培した野菜は当然より安全で、味がよく、滋養分が多いです。
nutrition [nju:tríʃən]〔名〕栄養

772 **produce** [prádjus] 〔名〕生産物、製品
Organic produce may cost a little more, but it's well worth it.
有機産物は少し値段が高いかもしれないが、その価値は十分あります。

773 **recommendation** [rèkəmendéiʃən]〔名〕お勧め料理

774 **refreshments** [rifréʃmənts] 〔名〕軽食、飲み物

775 **rotary sushi shop** 回転すし店
Do you think a rotary sushi shop would go over around here?
回転すし店はここら辺りで受け入れらると思いますか。

776 **skip** [skíp] 〔動〕飛ばす、抜きで済ませる
I was so exchausted that I skipped dinner and went straight to bed.
とても疲れていたので、私は夕食抜きで済ませ、すぐ寝ました。

777 **specialty** [spéʃəlti] 〔名〕名物料理、特別料理
The specialty of the house is corned beef and cabbage.
その店の特別料理はコーンビーフとキャベツです。

778 **to one's taste** ～の好みに合って
Some of the foods may not be to your taste but at least give them a try.
食べ物のいくつかは、あなたの好みに合わないかもしれませんが、少なくとも食べてみなさい。

779 **worry about** ～について心配させる
Consumers are naturally worried about reports that some frozen foods may be tainted.
冷凍食品には汚染されているものもあるという報告を、消費者はもちろん心配しています。

食材・調味

780 **cabbage** [kǽbidʒ] 〔名〕キャベツ
781 **carrot** [kǽrət] 〔名〕ニンジン
782 **cereal** [síəriəl] 〔名〕シリアル
783 **chop** [tʃáp] 〔動〕細かく切る
784 **flavor** [fléivər] 〔名〕風味
Indian food is all the rage for its spicy flavors.
インド料理はスパイスの効いた風味のため大流行しています。
　　be all the rage「大流行している」

785	**flour** [fláuər]	〔名〕 小麦粉
786	**garlic** [gáːrlik]	〔名〕 ニンニク、ガーリック
787	**green pepper**	〔名〕 ピーマン
788	**moldy** [móuldi]	〔形〕 かび臭い

When cleaning your refrigerator, throw away any food that is moldy, spoiled, or past the use-by date.
冷蔵庫を掃除するときは、かび臭いか、腐っているか、賞味期限の過ぎた食べ物は捨てなさい。

use-by date「賞味期限」

789	**mushroom** [mʌ́ʃruːm]	〔名〕 きのこ
790	**onion** [ʌ́njən]	〔名〕 タマネギ
791	**oyster** [ɔ́istər]	〔名〕 カキ
792	**prawn** [prɔ́n]	〔名〕 クルマエビ
793	**pumpkin** [pʌ́mpkin]	〔名〕 カボチャ
794	**radish** [rǽdiʃ]	〔名〕 大根
795	**salmon** [sǽmən]	〔名〕 サケ
796	**savor** [séivər]	〔名〕 風味

savory [séivəri] 〔形〕 味の良い
（反）savorless [séivərles] 〔形〕 風味のない

| 797 | **seasoning** [síːzəniŋ] | 〔名〕 調味料、香辛料 |

（類）condiment [kándəmənt] 〔名〕 香辛料、スパイス

798	**seaweed** [síːwiːd]	〔名〕 海草
799	**shrimp** [ʃrímp]	〔名〕 小エビ
800	**soybean** [sɔ́ibiːn]	〔名〕 大豆
801	**spicy** [spáisi]	〔形〕 スパイシーな

hot [hát] 辛い bitter 苦い

| 802 | **tuna** [tjúːnə] | 〔名〕 マグロ |

料理法

803 **bake** [béik] 〔動〕焼く
(類) broil [brɔ́il], roast [róust], toast [tóust]

804 **boil** [bɔ́il] 〔動〕煮る、煮立てる、炊く、ゆでる
(類) simmer [símər]

805 **burn** [bə́ːrn] 〔動〕焼く
I smell something burning in the kitchen.
台所で何かを焼いている臭いがします。

806 **crisp** [krísp] 〔形〕カリッとした

807 **dice** [dáis] 〔動〕さいの目に切る
shred [ʃréd] 細長く切る   slice [sláis] 薄く切る
chop [tʃáp] 細かく切る、切り刻む

808 **fry** [frái] 〔動〕油で揚げる、いためる
deep-fry 〔動〕たっぷりの油で揚げる

809 **go well with** ～によく合う

810 **grate** [gréit] 〔動〕おろす

811 **grill** [gríl] 〔動〕網焼きにする
(類) broil [brɔ́il] あぶる

812 **rare** [réər] 〔形〕レア、生焼きの
medium [míːdiəm] メディアムの、ふつうの
well done ウエルダン、十分焼いた

813 **slice** [sláis] 〔動〕薄切りにする

814 **sour** [sáuər] 〔形〕すっぱい
(類) vinegary [vínigəri]

815 **steam** [stíːm] 〔動〕蒸す、ふかす

10. 日常生活
生活

816 award [əwɔ́:rd]　　　　〔動〕与える、贈る
At the end of the summer reading program, prizes will be awarded in each age group for the most books read.
夏の読書プログラムの終わりには、最も多くの本を読んだ年齢グループに、賞が贈られるでしょう。

817 biological [bàiəláʤikəl]　　　〔形〕生物学的な
Depression may be a more biological than spiritual or emotional affliction.
うつ病は精神的、感情的苦悩というよりも生物学的なものであるかもしれません。

818 category [kǽtəgɔ̀:ri]　　　〔名〕カテゴリー、区分
"Gender" is commonly used to refer to social and cultural categories, while "sex" refoers to biological categories.
「ジェンダー」は社会的文化的なカテゴリーを言うために一般的に使われるのに対し、「性」は生物学上のカテゴリーに言及するために使用されます。

819 come through　　　　切り抜ける、乗り切る
I came through the painful experience with a renewed sense of hope and determination.
希望と決断の感覚を取り戻して、つらい体験を乗り切りました。

820 despair [dispéər]　　　　〔名〕絶望
Million of children are doomed to lives of want and despair.
何百万人の子供たちが貧困と絶望の生活を運命づけられています。
　　want「貧困」

821 expense [ikspéns]　　　　〔名〕費用
Local areas are trying to attract doctors by offering to pay their medical school expenses.
地元の地域は医科大学の費用を払うことを申し出ることで、医者を引きつけようとしています。

822 **independent** [ìndipéndənt] 〔形〕独立した、自立した
American teenagers wish to become independent from their parents as soon as possible.
アメリカのティーンエイジャーは、できるだけ早く親から独立することを望んでいます。

823 **laundry** [lɔ́:ndri] 〔名〕洗濯物、クリーニング店
(類) dry cleaner クリーニング屋

824 **pick up** 迎えに行く
I'll pick you up in front of your office building at 5:15.
5時15分にオフィスビルの前へあなたを迎えに行きます。

825 **under the weather** 気分がすぐれない、(酒に)酔った
You must be feeling a little under the weather after last night's celebration.
昨夜の祝賀会のあと、少し気分がすぐれないと感じているかもしれません。

826 **weather** [wéðər] 〔動〕風雨に耐える
The house had a warm and weathered look that attracted me as soon as I saw it.
その家は一目で私を魅了する暖かくて風雨に耐えた様子をしていました。

家庭

827 **adolescence** [æ̀dəlésns] 〔名〕思春期

828 **adopt** [ədápt] 〔動〕養子にする
The number of couples wishing to adopt from abroad will be increasing in the future.
海外から養子を迎えることを希望する夫婦の数は将来増えるでしょう。

829 **adoption** [ədápʃən] 〔名〕養子縁組
Adoption is the obvious solution for couples who cannot have children of their own.
養子縁組は自分の子供が持てない夫婦にとって、明白な解決法です。

830 **assisted living** 生活援助
An assisted living facility provides just the amount of care each resident requires.
生活援助施設はちょうどそれぞれの居住者が求める程度の世話を提供します。

831 **be born to** ～から生まれる
In the US, 30% of all babies are born to single mothers.
アメリカでは赤ん坊の30％が未婚の母から生まれています。

832 **benefit** [bénəfit] 〔名〕利益
The benefits of living at home with one's parents are primarily financial.
親と一緒に家で住むことの利益は、主として財政的なものです。

833 **bring up** 育てる
834 **detergent** [ditə́ːrdʒənt] 〔名〕洗剤
835 **discipline** [dísəplin] 〔名〕しつけ
836 **divorce** [divɔ́ːrs] 〔名〕離婚 〔動〕離婚する
837 **elderly** [éldərli] 〔名〕年配の人
838 **ex-husband** [èkshʌ́zbənd] 〔名〕前の夫、先夫
My ex-husband and I divorced several years ago, but we remain on good terms.
前の夫と私は7年前に離婚しましたが、良い関係のままです。

839 **femininity** [fèmənínəti] 〔名〕女性
840 **grow up** 成長する
841 **infant** [ínfənt] 〔名〕幼児
842 **living standard** 生活水準
843 **parenting** [péərəntiŋ] 〔名〕子育て
parenting skills 育児法

844 **raise** [réiz] 〔動〕育てる
845 **relative** [rélətiv] 〔名〕親類

846 **senior citizen** お年寄り、高齢者
Senior citizens who can no longer take complete care of themselves require some form of home assitance.
もはや自分自身の世話が完全にできないお年寄りは、何らかの形の在宅援助を必要とします。

847 **separation** [sèpəréiʃən] 〔名〕別離

848 **sibling** [síbliŋ] 〔名〕兄弟姉妹
Growing up with seven siblings, I had to learn to fight for myself very early.
7人兄弟で育ったので、私はとても早く自分で戦うことを学ばねばなりませんでした。

849 **single** [síŋgl] 〔形〕独身の
More and more women are choosing to remain single well into their thirties.
だんだん多くの女性が30歳になるまで独身でいることを選んでいます。

850 **youngster** [jʌ́ŋstər] 〔名〕若者

社会

851 **conventional** [kənvénʃənəl] 〔形〕因習的な、習慣的な
852 **diverse culture** 多様な文化
853 **domestic** [dəméstik] 〔形〕国内の、家庭の
854 **ethnic heritage** 民族遺産
855 **flock to** 〜に押し寄せる
Immigrants from all across Europe flocked to the United States in the late 19th and early 20th centuries.
19世紀の終わりから20世紀のはじめに、ヨーロッパ中からの移住者が米国へ押しかけました。

856 **folks** [fóuks] 〔名〕人々、皆さん
857 **generation** [ʤènəréiʃən] 〔名〕世代
Today's generation of young people focuses more on individuality than group consciousness.

今日の若者世代は、グループの意識よりも個人に焦点を合わせます。

858 **humanity** [hju:mǽnəti] 〔名〕人類

859 **ID card** 身分証明書
identification card, identity card の略

860 **majority** [mədʒɔ́:rəti] 〔名〕大多数
861 **religion** [rilídʒən] 〔名〕宗教
862 **resident** [rézidənt] 〔名〕居住者

ファッション

863 **alter** [ɔ́:ltər] 〔動〕手直しをする
He lost so much weight that he had to have all his suits and trousers altered.
彼は非常に体重が減ったので、スーツやズボンの手直しをしてもらわねばなりませんでした。

864 **apparel** [əpǽrəl] 〔名〕衣料
865 **attire** [ətáiər] 〔名〕服装
866 **classy** [klǽsi] 〔形〕おしゃれな、上品な
Her designs are sophisticated and classy, yet durable and versatile.
彼女のデザインは洗練され、おしゃれですが、長持ちして多機能です。

867 **coat** [kóut] 〔名〕コート
868 **collar** [kɑ́lər] 〔名〕えり
869 **dandy** [dǽndi] 〔名〕ダンディー、しゃれ男
He was quite a dandy in his youth, though you wouldn't know it to look at him today.
今日、彼を見ても分からないだろうが、青年時代はまったくダンディーでした。

870 **fashion-conscious** [fǽʃən kɑ̀nʃəs] 〔形〕流行に敏感な、流行を追う
When she was hired for the job, she was the least fashion-conscious member of the staff.

その仕事に雇われたとき、彼女は最も流行を追わない社員でした。

871 **inexpensive** [inikspénsiv]　　〔形〕安い、手ごろな値段の
（類）cheap [tʃíːp]　（反）expensive [ikspénsiv] 高価な

872 **informal** [infɔ́ːrməl]　　〔形〕インフォーマルな
A good black dress can be worn for both formal and informal occasions.
いい黒のドレスはフォーマルな場合にもインフォーマルな場合にも着ることができます。

873 **jacket** [dʒǽkit]　　〔名〕ジャケット、上着

874 **jewelry** [dʒúːəlri]　　〔名〕宝石類

875 **out of fashion**　　流行遅れの
be in fashion はやっている

876 **plain** [pléin]　　〔形〕無地の
a plain white shirt 無地の白のシャツ

877 **sewing** [sóuiŋ]　　〔名〕裁縫
sew [sóu]〔動〕～を縫う　sewing machine ミシン

878 **sleeve** [slíːv]　　〔名〕（衣類の）そで
a dress with short sleeves 半そでのドレス

879 **sweat shirt** [ʃə́ːrt]　　トレーナー

880 **try on**　　試着する
Why don't you try the jacket on for size in one of our changing rooms?
試着室の1つで、サイズが合うかどうかジャケットを試着したらどうですか。

881 **wear out**　　すり切らす
The elbows of this corduroy jacket were worn out, so I had leather patches put on them.
コーデュロイ（地）のジャケットのヒジがすり切れたので、レザーのあて布をしてもらい

ました。

882 **zipper** [zípər] 〔名〕ファスナー

風景

883 **amenity** [əménəti] 〔名〕生活を快適にする設備
884 **avenue** [ǽvənjùː] 〔名〕通り
885 **block** [blák] 〔名〕ブロック、街区
Chinatown is a ten-block walk from the main business district.
チャイナタウンは主なビジネス地区から歩いて10ブロックのところにあります。

886 **cathedral** [kəθíːdrəl] 〔名〕教会
887 **complex** [kɑmpléks] 〔名〕複合ビル
888 **curb** [kə́ːrb] 〔名〕（歩道の）縁石
889 **florist** [flɔ́ːrist] 〔名〕花屋
at the florist's 花屋で

890 **grocery store** 雑貨店
891 **high-rise** [háiràiz] 〔形〕高層の、高層建築
892 **landscape** [lǽndskèip] 〔名〕景色
（類）scenery[síːnəri]〔名〕景観　view[vjúː]〔名〕眺め　sight[sáit]〔名〕光景

893 **mall** [mɔ́ːl] 〔名〕ショッピングモール、商店街
894 **newsstand** [njúːzstæ̀nd] 〔名〕新聞スタンド
895 **overpass** [óuvərpæ̀s] 〔名〕歩道橋
896 **pay phone** [péifòun] 〔名〕公衆電話
897 **pedestrian** [pədéstriən] 〔名〕通行人
898 **rest room** 化粧室、トイレ
899 **sidewalk** [sáidwɔ̀ːk] 〔名〕小道、散歩道
（類）pathway

900 **skyscraper** [skáiskrèipər] 〔名〕摩天楼
901 **story** [stɔ́:ri] 〔名〕階
《英》storey （類）floor

902 **vending machine** 自動販売機
903 **well-built** [wèlbílt] 〔形〕頑丈な

休日

904 **approach** [əpróutʃ] 〔動〕近づく
With summer fast approaching, it's time we thought about where we should go on vacation.
夏休みがどんどん近づいているので、休みにどこへ行くべきかについて考えるときです。

905 **day off** 休暇
I had to take a few days off to deal with a family matter.
家庭の問題を処理するために数日休暇を取らねばなりません。

906 **national holiday** 国民の祝祭日
Independence Day 独立記念日　Labor Day 労働者の日
Veterans Day 復員軍人の日　Memorial Day 戦没者追悼の日

907 **paid holiday** 有給休暇

908 **three-day weekend** 3連休の週末
We have a three-day weekend coming up, so how about playing a couple of rounds of golf?
3連休の週末がやって来るので、2、3ラウンドのゴルフをするのはどうですか。

＜文法のまとめ 5＞

形容詞

1. 限定用法：形容詞＋名詞
   My uncle walks in the large park near our house on warm days.（名詞の前）
   （叔父は暖かい日には家の近くの大きな公園で歩きます）
   This is a country rich in natural resources.（名詞のうしろ）
   （これは天然資源が豊富な国です）
   -one, -thing, -body で終わる名詞の修飾はうしろ
   something special「なにか特別なもの」somebody reliable「誰か頼れる人」

2. 叙述用法：補語として、主語や目的語を説明
   I felt sad when he left for London.
   （彼がロンドンへ発ったとき寂しく感じました）

3. 叙述用法のみに用いられる形容詞
   afraid「恐れる」 alive「生存して」 asleep「眠って」 aware「気づいて」

4. 限定用法と叙述用法で意味が異なる形容詞
   Do you know her present address?
   （現在の彼女のアドレスを知っていますか）
   Many people I didn't know were present at the party.
   （見知らぬ人がたくさんパーティーに出席していました）

5. 数量：most, most of, many, much, few, little, some, any, enough, etc.
   Most people like to spend their time at home.
   （大部分の人々は家で時間を過ごすのが好きです）
   Most of her life was spent in Los Angeles.
   （彼女の人生の大部分はロサンゼルスで過ごしました）

6. 形容詞の語順
   冠詞＋数量＋大小＋形状＋性質＋新旧＋色＋材料

副詞

1. 頻度を表す副詞：always, seldom, sometimes, never, often, usually, etc. は一般動詞の前、be 動詞・助動詞の後
   My brother often goes to the library.

（弟はよく図書館へ行きます）
He is always busy.
（彼はいつも忙しいです）

2. **場所・時を表す副詞**：there, here, yesterday, today は場所＋時の順
   Michael happened to be there yesterday.
   （マイケルはたまたま昨日そこにいました）

3. **文全体を修飾する副詞：文頭に置く**
   Happily he did not die.〔文全体を修飾〕
   （幸いにも彼は死にませんでした）
   He did not die happily.〔動詞 die を修飾〕
   （彼は幸せな死に方をしませんでした）

4. **very と much**: very は形容詞・副詞の原級、much は比較級、最上級を修飾
   I wrote my paper very carefully.
   （とても注意深くレポートを書きました）
   Jessica's room is much bigger than mine.
   （ジェシカの部屋は私のよりもずっと大きいです）

前置詞

> 前置詞句（前置詞＋名詞）は形容詞句・副詞句として修飾語や補語になる。

1. **形容詞句として名詞を修飾**
   The man in the long-sleeved shirt is Matthew.
   （長そでのシャツを着た男性はマシューです）

2. **副詞句として動詞を修飾**
   Jack arrived at the airport just in time.
   （ジャックはちょうど間に合って空港に着きました）

3. **補語として文の要素**
   This microwave oven is of Japanese make.
   （この電子レンジは日本製です）

> 前置所の用法：時、場所、方法、原因・理由、手段、道具、単位、材料、目的、結果

4. 時：　　Ashley was born on September 5 in 2005.
         （アシュリーは2005年9月5日に生まれました）

5. 場所： There is a comic book on the desk.（デスクにマンガがあります）
6. 原因： I was surprised at his resignation.（彼の辞任に驚きました）
7. 手段： Mike goes to school by bus.（マイクはバスで通学します）
8. 材料： They make wine from grapes.（ブドウからワインをつくります）
9. 単位： The workers are paid by the month.（労働者は月ぎめで支払われます）

郡前置詞：2つ以上の語で1つの前置詞の働き

according to「～によれば」 as for, as to「～に関して」 at the cost of「～を犠牲にして」 because of「～のために」 for the sake of「～のために」 in addition to「～に加えて」 in case of「～の場合には」 instead of「～の代わりに」 in spite of「～にも関わらず」 on account of「～のゆえに」 thanks to「～のおかげで」 with regard to「～に関して」

The flight was delayed because of a blizzard.
（その便は猛吹雪のために遅れました）

仮定法

1. 仮定法過去：現在の事実に対して反対のことを仮定
   If + 主語 + 過去形 …, 主語 + should, would, could, might + 動詞の原形
   「もし…であれば、～であろう」
   If I had enough money, I would buy a new car.
   （もし十分なお金があれば、新しい車を買うでしょう）

2. 仮定法過去：be 動詞は主語の人称に関係なく were
   If I were a little younger, I'd take up tennis.
   （もしもう少し若かったなら、テニスを始めるでしょう）

3. 仮定法過去完了：過去の事実に対して反対のことを仮定
   If + 主語 + 過去完了 …, 主語 + should, would, could, might + have + 過去分詞
   「もし…だったならば、～していただろう」
   If he had not helped me, my business I would have failed.
   （もし彼が私を助けてくれなかったら、ビジネスは失敗していたでしょう）

4. I wish：願望を表す。

I wish + 主語 + 仮定法過去「～ならいいのに」(現実と異なる願望)
I wish I had more self-confidence.
(もっと自信があるといいのに)
I wish + 主語 + 仮定法過去完了「～だったらよかったのに」(過去の事実と異なる願望)
I wish I had been a better father.
(もっと良い父だったらよかったのに)

強調

1. 否定の副詞 + 助動詞 + S + V
   Never did I dream that such a tragic accident would occur.
   (そんな悲惨な事故が起こるとは夢にも思いませんでした)

2. do [does]、did で動詞を強調
   We do offer special service to customers who pay in cash.
   (現金で払うお客様には特別サービスを提供いたします)

3. it is ... that の間に強調するものを置く。
   It was the plant in Texas that caught fire.
   (火災になったのはテキサスの工場でした)

4. 倒置
   He didn't go. Neither did I. (彼は行きませんでした。私もです)
   She is intelligent, and so am I. (彼女は頭がいいです。私もです)

索引（見出し語）

A

a compulsory subject	235
a free pint of	259
abandon	26
ability	54
abortion	219
absorb	26, 173
abuse	73, 221
academic	232
accept	34
acceptable	141
access	137
access charge	152
accommodation	201
accompany	37
account	163
account for	130
accountability	177
accountant	124
accounting	133, 235
accounting department	118
accounting firm	118
accounts receivable	133
ache	217
achievement	179
acid rain	207
acting	226
action	74
activity	74
actor's agent	226
actress	50
ad	83
addict	43
addiction	222
addition	126
additive	211
adjourn	18
administration	120, 244
admission	240
adolescence	265
adopt	37, 265
adoption	265
adult education	235
advantage	54, 120
advertise	16
advertising	141
advertising agency	56, 141
aerospace	178
affair	241
affected	213
affiliate	118
affiliated station	56
affordable	168
after all	108
after-dinner speech	176
agency	201
agenda	173
agent	50
aggressive	213
agreement	140
air	226
air cleaner	254
air conditioner	254
air pollution	207
aircraft	60
airfare	203
aisle	80, 205
alcohol dependency	222
alert	18
all but	176
allergic	217
allergy	74
alliance	120
allied industries	118
all-important	174
allocate	128
allow	34
allowance	159
ally	243
alter	268
alternative	201
altitude	206
altocumulus	199
altostratus	199
alumni	256
ambulance	60, 219
amendment	247
amenity	270
amount	163
amusement	178
analyze	179
ancient	240
anecdote	174
animated movie	226
anniversary	86
announcement	87
anonymous	241
answering machine	157
antibiotics	221
antibody	219
antifreeze	62
anti-viral software	153
anxious	224
apartment	249
apologize	43
apology	171
apparatus	179
apparel	268
appear	16
appearance	87
appetizer	259
appliance	67, 254
applicant	127
application	127
apply	34, 140
appoint	128
appointment	137

276

appraise		133	audition		226	be exposed to	44
appraiser		124	auditor		133	be in need of	143
appreciate		140	auditorium		80, 228	be in trouble	44
approach		271	authentic		168	be prone to	39
appropriate		174	author		240	be rained out	22
approval		177	authority		241	be required to	39
approve		37	auto mechanics		125	be supposed to	20
apt		102	automatically		109	be unfamiliar with	20
area		199	automobile		186	beforehand	174
area code		157	available		98, 131	belt	206
argument		173	avenue		270	beneficial	213
arrangement		256	average		83, 133	benefit	57, 160, 266
arrest		247	award		74, 264	best before date	146
article		83	award-winning mural		240	beverage	257
artist		240				beverage company	118
as a result		177	**B**			bid	138
assault		243	bachelor's (degree)		235	bidding price	167
assembly		169	back issues		87	bike	22
assess		211	back up		44	bilateral	243
asset		167	background		127	bill	64, 70, 148
assignment		130	backpacking		237	billboard	64
assisted living		266	bacteria		74	bin	212
associate (degree)		235	baggage		203	biological	264
asthma		74, 217	baggage claim		204	biologist	180
astronomy		179	bake		263	biosphere	208
at least		108	balance		163	bird flu	214
at no charge		142	balance sheet		133	blanket	206
at the latest		108	balloon		64	bleed	217
at the moment		108	ban		247	blizzard	80
ATM card		163	banking service		163	block	270
ATM (=automated teller			bankruptcy		120	blockbuster	226
machine)		68	banner ad		143	blog	83, 152
atmosphere		196	banquet		257	blood	70
atomic number		179	barely		109	blood pressure	217
attach		154	bargain		146	board	206
attachment		154	base on		226	board member	172
attend		172	basement		250	board of directors	172
attendance		83, 228	basic pay		159	boarding pass	204
attention		159	battery		68	boarding gate	206
attire		268	be born to		266	boat	60
audience		174	be bound to		152	body	214
audit		132	be entitled to		160	boil	263

277

boiling point	87	budget price	146	call center	171
bond	167	buffet	257	call for	20
book	34	bug	74	call in sick	158
bookkeeper	125	built-in	254	call it a day	131
booklet	64	bulletin	131	call to order	173
bookmark	152	bulletin board	68	call-waiting telephone	158
bookshelf	64	bundle	131	caller	50
booming	182	bureau	245	call-in talk show	143
border	243	bureaucracy	120	calm down	224
bored	224	burn	263	calory	70
boring	226	burnable	212	campaign	245
borrow	133	bus stop	185	camper	237
boss	123	business	87	campsite	237
bother	42	business activities	120	cancel	34, 201
bottle	64	business administration	235	cancer	217
bottom line	138	business card	131	candidate	127
bound for	206	business community	121	canoeing	237
bow	18	business condition	168	capacity	180
box office	228	business day	131	capital	133
box office receipts	228	business hours	128	capital flight	141
box up	149	business is slow	182	capital gain	165
branch	55, 118	business management	121	capital investment	182
branch director	123	business meeting	172	car	61
brand	168	business partner	123	carbon dioxide	207
brand name	254	business trip	201	carcinogen	214
brand-new	102	businessperson	125	cardboard	135
break	34, 70	by all means	231	care for	45
break down	33, 150	by far	257	career	127
break room	81	by noon	186	carefully	107
breaking news	241	by snail mail	159	cargo	149
breathe	23	by the week	160	carousel	204
brew	23	by way of	186	carpenter	50
bride	50			carpool	184
bride and groom	257	**C**		car pool	63
bring up	20, 266	cab	186	carrot	261
broadband	152	cabbage	261	carry-on luggage	206
broadcast	241	cabinet	245	cash	65
brochure	143	cabinet reshuffle	243	cash cow	147
broker	167	cafeteria	259	cash on delivery (=COD)	148
browse	152	calculation	133		
brush	23	call	16	cash register	55
budget	57, 133	call back	157	cash substitute	148

cashier	50, 148	chemist	180	collaboration	128
casually	109	Chief Executive Officer		collaborator	123
catalogue	65, 143	(=CEO)	123	collapse	165
catch a movie	20	choose	16	collar	268
category	264	chop	261	colleague	52
cater	37	chore	131	collect on delivery	159
catering	257	cinema	77	collectible	147
cathedral	270	circular	143	collide	186
cause	171	cirrocumulus	200	cologne	68
cavity	217	cirrostratus	200	combine	18
ceasefire	243	cirrus	200	come through	264
celebrate	256	citizenship	245	come to terms	140
celebration	257	city bank	164	come up	20
celebrity	226	civil engineering	178	come up with	21
cell	208	civilization	240	come-as-you-are party	257
cellphone	65	claim	149	comfortable	222
cellular phone	158	clap	23	commemoration	256
Celsius	87	classical	240	commerce	121
ceramic	102	classified	143	commercial	83
cereal	261	classy	268	commercial bank	164
ceremony	172, 256	clean driving record	63	commercialize	169
certificate	162	clear up	196	committee	247
chair	172	clearance sale	145	commodities	167
chairperson	123	clerk	125	commute	184
chance	55	click	164	commute time	63
chance of rain	196	client	247	commuter	184
change	77	climate	196	commuter train	185
character	87	climb	23	commuting by bike	185
charge	37, 148	clinic	77, 214	compactor	254
chase	23	clip	26	company	118
chat	16	close the books	133	company brochure	131
chat online	154	close the deal	140	comparable	102
chat room	155	cloud	77	compartment	186
check	31, 163	cloudy	196	compatible	150
check in	204	coalition cabinet	245	compensate	171
check out	39	coat	65, 268	compensation	160
checking account	164	code sharing	149	competence	126
checkout	148	coffee maker	68	competition	121
checkup	219	cold	217	competitive	102
cheese	70	cold call	145	competitive edge	121
chemical	178	cold front	196	competitor	126
chemicals	211	collaborate	121	complaint	171

complete	37	consultant	165	index)	183		
completely	107	consume	37	credit	57, 164, 236		
completion	140	consumer	168	credit card	164		
complex	102, 270	consumption	222	credit to	149		
compliment	256	consumption tax	182	credit voucher	149		
complimentary	206	contagious	217	creditor	167		
comply with	141	contaminate	212	crew	206		
component	169	continent	198	criminal justice	247		
compromise	138	contract	57, 140	crisp	263		
concede	138	contribution	88	critic	52		
concentration	214	controllable	196	critical	211		
concept car	188	controller	123	cross-cultural	177		
concern	224	controversial issue	155	crosswalk	185		
conclusion	88	convenience	55	cruise	187		
condition	84, 196	convenient	103, 186	cuisine	259		
condominium	81, 250	conventional	103, 267	cumulonimbus	200		
conduct	26	convert	32, 187	cumulus	200		
conductor	180	cook	35, 259	cupboard	65		
conference	172	cooperate	141	curb	270		
conference call	158	cooperation	212	cure	70, 219		
conference room	57	coordination	214	currency	68, 165		
confidence	147, 227	cop	231	currency in circulation	165		
confidential	102, 159	copyright	156, 247	curricula	236		
confirm	138	corporate ladder	126	custom	259		
conflict	243	corporation	118	custom declaration	204		
conform	138	correct	131	customer	145		
confront	222	correspond with	155	customer service	171		
congest	186	correspondence course	235	customize	151		
conglomerate	118	corruption	247	customs	141		
Congress	245	cosmetics	178	cut taxes	183		
connect	158	cost	134	cut up	28		
connection	186	cost price	169	CV	127		
consecutive	167	costume	65				
consequence	222	cough	217	***D***			
conservation	210	counselor	50	damage	171, 231		
conserve	210	countryside	77	damage claim	204		
consideration	88	coupon	145	damage deposit	253		
consortium	118	courier	149	dandy	268		
Constitution	247	court	77	dangerous	98		
construct	233	coverage	162	dashboard	63		
construction	81, 178	co-worker	125	data	180		
consult	18	CPI (=consumer price		day off	57, 271		

daycare center	81	despair	264	disposal	212
dead end	185	destination	206	dispose of	210
deadline	138	destroy	23	disproportionately	207
deal	55	destruction	243	dispute	173
debate	172	detergent	266	disrupt	187, 218
debt	134	deteriorate	18	dissatisfied	171
debt relief	245	detour	185	distribuition	149
debt repayment	245	devastate	243	distribute	131
decide	18	developed nations	245	distributor	125
decision-making	137	developing nations	245	diverse culture	267
declare	183	development	81	diversify	121
decoration	257	diabetes	217	dividend	167
default	134	diagnosis	219	division	118
defective	103,171	diarrhea	218	divisional system	131
define	18	dice	263	divorce	266
deforestation	208	die out	21	dizzy	218
degree	84, 236	diet	71	do one's best	233
deinduslrialization	178	dig	23	do the dishes	30
delete	155	dinner	71	do well	151
delicacy	201	diploma	236	document	57, 131
delicious	260	diplomat	245	documentary	88
deliver	159, 252	diplomatic break	245	do-it-yourself	252
delivery	149	diplomatic corps	245	dolphin	77
delivery charge	74	diplomatic privilege	245	domain	155
demand	183	direction	84	domestic	267
demographic	88	directory	74	donate	37
demotion	126	disadvantage	201	donation	75
dental	55	disappoint	44	dose	221
depart	26	disappointed	224	doubles	71
department	55, 118	disarmament	243	down in the mouth	224
departure	206	disaster	208	down payment	253
depend	35	discharge	212	download	32
dependent	162	discipline	214, 266	downpour	81
deposit	164	disclosure	173	downshift	27
depreciation	134	discomfort	156	downsize	129
depression	183, 217	discount	71, 145	downtown	78
deregulation	165	disembarkation	204	dozens of	201
describe	137	dish	65	draft	131
desertification	210	dishwasher	65	drastically	109
design	147	dismiss	128	drawer	136
designate	128	disorder	218	dress code	131
desired	254	display	84	drink	71

drinking	222	electric gadget	254	evaluate	233
drive	24	electrician	125	evaluation	57
driver	61	electricity	68	even then	109
driver's license	188	element	180	evidence	247
drive-through	63	elementary school	236	evolution	180
drive-thru / drive-through		e-mail	31, 155	exceed	241
	103	embarrassed	225	excellent	103
drizzle	196	embassy	201	excessive repetition	157
drop out	28	emergency	219	exchange	147
drunk driving / DUI	223	emergency leave	160	exchange rate	165
due	98	emergency room	214	exclusive	142
during working hours	129	emission	212	excursion	237
duties	141	emotion	225	excuse	225
duty-free	204	emotional uplift	88	executive	58, 123
dweller	52	employer	123	exercise	24
		employment	127	exhaust	212
E		employment agency	118	exhibit	240
earn	35	empty	98	exhibition	168
earned run average	88	enclose	131	ex-husband	266
earnest money	253	encourage	233	exit	151
earning	134	endangered species	208	expansion	121
earthquake	208	energy	180	expect	44
easy-to-use	155	engagement	256	expenditure	134
eat	35	enroll	233	expense	264
eat out	260	enrolment	172	expenses	169
ecology	208	enterprise	118	expensive	98
e-commerce	137	entrée	260	experience	84
economic	183	entrepreneur	125	experiment	180
economic climate	245	envelop	65	expert	214
economic unification	121	environment	81	expert commentary	240
economics	236	environmental	210	expert haggler	52
ecosystem	208	environmentalist	210	expiration date	142
eco-tour	81	environment-friendly	210	expire	38, 204
editorial department	241	envy	42	explain	16
education	233	equip	38	explicit	231
educational institution	236	equipment	136	explore	27
effect	223	era	240	export	149
efficiency	250	establish	121	express	159
efficient	254	estate agent	250	expression	177
elderly	266	estimate	252	extension	158
election	245	estimated	103	exterior	88
electric blanket	68	ethnic heritage	267	extinction	82

eye contact	55, 174	fine	89		141
Eye of Providence	89	finest	98	forget	43
eye-catching	142	firm	119, 140	formal	98
		fiscal deficit	166	forward	155

F

		fiscal policy	183	forwarder	149
face	246	fiscal year	134	fossil fuel	208
facility	229	fishery	178	fragile	159
factor in	229	fit	35	franchise	121
factory	78	fitness center	82	frankly speaking	109
faculty	236	fitness fad	237	fraudulent use	156
fad	142	fix	254	free	98
Fahrenheit	89	fixed assets	134	freebie	143
fare	204	flag	66	freeway	185
farmhouse	78	flair	127	freeze	197
fashion-conscious	268	flaw	171	freezer	254
fasten	206	flat	188	freight	149
fault	84	flavor	261	frequently	157
favor	257	flexible	185	freshly	107
fax	31, 159	flier / flyer	89	from now on	110
feathery	200	flight	61	front desk	56
feature	243	flight attendant	206	front page	242
federal law	247	flock to	267	fry	263
fee	252	florist	270	fuel	180
feel	42	flour	262	fulfill	138
feel like	45	flu	218	fulfillment	156
femininity	266	fluctuate	166	full-time	129
ferry	61	flue shot	75	fun	237
fertilizer	180	fluffy	103	function	250
fever	218	focus	19	fund	134
fiber optics	152	fog	78	fundamental	233
field	127	foggy	197	fundamentals	183
figure	89	folk arts and crafts	69	furniture	250
file cabinet	136	folks	267		
film	78	follow suit	246		

G

film director	227	footage	227	gadget	170
finalist	52	for good (and all)	109	gain	134
finance	134	for the first time	109	game	71
financial	133	forbid	19	garage	61
financial director	123	forecast	83	garlic	262
financial institution	165	foreign currency reserves		gas station	61
financial policy	166		166	gasoline	61
financing	166	forex(=foreign exchange)		gene	208

283

general public	231	go-kart	63	head	84
generation	267	government	246	headline	242
generic	168	governor	246	headquarters	119
genetically modified foods		grade	71	headset	206
	180	graduate	233	heal	219
genre	227	grant	142	healing power	215
get along	45	grate	263	health care	215
get along with	45	green pepper	262	health insurance	162
get down	45	greenhouse gas	207	heavy rain	197
get fed up with	45	grief	84	heavy traffic	187
get in touch with	158	grieve	225	heavy-duty	103
get it off one's chest	45	grill	263	herald	153
get off	39	grocery store	270	heredity	215
get oneself posted to	28	gross margin	134	heritage	240
get rid of	28	grow up	266	hierarchy	126
get sick of	45	grown-up	50	high	197
get tired of	45	growth rate	183	high tide	197
get to	28	guarantee	172	higher education	236
get together	29	guaranteed	103	highest-grossing	227
get under way	257	guest	258	high-powered	254
get used to	45	guideline	156	high-pressure	197
get-together	75	guilty	248	high-profile	169
gimmick	143	gust	197	high-rise	270
give a speech	174	gym	78	highway	185
give away	21			hiker	238
glacier	207	**H**		hire	127
glance	174	habitat	208	hit	153
glare-free screen	151	hacker	154	hold a meeting	172
global warming	207	haggle	138	hold on	158
gloomy	225	hall	250	hold up	187
go bankrupt	121	handle	38	home care	219
go fishing	237	handout	173	home caregiver	53
go for	29	hang up	158	home-delivery service	63
go for a ride	61	hangover	218	homemaker	143
go into business	121	harass	248	hood	188
go into effect	248	harassment	89	horn	188
go on line	152	harmless	75	horror film	227
go out	29	have … in common	40	horseback riding	238
go over very well	39	have … on board	29	hospital	78
go to bed	29	have no choice but to	253	hospitalization	219
go well with	263	have nothing to do with	21	hot spring	215
go with	40	hazardous	211	hourly	99

284

hourly pay	160	income tax	164	intellectual property rights	
household	250	incoming	155		142
housewarming party	258	inconvenience	242	intelligent design	233
housewife	51	inconvenient	172	intensive	236
hub	149	incorporate	122	intensive care	89
human interest stories	242	incredibly	254	interest	85, 164
human resources	127	independence	246	interest rate	164
human rights	248	independent	265	interesting	99
humanities	236	index	156	intermission	240
humanity	268	indicate	223	international call	158
humid	197	indoors	107	interrupt	27
humidifier	254	industrial	178	intersection	185
humidity	197	industrial purpose	58	interview	127
hurricane	78	industry	122	invent	255
hybrid	188	inexpensive	269	inventory	150
hyperlink	58	infant	266	inventory adjustment	145
hypertension	218	infection	154	invest	38, 167
hypothesis	181	inform	16	investigation	242
		informal	269	investment	135
I		information	84	invitation	258
icon	151	ingredient	260	invite	256
ID card	268	initial payment	145	invoice	150
illegal	248	initialize	151	invoicing	135
illegal copy	156	inland	199	involve	35
illness	218	innovation	170	IPO (=initial public	
immediately	107	inquire	17	offering)	167
immigration	204	insider dealing	167	issue	246
immune system	75	insightful	104	itchy	218
import	149	insomnia	218	item	147
impress	175	inspect	170	itinerary	201
impressive	104	inspire	38		
imprisonment	248	install	32, 156	*J*	
improve	19	installment payment	149	jacket	269
improvement	250	institution	119	jail	248
in a row	197	instruction	177, 233	jam	187
in charge of	131	instructions	89, 255	jet lag	207
in line	229	instrument	240	jewelry	269
in progress	170, 229	insurance	162, 253	job opening	128
in response to	231	insurer	162	job-hop	129
inclement	197	insurgent	244	join	35
include	35	intake	211	journal	71
income	134	integrated circuit	181	judge	248

junior	51	leave	160	logistics	150
jurisprudence	236	leave a message	158	long-term	250
jury	248	leave for	202	look alike	21
justify	151	led the way	129	look for	21
juvenile	248	legal	248	look forward to	46
		legendary	104	look over	21
K		legislation	248	look through	21
kayaking	238	leisure	238	look up	22
keep	36	let down	225	looked-up word	90
keep an eye on	154	let out	21	lost	90
keep in mind	46	let ... go	29	lost and found	202
keep up	40	lethal impact	210	lot	227
keep up with	40	letter pads	137	low-seniority	53
key money	253	level	211	loyal	99
kidney	219	liability	142	loyalty card	145
kidney infection	75	liberal arts	236	luck	85
		librarian	234	luggage	66
L		licensor	138	lunch break	56
laboratory	181	lie	24	luncheon	260
ladder	66	lift	32	lung cancer	223
land	32	limited-time offer	145	luxury	104
landfill	212	line	58		
landscape	270	link	84	**M**	
lane	185	liquid crystal	255	machine	66
lap	75	list	204	machinery	179
last minute notice	90	list price	147	magnify	144
late fee	232	listed company	119	mail order	145
lately	107	litter	212	mailing list discussion	153
latest	99	live-alone senior	53	maintenance	136
launch	131	liver function	223	major	104, 236
laundry	265	living standard	266	majority	268
law enforcement	58	living thing	209	make ends meet	166
lawmaker	246	load	24	make one's way	40
lawn mower	255	loading	150	make up one's mind	46
lawyer	248	loan	166	make use of	40
lay off	29	local	99	mall	270
layer	200	local call	158	malnutrition	211
layout	58	local industry	178	manageable	131
lead actor	227	local government	246	management	122
lead the way	129	location	79	manager	123
leading	240	lodging	202	managing director	123
lease	71	logging	209	manifest	150

manual	85, 129	military strength	244	naive	223
manufacturer	119	mind	43	name tag	256
manufacturing	170	mine	179	national holiday	271
mark down	145	minimum wage	129	national park	209
mark up	135	ministry	246	nationalize	246
market	79	minutes	173	natural	99
market share	169	miracle drug	222	natural recourses	209
marketing	169	miss	43	natural resources	82
mass transit	185	mistake	85	natural surroundings	82
masterpiece	241	misunderstanding	90	nauseous	218
master's (degree)	237	misuse	172	negotiate	139
match	238	mobil	66	neighborhood	79
material	179	modify	140	nervous	225
maternity leave	58	moldy	262	net	135
matinee	229	molecule	178	net sales	135
maximize	142	mom-and-pop	119	new release	232
mean business	46	money order	141	newscaster	242
mechanic	179	money supply	166	newsstand	270
medical benefits	162	monitor	151	niche	169
medical insurance	162	monopoly	122	nicotine gum	69
medication	75	monotonous	175	nicotine-free	223
medium	181	monthly	72	nicotine patch	223
megahit	227	more often than not	110	night shift	132
member	51	mortgage	253	nightfall	82
memo pads	136	motion	177	nimbostratus	200
memorandum	132	move	24, 252	no matter what	238
menu	72	move into	252	noisy	99
merchandize	145	movie critic	227	nominal fee	90
merger	122	movie memorable	232	nominee	227
meritocratic	129	moviegoer	227	non-performing loans	166
merit system	132	moviemaker	227	North Star	82
message	85	MP3 player	69	no-smoking rule	223
metal detector	205	multinational	119	not once	110
meteorologist	197	multiplex	82	note	56
meteorology	197	multiplex cinema	229	nothing but	215
microphone	258	multi-purpose	104	notice	17, 56, 258
microwave	69	municipal	246	notify	132
mid-career manager	53	mushroom	262	novel	241
mid-level executive	124	mutual funds	167	nurse's helper	53
mild	197			nursing care	220
military	58	**N**		nutritious	260
military personnel	244	nagging	219		

O

obesity	218
obey	248
objective	177
obligation	142
obstacle	238
occasional rain	198
occasionally	107
occupant	250
offend	139
offense	249
offer	36
office machinery	137
office party	258
office personnel	53
office supplies	137
office work	132
official	246
official bank rate	164
ominous-looking	198
on account of	238
on behalf of	175
on business	202
on foot	202
on hold	158
on leave	202
on sale	145
on schedule	132
on the shelves	147
on time	187
once and for all	110
one-way	202
onion	262
online	110
on-site	250
op-ed	242
open for business	122
operate	32
operating profit	135
operating room	220
operation	170, 220
opinion poll	144

opportunity	128
opt for	40
optical	181
optical communication	153
optimistic	175
optimization	151
order	36
ordinary income	135
organ	220
organic	209
organism	181
organize	175
organized votes	246
out of	137
out of fashion	269
out of order	104
out of shape	215
out of stock	137
outdoor	99
outlet	145, 255
outline	173
output	170
outside	229
outskirts	250
outsourcing	141
overcharge	149
overcome	44
overdo	27
overdue	104
overnight	205
overpass	270
overtime	58
overtime compensation	160
overtime pay	160
overweight	72
overwork	27
oveseas	202
oxygen	181
oyster	262
ozone	207

P

pack	24, 27, 150
pack up	187
pack with	29
package	72, 159
package deal	150
pact	246
paddle	238
paid holiday	271
paid leave	160
paid vacation	160
pale	99
paleontologist	181
paper	237
paper clip	137
paperwork	132
parent company	119
parenting	266
parking lot	188
parking ticket	63, 189
participant	172, 238
participate	256
partner	256
party	72, 246
passbook	165
passenger	51
passerby	53
passport	205
past sell-by date	147
pastime	202
pat	27
patent	142
patient	51, 205
pavement	79
pay	36
pay increase	161
pay off	166
pay phone	270
paycheck	161
payer	166
payment	166
PBX (=private branch	

exchange)	158	plaintiff	249	presentation	90
peacekeeping	244	plan	17	preserve	132
peak months	202	plant	119	president	124
pedestrian	185, 270	plastic	69	press	242
penalty	90	play	72	prevail	242
peninsula	199	pleased	225	previous position	59
pension	162	plug	66, 151	price	66
perfect	100	plumber	125	prime time	242
perform	140	PO Box	159	principal	134, 234
performance	76, 126	podium	175	privatize	183
periodical	242	point	24	procedure	205
periodic pay raise	129	point out	41	proceed	167
peripheral	151	poise	175	procure	147
perk	161	policy	162, 215	produce	260
permission	132	political climate	246	product	170
permit	19	politician	246	productive	216
personal belongings	202	poll	246	productivity	170
personal journal	90	pollution	208	professor	234
personel ad	59	popcorn box	229	proficiency	177
personnel	53, 119	popularity	227	profit	135
personnel department	124	pop-up ad	144	profit margin	135
personnel manager	124	portion	72	profit ratio	145
personnel transfer	126	pose	24	profitable	135
petroleum	179	position	126	program	242
petty crimes	249	post	242	prohibit	38
pharmaceutical	179	postage	159	promising	129
pharmaceutical company		postgraduate	234	promote	126
	119	Post-it	137	promotion	169
pharmacy	222	potential	183	promotional idea	59
phone	66	powerful	100	pronunciation	176
physical	215	practical	105	proof	176
physician	220	practically	110	proofread	132
pick out	40	prawn	262	proper	100
pick up	29, 41, 265	precaution	220	property	251
pickpocket	202	precipitation	198	propose	139
pill	222	prefer	43	prose	241
PIN (=personal identification number)		pregnant	215	prosecutor	249
		premises	250	protect	211
	165	premium	163, 232	prove	19
piracy	156	prepare	17	provide	239
place an order	147	prescription	222	provider	59
plain	269	presence	244	province	246

provisions	239	rack up	41	recycling law	213
psychiatrist	220	radiation	181	recycling site	213
psychology	237	radish	262	reduce	19
public relation department		rafting	239	refer to	176
	59, 144	rain forest	209	reference	128
public relations (=PR)	144	raincoat	67	reflect	151
public transportation	62	raise	161, 266	refreshing	100
public works	183	rambunctious	105	refreshments	261
publication	241	rare	263	refrigerator	67
publicize	132	rash	218	refugee	244
public-service corporation		rat race	128	refund	166
	119	rate	166, 232	refurbish	248
publish	179	rate of return	136	regarding	155
pull out	30	rating	232	regards	90
pump	33	raw material	170	region	199
pumpkin	262	ready	100	register	38
punishment	249	real estate	251	registered	159
purchase	36, 72	real estate agent	125	registration	234
purchase order	147	real estate company	129	regret	225
purse	66	realize	17	regular	100
put an ad	144	realtor	251	regular mail	76
put back	30	rearview mirror	189	regularly	255
put in charge	132	reasonable	105, 224	regulate	247
put up	41	reasonably-priced	144	rehearse	176
		rebound	167	re-heat	33
Q		receipt	72	reimbursement	165
qualification	128	receive confirmation	155	relative	266
qualified	128	reception	258	relax	225
quality	139	reception desk	202	release	146
quantity	139	receptionist	125	relieve	19, 220
quarter	67, 136	recession	183	religion	268
questionnaire	169	recipient	163	relocate	126, 252
quiet	100	reckless driving	187	relocation	252
quietly	117	recognition	169	remains	241
quit	27	recommend	220	reminder	166
quota	132	recommendation	260	remittance	159
quotation	176	reconcile	138	remote processing	151
quote	139	record	17, 85	removable	255
quoted company	119	recovery	183	removal company	253
		recyclable	212	remove	24
R		recycled	105	renew	38
rack	255	recycling	212	renewal	91, 156

renovate	251	retirement	161	safe and sound	154
rent	251	retirement age	59	safeguard	179
rental charge	232	retirement benefits	161	salary	161
repair	36, 137	retrench	136	sale	72
replace	172	retrieval system	153	sales	136
replacement	126	retrieve	153	sales forecast	146
reply	155	return	232	sales manager	124
report	17	reunion	257	sales network	146
representative	54	reusable	147	sales promotion	146
reprimand	44	revenue	136	sales representative	146
reproduce	209	review	91	salespeople	51
reputable	144	revolutionary	105	salmon	262
reputation	227	reward	161	satellite navigation	189
requirement	254	rewarding	105	satisfaction	91
research	234	rice cooker	69	satisfy	43
research vessel	82	right	249	save	155
researcher	181	right angle	157	savings account	165
reservation	61	risk management	154	savor	262
reserve	189	robbery	249	saw	91
reserve for	41	robust	184	say-so	243
residence	251	rocket attack	244	scale	200
resident	268	rocky	100	scalpel	220
resign	126	rotary sushi shop	261	scan	221
resolution	91	roundabout	186	scared	225
resort	249	round-the-clock	220	scholarship	234
resource	209	round-trip	202	school board	234
respondent	169	routine	132	school phobia	234
responsibility	213	royalty	142	science	73
responsible	105	RSVP	257	scientific	105
rest room	270	ruin	19	score	85
restaurant	79	ruler	136	screenplay	59
restrict	142	ruling	247	script	230
restriction	232	rumor	243	sculpture	241
restructure	122	run	132	search engine	153
result	85	run an errand	30	seasonal affective disorder
result from	41	run high	239	(=SAD)	218
résumé	59	run out	41	seasoning	262
retail	146	runny nose	218	seat	230
retailer	54	runway	205	seaweed	262
retained profit	136			second	178
retire	39	**S**		secondhand	232
retiree	54	safe	100	secondhand smoke	224

secretary	51	shoot	33	sluggish	184, 218
section	76, 119	shoot the film	227	small business	120
sector	119	shortcut	186	small part	59
secure	154	short of	137	smoke-free	73, 224
securities company	120	shortage	147	smoking-related cause	224
securities investment	168	shot	221	snack	258
security	161	shot in the arm	203	snapshot	76
select	36	shoulder-width	176	sneak preview	230
selection	232	show	17, 251	sneeze	219
self-confidence	176	show up	172	snowstorm	198
self-improvement	176	shower	198	soak	19
semester	234	shrimp	262	soak through	197
semiconductor	181	shut down	122	social issue	234
seminar	234	sibling	267	social security	163
Senator	247	sick leave	161	soil	209
senior	51	sick pay	162	solar cell	211
senior citizen	267	side effect	222	solemn duty	247
senior management	124	sidewalk	270	solvent	139
seniority	126	sign	86	some other time	110
sense	91	sign up	41	sophisticated	182
sentence	246	sign up for	151	sort out	132
separate branch	181	signal	198	sort through	42
separation	267	signature	139	sound	43
serious	225	silver lining	184	soundproof viewing room	
serve	25	similar	101		230
server	153	simulator	182	sour	263
session	169, 234	simultaneously	110	source	243
set off	216	single	267	souvenir	203
settle down	30	sink	251	sovereign	247
settle in	253	site	82, 153	soybean	262
sewage	213	skid	189	spacious	251
sewing	269	skill	177	spam	156
sexist remark	177	skip	33, 261	spank	28
shake hands	30	skyrocket	166	spare	170
shareholder	168	skyscraper	271	spawn	209
shark	79	sleep on	46	speak my piece	178
sharp	230	sleeve	269	special	101
shelf	67	slice	263	special effect	60
shiny	198	slightly	108	special fare	203
ship	253	slip	28	special offer	232
shipment	150	slow cooker	69	specially	108
shipping	150	slowly	108	specialty	237, 261

specific purpose		177	stranger	52	survey		169	
specifications		170	strategy	122	suspect		249	
speech		86	stress	20	suspicious		106	
speed		25	strict	106	sweat shirt		269	
speeding		189	strictly	110	sweater		67	
spicy		262	strike out	30	sweep		25	
sponsor		20	stroller	64	symbiosis		211	
sponsor a booth		146	stub	230	sympathetic		106	
spouse		162	studio	79	sympathy		225	
stack		133	study abroad	234	symptom		219	
staff		125	subcontract	171	syndrome		224	
stage		39	subject	156	synthetic		182	
stand for		22	submit	39				
stapler		136	subordinate	126	***T***			
star	79,	228	subscribe	39	tab		76	
start up		152	subscriber	153	table		176	
state		247	subscription	148	tablet		222	
statement	91,	165	subsidiary	120	tableware		259	
state-of-the-art		171	substance	209	tactical withdrawal		244	
stationary		137	subtitles	228	actics		122	
stationary department		146	suburb	80	tag price		146	
statistics		91	subway	80	take a leave of absence		216	
steak		73	successive	106	take a walk		30	
steam		263	succinctly	111	take care of		42	
steering wheel		189	suggest	235	take effect		139	
step up		205	suggestion	178	take it easy		225	
stiffen up		157	suit	249	take off		33	
stimulate		234	suitable	232	take over		42	
stimulus package		184	sum up	22	take part in		31	
stock	56, 148,	168	summarize	177	take the day off		22	
stock exchange		168	summit conference	247	take the minutes		173	
stock market		168	sunbathe	25	take up	22,	31	
stockbroker		125	sunglasses	67	take ... up with		22	
stockholder's equity		168	supervisor	124	takeoff		207	
stop	25,	187	supplement	216	takeover		122	
stop off		30	supplier	171	talent scout		228	
stoplight		62	supply	211	talk		17	
storage		253	surface transport	150	tap		25	
story		271	surgeon	221	target		169	
straight		101	surgery	221	tariff		141	
strain		157	surprisingly	111	tax		162	
strange		101	surrounding	251	taxation at sources		136	

tech-nerd	152	to be on the safe side	205	treatment	76
technology	152	to one's taste	261	treaty	249
telecommunication	158	toast	259	trial	143, 249
telecommuting	185	tolerate	224	trick	259
telegraphic transfer	165	toll	186	trolly car	188
telemarker	54	tollbooth	186	troop	244
telemarketing	146	toll-free dial	146	tropical	199
temperature	86	top-notch	128	troublesome	106
temporary	129	top-of-the-line	106	trouble-spot location	244
tension	157	tornado	198	trout	80
tentative	139	toss	25	trust	259
tenure	130	tough	101	trustworthy	106
term	140	tourist attraction	203	try on	269
terminal	205	tow	32	try one's hand at	42
terminate	140	tow away	33	tuition	235
terms	142	toxic	213	tuna	262
terrible	101	track	62	tune	241
terrific	101	tracking number	150	turbulence	207
territory	244	trade	140	turn around	132
textile	179	trade imbalance	179	turn down	33
that was that	148	trade surplus	141	turn in	133
the polar ice cap	209	trademark	143	turn off	31
the World Health Organization	216	trading firm	120	turn out	33
the yen	60	traditional	106	turn around	31, 133
theater	80	traffic	62	turnaround	184
theme	86	traffic congestion	188	turnover	136
theory	182	traffic jam	64	tutor	235
therapy	221	traffic light	64	TV ads	56
thermometer	198	trail	239	type	25
thermos	255	train	62	typographical	128
think twice	46	train in	153	tyranny of advertising	143
this time	111	train schedule	188		
three-day weekend	271	tram	188	**U**	
throughout	108, 216	transaction	139	ultrasonic	182
thunderstorm	198	transfer	28, 126, 165, 188	uncertainty	184
ticket	188	translation	60	under the weather	265
time frame	253	transmission rate	153	undergraduate	235
time deposit	165	transmit	216	unemployment	130
timesaver	255	transport	28	unemployment rate	184
timetable	187	transportation	150, 188	unforgettable	106
tip	73, 86	trash bin	152	union	120
		treat	221	unit	148

294

unleash	228
up to date	153
update	152
upgrade	156
upright position	207
upset	44
up-to-the-minute	182
urban	251
use	36
used title	76
user	152
user authentication	152
utilities	253
utility	69

V

vacancy	128
vacate	253
vaccination	221
vacuum cleaner	70
valid	166
validity	182
valuables	203
valued client	172
veggie /vegetable	73
vehicle	62
vending machine	271
vendor	171
venture	179
verdict	249
vessel	150
vice president	124
vicinity	251
vicious circle	184
virus	210
visibility	198
visual aids	70
vital sign	76
vote	73, 247

W

wage	92
wage differential	130
wage increase	130
wage in kind	130
wage reduction	130
wait for	31
wait tables	42
waitress	52
wake-up call	203
walk	25, 62
walkout	184
war zone	244
warehouse	150
warm	101
warn	17
warning	198
warranty	255
washer	67
washing machine	255
waste	86, 213
water shortage	198
waterfall	239
wave	26, 80
wear	26
wear out	269
weather	86, 265
weather report	198
wedding shower	259
weight	73
welfare	161
welfare facilities	130
welfare-to-work	163
well-being	217
well-built	271
well-known	230
wet to the skin	199
wheelchair	221
wheels	62

white-water ride	239
wholesale	146
wilderness area	211
willing	101
windshield	189
windy	199
wire sculpture	241
wireless	156
withdraw	165
withdrawal	219
witness	54, 249
work	26
work condition	130
work flexible hours	130
work on	133
work out	34
work overtime	130
worker's compensation	162
workforce	130
workout	77, 239
workshop	60
workweek	130
worldwide	211
worry about	261
wrapping paper	259
wrong	101
wrong number	158

X

X-ray	221

Y

yield	168
youngster	267
youth	52

Z

ZIP code	159
zipper	270

新 TOEIC® テスト ズバリ出る英単語ファイル

2009年7月27日　1刷

著　者────三原　京
　　　　　　© Kei Mihara, 2009

発行者────南雲一範

発行所────株式会社　南雲堂
　　　　　〒162 東京都新宿区山吹町361番地
　　　　　電　話　（03）3268-2384（営業部）
　　　　　　　　　（03）3268-2387（編集部）
　　　　　FAX　　（03）3260-5425（営業部）
　　　　　振替口座　00160-0-46863

印刷所／日本ハイコム株式会社　　製本所／松村製本所

Printed in Japan　〈検印省略〉
乱丁、落丁本はご面倒ですが小社通販係宛ご送付下さい。
送料小社負担にてお取替えいたします。

ISBN 978-4-523-26482-8　C0082〈1-482〉
E-mail nanundo@post.email.ne.jp
URL http://www.nanun-do.co.jp